File Handling on the BBC Microcomputer

Macmillan Microcomputer Books
General Editor: Ian Birnbaum (Adviser for Microelectronics in Education, Humberside LEA)

Advanced Graphics with the Acorn Electron
  Ian O. Angell and Brian J. Jones
Advanced Graphics with the BBC Microcomputer
  Ian O. Angell and Brian J. Jones
Interfacing the BBC Microcomputer
  Brian Bannister and Michael Whitehead
Assembly Language Programming for the Acorn Electron
  Ian Birnbaum
Assembly Language Programming for the BBC Microcomputer,
second edition
  Ian Birnbaum
Using Your Home Computer
  Garth W. P. Davies
A Science Teacher's Companion to the BBC Microcomputer
  Philip Hawthorne
Beginning BASIC with the ZX Spectrum
  Judith Miller
Using Sound and Speech on the BBC Microcomputer
  M. A. Phillips
File Handling on the BBC Microcomputer
  Brian J. Townsend
Good BASIC Programming on the BBC Microcomputer
  Margaret White

Also from Macmillan

Advanced Graphics with the IBM Personal Computer
  Ian O. Angell
Advanced Graphics with the Sinclair ZX Spectrum
  Ian O. Angell and Brian J. Jones
Advanced Programming for the 16K ZX81   Mike Costello
Beginning BASIC   Peter Gosling
Continuing BASIC   Peter Gosling
Practical BASIC Programming   Peter Gosling
Program Your Microcomputer in BASIC   Peter Gosling
More Real Applications for the ZX81 and ZX Spectrum   Randle Hurley
Programming in Z80 Assembly Language   Roger Hutty
Microprocessor and Microcomputer Technology   Noel Morris
Understanding Microprocessors   B. S. Walker
Assembly Language Assembled – for the Sinclair ZX81   Anthony Woods

File Handling
on the
BBC Microcomputer

Brian J. Townsend

Senior Lecturer in Computing
Havering Technical College
Romford, Essex

MACMILLAN

First published 1985

Published by
Higher and Further Education Division
MACMILLAN PUBLISHERS LTD
Houndmills, Basingstoke, Hampshire RG21 2XS
and London
Companies and representatives
throughout the world

Printed in Great Britain by
Camelot Press, Southampton

British Library Cataloguing in Publication Data
Townsend, Brian J.
  File handling on the BBC Microcomputer.—
  (Macmillan microcomputer books)
  1. BBC Microcomputer   2. Data base management
  I. Title
  001.64'42   QA76.8.B35

  ISBN 0–333–36808–8

Associated software cassette: 0–333–38921–2

Contents

Preface

Many people who are responsible for the control of small organisations are aware of the fact that using a computer can make the difference between the success or failure of that organisation. Unfortunately, the introduction of a computer to carry out data processing activities does not guarantee the continued viability of that organisation.

This is because a large number of the programs that are supposed to carry out such tasks fail to do so in the way that is required by the user. Such programs are produced to satisfy the largest number of potential users, in order to sell as many programs as possible, and thus represent a solution to what is seen by their writers as a general problem. The continued existence of many small organisations is often due, however, to the special nature of the service provided, or the way in which it is provided, and thus its problems may be difficult or impossible to solve using a general-purpose program.

Even if a user feels confident enough to attempt a modification, such programs may have been written so as to prevent user-modification and the cost of modification by the writer may be prohibitive. An approach to organisations that have solved similar problems may be considered as unwise from the aspect of having to reveal sensitive information to a possible competitor. This book provides a means whereby such problems may be solved within the organisation.

It is not, however, necessary to be a computer programmer in order to use this book because readers are taken, in easy steps, through the development of a typical file-handling program. Self-test questions are provided to enable readers to check their understanding of each new concept and model solutions to those questions are provided. As each new user-requirement is identified, a routine is developed and tested on the computer and then the results are analysed in order to establish whether or not the routine is satisfactory.

The initial development is carried out on a basic system comprising a BBC microcomputer, an audio

cassette recorder/player and a TV receiver. As the
development progresses, so readers will become aware of
the limitations of the basic system for certain types
of data processing activities. It is stressed, however,
that this basic system can be used for a number of
activities in which a printed output or a rapid
response to a requirement is not important.

A method of creating records and files on the
computer is developed and this is followed by routines
for sorting, searching and updating files. As the
production of a printed output is likely to be the next
most important aspect, this is dealt with before
considering how floppy discs can be used for the
various aspects of file-handling. Finally, although the
development has been carried out in a logical and
sequential manner, the results need to be combined into
a self-contained package of routines that can be
selected by the user. Such a combination is described,
developed, tested and analysed.

This package is not meant to be the answer to the
file-handling requirements of an organisation but it
provides the framework on which the development of an
appropriate package can be based. Suggestions for
incorporating possible user-requirements are made and
the various types of printer and floppy disc equipment
are analysed.

Thanks and appreciation are due to my wife Marian
for her patience and encouragement during the writing
of this book.

Brian Townsend
Stow Maries
November, 1984

Program Cassette
All of the program listings given in the book are
available on a cassette, which will overcome the need
to enter programs from the keyboard - and eliminate
typing errors. The cassette is obtainable from major
bookshops, but in case of difficulty order direct from

Globe Book Services
Houndmills, Basingstoke, Hampshire RG21 2XS

ISBN 0-333-38921-2   Price £9.00 inc VAT

Important Note
Readers are asked to note that users of data processing
programs may be affected by the 1984 Data Protection
Act.

1 Simple File Processing on the BBC Micro

This book explains how the BBC microcomputer can be
used to set up and manipulate files of data. It is
essential that access to a BBC micro, as it is usually
called, is readily available so that the program
listings and self-test questions given in each chapter
can be tried out while the theory is still fresh in the
reader's mind.

The minimum additional equipment required is a TV
receiver and an audio cassette recorder, as explained
in the User Guide. It will be realised, as the reading
of the book progresses, that this minimum equipment
will be insufficient to carry out the fast processing
of data that would be required for business purposes.
The use of a printer and a disc (disk) drive unit will
enable the rapid sorting, searching and updating of
information and the output of results such as invoices,
orders, stock lists, etc. to be carried out.

It will be recalled that the WELCOME tape supplied
with the BBC micro contained a number of programs which
demonstrated many of the features of the computer. The
programs on the WELCOME tape are sometimes referred to
as files although they may not seem very much like the
files with which most readers will be familiar. Such
files are, perhaps, best exemplified by the author and
subject indexes in libraries, by address books, by
telephone number lists and stock lists, etc. In each of
these examples, a list of similar items of data has
been compiled in order that rapid reference can be made
to any specific item. A necessary feature of such files
is that the data contained is sorted into some order,
usually alphabetic.

When using computers, the word "files" is sometimes
given an extended meaning so as to include any
information kept, or stored, outside the computer.
Thus, the programs stored on the WELCOME tape are files
in this sense. However, as the aim of this book is to
provide the reader with the basic skills for developing
his or her own data processing requirements into usable
programs for the BBC micro, the meaning given in the
User Guide will be used throughout this book.

1

Therefore, a cassette recorder will be used to store both programs (of instructions) and files (of data), but the methods of control are different. Programs are stored or SAVEd on tape and retrieved or LOADed from tape, whereas files are stored on tape using the PRINT# statement and retrieved using the INPUT# statement. In addition, certain statements must be used before and after working with files - these will be introduced later.

There now follow examples of two different methods of use of the cassette recorder with the computer.

Using a Cassette Tape for Program Storage
Listing 1.1 is for a program that will create a file consisting of five items of data from a sales catalogue.

```
LISTING 1.1
 10 REM FILE DEMONSTRATION NC.1
 20 N$="FILE1"
 30 FILE=OPENOUT(N$)
 40 READ NUMBER
 50 PRINT# FILE,NUMBER
 60 FOR V=1 TO NUMBER
 70 READ NAME$,C
 80 PRINT# FILE,NAME$,C
 90 NEXT V
100 CLOSE# FILE
110 DATA 5
120 DATA "PLATES,LARGE",1278
130 DATA "PLATES,SMALL",1279
140 DATA "GLASSES,SHERRY",823
150 DATA "CUP",771
160 DATA "SAUCER",772
170 END
```

Before the program is entered into the computer and RUN, a few words of explanation about the various parts of the program will be given.

Line 10 is the title of the program and will not be taken as an instruction because the first word after the line number is REM (meaning REMark).

Line 20 allocates the name "FILE1" to the file that is to be created to hold the five catalogue items. Notice that there are no spaces in the file name but up to ten other characters may be used for cassette file names. N$ is a string variable whose value is "FILE1".

Line 30 tells the computer that a channel called FILE is to be OPENed for OUTput from the computer. Note that lines 20 and 30 could be combined as FILE=OPENOUT"FILE1" but this form is not so useful for future work.

Line 110, being a DATA statement, holds data that can be used by the program when obeying READ statements such as lines 40 and 70. The first READ statement in the program will copy the item that is identified by the data pointer, whether a string variable which is enclosed in quotation marks or a numeric variable such as 12, 1023, etc. Thus line 40 causes the computer to create a variable called NUMBER with the value (read from line 110) of 5.

Line 50 causes the value of NUMBER to be PRINTed, or written, onto the file.

Lines 120 to 160 inclusive are five DATA statements, each holding a sales catalogue item. Each item consists of a name, such as cup (which, because it is a string variable, must be enclosed in quotation marks) and a number. A comma must separate the individual items in a DATA statement.

After obeying the instruction in line 40, the computer will move its data pointer to the item PLATES,LARGE and this will be the next item to be copied by a READ statement. A READ statement will move the data pointer along by one data item for each of the variables itemised in that READ statement. Thus, the data pointer is moved once by the READ statement in line 40 but moved twice by that in line 70. What is required is that each catalogue item is written onto the file in the sequence given in lines 120 to 160 inclusive and this is achieved by lines 60, 70, 80 and 90.

Line 60 sets up a FOR...NEXT loop which causes the computer to repeat one or more statements a certain number of times. In this case, the number of repetitions is given by the value of NUMBER, that is 5.

The statements which will be repeated 5 times are in lines 70 and 80. Line 70 READs two data items; the first will be called NAME$ and will thus be a string variable and the second will be called C and be a numeric variable. Thus, in each repetition of the FOR...NEXT loop, a complete catalogue item will be copied from a DATA statement.

Line 80 causes the variables NAME$ and C to be written onto the file and this will be repeated each time that the FOR...NEXT loop is obeyed.

As indicated above, after each READ statement has been completed, the data pointer will be positioned at the first item in the next DATA statement. Two important points arise from this fact. If the value of NUMBER is less than 5, not all of the DATA items will be copied (and then written onto the file). Conversely, if the value of NUMBER is greater than 5, the data pointer cannot be moved and the computer will display a

message to indicate that no more DATA items are
available to be copied and written onto the file.

Line 90 is a necessary part of the FOR...NEXT loop
but the control variable, V in this case, is optional -
see page 305 of the User Guide. The use of a control
variable with the NEXT statement is advocated, however,
because programs are then more easily comprehended,
particularly when several FOR...NEXT loops are used.

Finally, line 100 informs the computer that the file
called "FILE1" is to be CLOSEd. Such a statement has to
be used whenever the reading from a file or the writing
to a file by a program is completed. The problems
created by not carrying out this requirement will be
dealt with later when disc-based files are discussed.

This program should now be entered into the computer
after first typing NEW to prevent any previous program
statements from interfering with the new program. If
the cassette of programs that complements this book is
available, load the program given in listing 1.1 by
using LOAD "L1.1" after placing the cassette in the
recorder. Do not attempt to RUN the program yet.

If the cassette of programs is not available, the
keyed-in program should be saved, using SAVE"DEMO1", on
a blank cassette tape. This is an important step to
take when developing programs because a power supply
failure will cause all program statements to be erased
from the computer's memory. Note that although the
title of the program is given in line 10 as "FILE
DEMONSTRATION NO.1", this title is too long to be used
as a cassette file name and, in addition, it also
contains spaces.

Note that recording must be carried out on the brown
part of the tape. The recording should then be verified
by using *LOAD"DEMO1"8000 and playing the tape again.
An incorrectly saved program will be indicated and can
then be saved again because the program is still in
memory.

Creating a File on a Cassette Tape

When the program has been saved, remove the cassette
from the recorder, WITHOUT rewinding the tape, and
identify it as FILE DEMONSTRATION. Now insert a blank
tape, correctly positioned for recording, and type RUN
before pressing the RETURN key. The computer will
respond with the usual RECORD then RETURN message and,
after this has been done, the recorder will operate for
a few seconds.

The program run has ended and a file containing the
five catalogue items has been created on the cassette
tape. Now rewind the tape, remove the cassette from the
recorder and identify it as FILES.

Before dealing with the procedure for using the stored data files, it is important that readers should test their understanding of the previous material. The following self-test question should now be attempted and the answer checked with that given at the end of the book.

Self-test 1.1
Write a program called "Test Program 1" that will create a file named "TESTFILE1". The file is to hold the ten sales catalogue items listed below but **not** the three column headings.

Description of Item	Catalogue Number	Delivery Time
PLATES,LARGE	1278	EX STOCK
PLATES,SMALL	1279	4 WEEKS
GLASSES,SHERRY	823	SPECIAL ORDER
CUP	771	EX STOCK
SAUCER	772	EX STOCK
BOWLS,SOUP	473	2 WEEKS
BOWLS,FRUIT	1280	3 WEEKS
SPOONS,DESSERT	079	SPECIAL ORDER
SPOONS,TEA	080	EX STOCK
SPOONS,SOUP	081	SPECIAL ORDER

It is recommended that readers´ programs should be tested on the computer, but using two different tapes from those already used. The program is a logical extension of that given in listing 1.1 and if the explanation of that program was followed without difficulty, no problems should be found in answering the question.

Retrieving Files from Cassette Tape
In the previous section, the program given in listing 1.1 was used to store a file of data on a cassette tape. The program given in listing 1.2 may be used to retrieve, or put back into the computer´s memory, that data.

LISTING 1.2
```
10 REM FILE DEMONSTRATION NO.2
20 N$="FILE1"
30 FILE=OPENIN(N$)
40 INPUT# FILE,NUMBER
50 FOR V=1 TO NUMBER
60 INPUT# FILE,NAME$,C
70 PRINTTAB(3);NAME$;TAB(20);C
```

```
 80 NEXT V
 90 CLOSE# FILE
100 END
```

Line 20 tells the computer that the file that is to be retrieved is called "FILE1". Line 30 OPENs a channel called FILE for INput to the computer. In the same way that lines 20 and 30 in listing 1.1 could have been combined, so lines 20 and 30 in listing 1.2 could be combined as FILE=OPENIN"FILE1". Again, it is better to use the form given so that future work can be carried out more easily.

Line 40 causes the value of the variable called NUMBER to be obtained from FILE1 and stored in the computer.

Line 50 uses this value to set up a FOR...NEXT loop with control variable "V". For each repetition of the loop, lines 60 and 70 will be obeyed.

Line 60 causes the string variable NAME$ and numeric variable C to be stored in the computer. Line 70 will cause the text contained in NAME$ to be printed, on the screen, starting at TAB position 3 and the value of C to be printed at TAB position 20.

Line 80 should need no explanation but it should be noted that, on repeating line 60, the existing values of NAME$ and C will be replaced by the new values obtained from the file.

Line 90 will cause the file access channel to be CLOSEd.

The program given in listing 1.2 should now be keyed in, after first entering NEW, and then saved with SAVE "L1.2". (If the cassette of programs is available, then the preceding action will not be necessary; just use LOAD "L1.2".)

The tape identified previously as FILES should now be placed in the recorder and rewound. Entering RUN and RETURN will not produce the "Searching" message which might be expected. The PLAY key on the recorder should now be pressed and then the recorder will start. After a few seconds the screen will display the data that was recorded on FILES using listing 1.1 and the recorder will stop.

In this introductory chapter on using the BBC micro, a method of using an audio cassette recorder for creating and retrieving data files has been given. Considerable scope exists for improving the operating speed of the programs but the programs given are so short that this aspect does not require treatment at this stage and can be left until later.

As a check on understanding, readers should now consider how listing 1.2 needs to be altered to make it

suitable   for retrieving the data that was stored using
the program developed as an answer to Self-test 1.1.   A
model   answer   for   the retrieval program, based on the
answer given for Self-test 1.1, is given in appendix I.
Note   that   the   screen   display   obtained   when   the
retrieval   program   is   RUN   will   not have the leading
noughts for the catalogue   numbers   of   SPOONS,TEA   and
SPOONS,SOUP.   This is a feature that will be dealt with
later.

2 Data Structures

Before any real attempt at writing programs for data processing can be made, it is important that clear ideas about the composition of data exist. The name normally given to this composition is "data structure".

An Example of a Data Structure
An easily understood example of a data structure is a card index kept by a retailer to hold details of all the customers who have accounts with him. Each card will contain a customer´s name, address, account number, credit limit, discount rate and, possibly, a telephone number. A normal procedure would be to keep the cards in alphabetical order so that finding a particular customer´s card would be quite easy.The card index is, therefore, a data structure containing the required information about the retailer´s account customers.

The complete card index consists of a number of cards, each of which contains a name, address, etc. The name will consist of letters, punctuation marks and spaces, whereas the address will most probably contain a number in addition to the previously mentioned characters. Now each character conveys certain information to the reader and thus it can be seen that a composite data structure can be formed from a number of more simple data structures. Individual characters (letters, spaces, digits, etc.) are used to form groups of characters (name, telephone number, etc.) which are then used to form an individual customer card. Finally, all the cards are kept together in, say, alphabetical order.

Information Relationships
Relationships between different items of information are recorded in data structures because, in the present example, each customer´s card holds his name, his address, his account number, etc. Although these are different items of information, they have an implied relationship because they all belong to the same customer.

The information contained in the card index can be used or changed easily. For example, a customer who is known to the counter staff may make a purchase and give only his name and account number. The staff responsible for compiling and despatching the invoice to the customer will need information on address and discount rate. This can be obtained by searching the card index for a card with the correct name on it and then checking that the account numbers agree. Further, if a customer closes his account, then his card can be removed from the card index and, conversely, the card for a new customer can be inserted into the index. Such alterations as change of address or of discount rate can be made without difficulty.

The three properties of the manual card index system discussed above, that is

(i)   the combination of simple data structures to
      form composite data structures
(ii) the recording of relationships between different
      items of information and
(iii) the organisation of data structures so as to
      allow ease of use or change

are properties that are common to those structures used to store information for processing by computer, sometimes called "electronic data processing".

Structured Data Types

If a data structure contains only a number or only an address, then the data structure is called "type number" or "type address" respectively. When such simple data structures are combined, as on the customer card, then the name "structured data type" is used. It is common to refer to four structured data types, that is

          arrays
          records
          sequences
          trees

but examination of the index for the User Guide will reveal that only the first type in the above list is dealt with. It should not be assumed that this is a serious impediment to using the BBC micro for data processing, because there is not, at the time of writing, any high level language that allows users to have direct access to sequences and trees. Such abstract data structures, as they are called, are usually obtained by careful organisation of those data structures that are available in the language. An example of such organisation is the creation of records by the use of arrays.

Fields and Records

Referring to the card index system again, each customer card is a "record" and each individual item of information on a card is referred to as a "field". Thus each record in the card index has the following fields

>   name
>   address
>   account number
>   credit limit
>   discount rate
>   telephone number

The order of listing the fields is not important in a manual system since it is unlikely that anyone using a card for making out an invoice for a customer will confuse the telephone number with the discount rate or the name with the address, even if the items have been entered on the card in the wrong order.

Thus, the following two examples of cards would not create any particular difficulty for a user who is familiar with the types of information contained on the card.

Bill Smith	Joe Bloggs
27 Long Street	B703
Anywhere	0374 5630
CX27 4PN	3A Fort Road
S347	Nowhere
1500	CX35 3SJ
12.5	15
0374 1279	2000
Example 1	Example 2

Using example 1, the fields can be specified by giving each one a particular identifier and information type as follows

Field No.	Field Identifier	Information Type
1	Customer Name	Number
2	Customer Address	Address
3	Account Number	Number
4	Credit Limit	Number
5	Discount Rate	Number
6	Telephone Number	Number

Note that to keep things simple at this stage, field 3 has "Number" as its Information Type even though it contains a letter. This classification would be unacceptable to a program written for the BBC micro, however.

Thus, a structured data type has been produced for the format of example 1 and, for computer use, such a structure must be adhered to. Example 2 would not be acceptable, therefore, to a computer because some of the Information Types are incorrect.

In field 2, for example, the computer expects to find an address but finds only a number. Even if a field is of the correct type, a well-designed computer program would reject an item if it did not meet a specified format such as, for example, no more than four digits for credit limit. It is possible, although very unlikely these days, that a customer does not have a telephone although field 6 is expected to contain a number. Under such circumstances, a dummy number could be used or else the program could be designed to take this feature into account.

A record can be described as a data structure with a number of fields, each in a certain, fixed, order with an unambiguous identifying name and containing a pre-defined information type.

To test your understanding of these ideas, try the following self-test question.

Self-test 2.1
A record structure for details of temporary staff services provided by an employment agency is given below.

Field No.	Identifier	Type
1	Customer	Name
2	Starting Date	Date
3	Duration	Number
4	Cost	Price

Which of the following sets of data are valid records and what is incorrect about those that are invalid?

(a)	J.Smith	(b)	Craig Plc	(c)	Vine´s
	14/7/82		5		10-50
	10		12-00		4/5/81
	8-50		Miss Morris		11/5/81

Self-test 2.2
Draw up a record structure for members of a Video Film Hire Club.

Creating a Record on the BBC Micro

The meaning of the word "record" should be quite clear by now and as record keeping and processing is a very important function in any organisation, a way in which a record can be created on the BBC micro will now be investigated.

Referring to the record structure given in self-test 2.1, a suitable set of data for it is

```
            Bloggs
            14/1/83
            5
            75-00
```

Listing 2.1 is a program that displays, on the screen, this data in the format of the record structure given above and also displays this data in a similar format to that used when creating records using BASIC.

LISTING 2.1

```
 10 CLS
 20 DIMA$(4)
 30 FOR I=1 TO 4
 40 READ A$(I)
 50 NEXT I
 60 FOR I=1 TO 4
 70 PRINTA$(I)
 80 NEXT I
 90 PRINT
100 PRINT
110 PRINT
120 FOR I=1 TO 4
130 PRINTA$(I);
140 NEXT I
150 PRINT
160 DATA BLOGGS    ,14/1/83    ,5     ,75-00
170 END
```

How the Program Works

Line 160 is a DATA statement containing the details for the above record. Notice that the first three items have four spaces as part of the data - this is necessary only for this demonstration.

Line 20 sets up a one-dimensional string array or, more simply a string array, with four elements.

Now string arrays on the BBC micro can consist of numbers, such as "5", or of dates, such as "14/1/83", or of account numbers, such as "B703", as well as

names, such as "Bloggs". Thus the problem of dealing
with different information types on a record when using
the BBC micro is taken care of by describing all data
items as string variables. This ploy may create other
problems in later work but, as usual, there are ways of
overcoming them.

Lines 30 to 50 inclusive cause each of the four data
items to be read and identified as array element
1,array element 2 and so on. The element number is
given by the value of "I" and the array is called "A$".
The result is a data structure called an ARRAY which
has the following format

ARRAY A$(4)   Bloggs   14/1/83   5   75-00

            Element 1 Element 2 Element 3 Element 4

It is obvious that this one-dimensional array is
just a different way of presenting the information
contained in the previous record structure.

Lines 60 to 80 inclusive will verify this fact by
printing the contents of the array, with each element
on a separate line and in the correct order for the
record structure. Notice that the order is determined
by what the array elements consist of. Thus, if the
data in line 160 is not correctly ordered or
positioned, neither will the contents of the array and
the record be correctly ordered or positioned.

Lines 120 to 140 inclusive are used to print the
contents of the array again but this time, because of
the ";" at the end of line 130, all the items are
printed on the same line, separated by the four spaces
inserted in the DATA statement. Note that there are
more elegant ways of achieving this printing format but
this is not of importance at the moment.

The program given in listing 2.1 should now be
entered and RUN before continuing with the chapter.
This is L2.1 on the cassette of programs.

Creating Multiple Records

It is now necessary to consider what is required in
order to deal with a number of records because this is
a more realistic use of a computing system. To keep the
work to a manageable level, only four records will be
considered but the principle is the same for as many
records as are required, within the limits of the
memory capacity of your system.

The single record dealt with so far was created from
a one-dimensional string array and four such records

would, if put into an array format, look like

```
ARRAY A$(4,4)
      Customer    Start Date    Duration    Cost
        Bloggs    14/1/83          5        75-00
        Smith     20/12/82         2        25-00
        Jones     4/1/83          10        300-00
        Green     22/2/83         20        500-00
```

Now again, terminology for this structure varies among
users and terms such as "matrix" and "table" are used.
The term used here, in order to maintain the status of
the User Guide, is "two-dimension string array". The
number of elements in this array is four in each of the
four fields, that is 4x4=16 elements, and the four
elements in a row are the data items for a record.
    Using four DATA statements, one for each record, a
two-dimension string array can be set up and then used
to create four records with the required structure. The
program is given in listing 2.2 (L2.2 on the program
cassette).

LISTING 2.2

```
 10   CLS
 20   DIM A$(4,4)
 30   FOR Y=1 TO 4
 40     FOR X=1 TO 4
 50       READ A$(X,Y)
 60       NEXT X
 70     NEXT Y
 80  PRINT
 90  PRINT"EXAMPLE OF FOUR RECORDS"
100  PRINT
110  FOR Y=1 TO 4
120  PRINT
130    FOR X=1 TO 4
140      PRINT A$(X,Y);
150      NEXT X
160    PRINT
170    NEXT Y
180  DATA BLOGGS     ,14/1/83    ,5     ,75-00
190  DATA SMITH      ,20/12/82   ,2     ,25-00
200  DATA JONES      ,4/1/83     ,10    ,300-00
210  DATA GREEN      ,22/2/83    ,20    ,500-00
220  END
```

The Use of Indentation in Program Listings
The format of the listing allows for an easier
understanding of the program because the FOR...NEXT

loops are indented. There is no need to indent the
program statements when entering the program via the
keyboard because using "LISTO7" before "LIST" will
produce the indentation. Similarly, "LISTO0" will
return the listing to the previous format. If entering
the program from the program cassette, it will be found
that this program, together with the rest of those on
the cassette, do not contain any spaces between the
line number and the first letter of the instruction.
This format saves storage space on the cassette, and in
the micro´s memory, and is a means of accommodating
larger programs. It is, of course, possible to save
even more space by not using any separation between the
parts of an instruction but this produces a program
that humans have difficulty in understanding and so it
is not recommended. When listing the programs in this
book, the space between the line number and first
letter of the instruction will be retained for clarity.

How the Program Works
Line 20 dimensions the array so that 16 elements can be
held in it, but dimensioning will be referred to again
later. Lines 30 to 70 inclusive allow an element of the
array A$ to be given a value from the DATA statements.
The particular item from the DATA statements will be
determined by the values of the two parameters, X and
Y. The first values are Y=1 and X=1 as given by lines
30 and 40 respectively. Thus the first data item read
will be for A$(1,1) and this will be "BLOGGS".

Line 60 will make the value of X increase by 1
because the "NEXT X" instruction returns the program to
line 40. The next array element to be given a value
will be A$(2,1) and the value will be "14/1/83".
Parameter X will be increased twice more and the result
will be that A$(3,1) takes the value "5" and A$(4,1)
the value "75-00". As parameter X is now equal to 4,
line 60 will not cause a return of the program to line
40, as previously, but instead it will obey the
instruction in line 70 and return to line 30.

Here, the parameter Y is increased by 1 to give Y=2.
The next instruction starts the FOR...NEXT loop for
parameter X again, that is X=1. Thus the fifth element
of the array to be given a value will be A$(1,2) and
the value will be "SMITH". Again, parameter X will be
increased up to the value 4 and then Y will be
increased to 3. The function of the nested FOR...NEXT
loops is, therefore, to READ each DATA item in turn and
to put the item into the element (X,Y) of the array A$.
A "picture" of the array after completing this part of

the program is given below.

0					
1		BLOGGS	14/1/83	5	75-00
VALUES 2		SMITH	20/12/82	2	25-00
OF Y 3		JONES	4/1/83	10	300-00
4		GREEN	22/2/83	20	500-0

```
        0       1        2        3       4
```

VALUES OF X

Inefficient DIM Statements
The reason for the nine blank elements is that DIM
A$(4,4) actually sets up an array A$ with a size of 5
by 5 because the first element is at position X=0,Y=0.
This fact should be taken into account if a large
number of small arrays are to be used because the
reserved, but unused, storage space will be denied to
the program. In this case, 9 of the 25 elements are not
being used, that is 36 per cent, but for an array
dimensioned as (2,2), there will be 5 out of 9 unused
locations - nearly 56 per cent wastage. There is, as
always, an alternative approach and that is to replace
lines 20, 30 and 40 by

```
20 DIM A$(3,3)
30 FOR Y=0 TO 3
40 FOR X=0 TO 3
```

However, it is unusual to start counting at zero and
this alternative may not be attractive to many people.
For larger arrays, say 100 by 100, the use of DIM
A$(100,100) and FOR...NEXT loops with values of 1 to
100 would result in 201 out of 10201 elements not being
used, that is less than 2 per cent wastage.
    Lines 110 to 170 use the same arrangement of
FOR...NEXT loops again but, in this case, a PRINT
statement replaces the former READ statement. The
result is that the array A$ is accessed, element by
element, and the value obtained is printed on a new
line. Thus, as X increases from 1 to 4, with Y=1, the
four separate items in line 180, now stored in the
array, will be printed as a record. For each value of
Y, line 120 will be obeyed and the result will be a
blank line between each of the four records.
    Notice that the four DATA statements include spaces
before each comma in order that the correct format is
obtained - the same technique was used in listing 2.1.
Thus, when the program is RUN, it will be seen that, as

stated previously, the lack of a RECORD structure in the language used by the BBC micro does not prevent the use of RECORDS in the processing of data.

Some Criticisms of the Program

The program in listing 2.2 would not make a great deal of sense without the accompanying explanation. Firstly, there are no REM statements and secondly, without a knowledge of graph terminology, the use of X and Y for the horizontal and vertical positioning of the array elements will not have much meaning. It would be much better if the program variables, such as X and Y, could be replaced by meaningful phrases using ordinary words from the English language.

A third, and no less important, criticism of the program is that if it was required to deal with fifteen records, each with ten fields, the program would need to be written again. Rewriting will be necessary whenever the number of fields and/or records change. To accommodate changing requirements by the user the program would probably grow in a very haphazard way, possibly understood only by the writer and then only for a short time unless it contained a large number of REM statements.

Overcoming the Criticisms

The program can be considered as two separate parts, that is one part to set up the array with items from the DATA statements and a second part to print the contents of that array. The requirement can be stated as follows

1. Set up the array
2. Print the contents of the array.

Taking requirement 1, this can be broken down into two further requirements, stated as

1.1 Dimension the array
1.2 Set up the array.

Similarly, requirement 2 can be separated into two parts, that is

2.1 Print the explanatory heading
2.2 Print the contents of the array as records.

Using Procedures

The original design has been refined to a level where each of the four separate parts is self-contained and, therefore, can be changed without having any effect on the other parts. The four parts can be written as PROCedures (see the User Guide) and thus the program becomes

```
10 PROCinitialise
20 PROCset_up_array
30 PROCprint_heading
40 PROCprint_records
50 DATA BLOGGS,14/1/83,5,75-00
60 DATA SMITH,20/12/82,2,25-00
70 DATA JONES,4/1/83,10,300-00
80 DATA GREEN,22/2/83,20,500-00
90 END
```

This program will not RUN however because the PROCedures have not been defined. DEFining the PROCedures will follow from line 100.

Note that procedure names consist of sensible words that are joined by what looks like a hyphen which has been lowered to the letter line. It is, in fact, the symbol that appears on the pound sign key which is just above the RETURN key and will appear as a hyphen on the screen.

Defining Procedures

The job of defining the procedures can now begin. PROCinitialise must clear the screen and dimension the array and, looking ahead to future work, it will be advantageous to input the array dimensions from the keyboard. To make the micro seem less remote from the user, a question will be asked by it such as "How many fields in each record?". This is, in BASIC, PRINT"How many fields in each record". There is no need to include the question mark because this is generated by the micro in response to the INPUT statement which follows, that is INPUT number_of_fields.

To illustrate another input method, the required quantity of records will be obtained using the following.

```
INPUT"How many records ",number_of_records
```

Again, the question mark is produced by the INPUT statement which contains the question. The size of the array is now given by "number_of_fields" and "number_of_records" and the DIM statement must use these new names. The complete procedure, starting at line 100, is now given.

```
100 DEFPROCinitialise
110 CLS
120 PRINT"How many fields in each record"
130 INPUT number_of_fields
140 INPUT"How many records ",number_of_records
150 DIM R$(number_of_fields,number_of_records)
160 ENDPROC
```

The next procedure is required to put the DATA items into the array and this was done in the previous program by using nested FOR...NEXT loops. Apart from using the new names and replacing X and Y by "field" and "record" respectively, the program segment is no different - it is given below.

```
170 DEFPROCset_up_array
180 FOR record=1 TO number_of_records
190   FOR field=1 TO number_of_fields
200     READ R$(field,record)
210     NEXT field
220   NEXT record
230 ENDPROC
```

The next procedure hardly merits that name but to maintain the design philosophy it will be defined as follows

```
240 DEFPROCheading
250 PRINT"EXAMPLE OF FOUR RECORDS"
260 ENDPROC
```

The final procedure, that for printing the array contents, will not use nested FOR...NEXT loops but, instead, nested REPEAT...UNTIL loops - see below.

```
270 DEFPROCprint_records
280 record=1
290 REPEAT
300   PRINT
310   field=1
320   REPEAT:PRINT R$(field,record)
330     field=field+1
340     UNTIL field=number_of_fields+1
350   record=record+1
360   UNTIL record=number_of_records+1
370 ENDPROC
```

Indentation, using LISTO7, indicates that there are two levels of nesting in the procedure. The inner loop, lines 320, 330 and 340, will cause the array to be accessed element by element, using the values given by "field" and "record", followed by the printing of that element. Line 320 actually contains two commands which are separated by a colon. This emphasises the main activity which is being repeated, the printing of the array contents. Another advantage is that the listing of the program will not take so many lines on the screen or paper.

The inner loop will terminate when the condition "field=number_of_fields+1" is reached. Thus, if "number_of_fields" is equal to 4, then the loop ends when "field" reaches the value 5. This may seem a rather strange arrangement but it is necessary because the termination condition cannot be checked until after the activity of the loop has been carried out. If the condition was "field=number_of_fields", then only 3 of the 4 fields would be printed. The value of "field" is incremented after each printing of an element - line 330.

When the inner loop ends, the program obeys line 350 which increments the value of "record". The outer loop will end when the UNTIL condition - line 360 - is satisfied but this will not happen before the required number of records has been printed. The comments regarding the inner loop format apply to the outer loop as well.

The complete program is given in listing 2.3 below (L2.3 on the program cassette).

LISTING 2.3
```
 10 PROCinitialise
 20 PROCset_up_array
 30 PROCprint_heading
 40 PROCprint_records
 50 DATA BLOGGS,14/1/83,5,75-00
 60 DATA SMITH,20/12/82,2,25-00
 70 DATA JONES,4/1/83,10,300-00
 80 DATA GREEN,22/2/83,20,500-00
 90 END
 95
100 DEFPROCinitialise
110 CLS
120 PRINT"How many fields in each record"
130 INPUT number_of_fields
140 INPUT"How many records ",number_of_records
150 DIM R$(number_of_fields,number_of_records)
160 ENDPROC
165
```

```
170 DEFPROCset_up_array
180 FOR record=1 TO number_of_records
190   FOR field=1 TO number_of_fields
200     READ R$(field,record)
210     NEXT field
220   NEXT record
230 ENDPROC
235
240 DEFPROCprint_heading
250 PRINT"EXAMPLE OF FOUR RECORDS"
260 ENDPROC
265
270 DEFPROCprint_records
280 record=1
290 REPEAT
300   PRINT
310   field=1
320   REPEAT:PRINT R$(field,record)
330     field=field+1
340     UNTIL field=number_of_fields+1
350   record=record+1
360   UNTIL record=number_of_records+1
370 ENDPROC
```

The use of lines 95, 165 and 235 as separators allows the four procedures to be clearly identified and is a further aid to understanding what a program does. Once again it must be stressed that this feature, like indentation, does not make the program any more efficient, it only helps those who need to follow how the program works.

RUNning the program with values of 4 being input in response to the two question mark prompts will result in the four records being printed in a column format, as before.

The program given in listing 2.3 is called a "structured program" because it consists of a number of PROCedure calls, lines 10 to 40 inclusive, usually called the "main" section. Each procedure is self-contained and was developed using the "top-down-design" method of successive refinement dealt with peviously. Each procedure can be developed and debugged, or made to work correctly, separately and can then become part of a procedure library to be used in future programs. As each procedure is developed satisfactorily, it is included in the remaining section of the program which contains the defined procedures.

Although it was not necessary in the program, it is possible for one procedure to call other procedures. There is, of course, much more to structured programming than has been covered in this introductory

treatment and, as the book progresses, other features
be dealt with.

Self-test 2.3
1. Referring to the program in listing 2.3, what will
be the effect of keying in the following values in
response to the questions appearing on the screen? Try
to work out the answers before running the program.

	FIELDS	RECORDS
(a)	3	4
(b)	2	6
(c)	16	1
(d)	1	16

2. From the results of part 1, it should be possible to
state what the results of the following responses will
be before the program is run.

	FIELDS	RECORDS
(a)	4	5
(b)	6	4
(c)	1	17
(d)	3	6

3. The actual results to part 1 should indicate that
the program can be made to give meaningless output. Try
to formulate a constructive criticism of the program
concept.

3 Creating Files

Now that a method of creating a fixed length file of records has been demonstrated, consideration will be given to the problem of creating a file whose length is variable. Any file will start with zero contents, will grow as records are added to it and shrink as records are deleted from it. It would be unusual if records came into existence in alphabetical order but that will be a probable requirement for the file.

The searching of a file for records containing certain features is a common requirement and this must be catered for. Users must also be able to amend or delete an existing record should the need arise. An example will be developed in which these and other requirements are catered for.

The example used will be for a file of employee records that holds details of employees including such information as employee number, department number, date of starting employment, etc. The number of attributes for the employee record will be limited in order to keep the example to a reasonable size. The principle to be developed is, however, capable of extension to any file handling requirement.

The fast processing of data that is required can only be achieved if the data is dealt with in the micro's memory and thus an array will be set up to hold the records as they are created. When all the initial records for the file exist, the array will be stored on tape.

For development purposes only, the number of records will be limited to 20. The real limit on file size is governed by the fact that the micro's memory holds the file during processing and thus the memory capacity available will determine the total number of characters in the file. As the result of multiplying the number of characters in a record by the number of records in the file cannot be greater than that total number of characters, it will be obvious that as the size of a record increases, so the number of records in a file must decrease.

In practice, files created in this manner can hold many records provided that the records are not too large. A way of calculating the limit will be given later.

Now that the problem has been defined, the first level in the top-down-design is

1. Set up the file in memory
2. Save the file

Refining this design will give

1.1 Initialise all variables
1.2 Put dummy data into all records on the file
1.3 Put actual data into records
2.1 Display the file size message
2.2 Request the file name
2.3 Store the file
2.4 Inform the user that the file has been stored

Before item 1.2 can be dealt with, it will be necessary to specify the field details for a record and these are as follows.

Field No.	Field Identifier	Type	Field Length
1	Employee No.	Numeric	3
2	Surname	String	16
3	Initials	String	2
4	Sex	String	1
5	Date of Birth	Numeric	6
6	Department No.	Numeric	2
7	Employed Since	Numeric	6
8	Job Code	Numeric	2
9	Salary	Numeric	5

This information will be used when creating and updating records via the screen, and to produce a screen format that is condensed without being misleading may require that the information is presented differently.

Level 1.2 can now be refined to give

1.2.1 Define dummy record details
1.2.2 Repeat
1.2.3 Place dummy data on a record
1.2.4 Until all records are initialised

Refining level 1.3 will produce

1.3.1 Initialise keyboard for data entry
1.3.2 Repeat
1.3.3 Input actual data
1.3.4 Until all data is on record

Consideration of level 1.2.1 will reveal that the dummy data for each field can be treated separately from the field names. This result arises from the realisation that there is no need to store the field name details on the file because they are only relevant to the presentation of records to users. Thus a further refinement of level 1.2.1 will give

1.2.1.1 Define the field names
1.2.1.2 Define the initial field values

To input the actual record data, it will be necessary to present the user with a picture of the record, complete with dummy data, on the screen. Each data field should be presented in such a way that the user is guided towards the correct response and if an incorrect data entry is made, the fact must be indicated to the user. An error in data entry must not have catastrophic results on the data entered previously and this must be catered for in the program.
It is important to maintain the confidence of users and thus, when all data for a record has been entered it must be presented for a visual check. Only when the user is satisfied with the contents of a record should that record be passed into the file. Note that the file is still held in the micro´s memory at this stage.
This process is repeated for all the records are to be created initially and this leads to the following refinement of level 1.3.3

1.3.3.1 Display dummy record on the screen
1.3.3.2 Repeat
1.3.3.3 Enter the field data
1.3.3.4 Verify the data visually
1.3.3.5 Store the record
1.3.3.6 Until all the records are created

The validation of a data entry must recognise the type of character, whether or not the correct quantity of such characters has been entered, whether or not the range of a numeric entry has been exceeded and so on. In addition, certain keys must be excluded from entry, either for formatting reasons or to prevent corruption of the records already entered. An example of the latter is the ESCAPE key which could be pressed in mistake for the ´1´ key.

Taking these requirements into account allows the following refinement of level 1.3.3.3

1.3.3.3.1 Repeat
1.3.3.3.2 Input a character
1.3.3.3.3 Validate the character
1.3.3.3.4 Until the field data is valid

Self-test 3.1
To demonstrate an understanding of the above refining process, the reader should now construct a complete ordered list of all the refinements.

The model answer to Self-test 3.1 shows that the refinements provide enough information for the file creation program to be written. It may be found that further refinement is necessary to cater for new requirements but this should not be difficult to achieve.

Procedures used in the Main Program
The main program contains five procedures, these being

                PROCdefine_field_names
                PROCdefine_initial_values
                PROCinitialise_file
                PROCcreate_record
                PROCsave_file.

The procedures are listed in the same order as that in which they will be used in the program. There are, of course, commands in the main program and the reason for these will become apparent as the procedures are defined. Readers should not try to enter the procedures as separate programs - they are meant to be used by the main program and will not necessarily produce useful output if used differently.

PROCdefine_field_names
This procedure, given in listing 3.1, sets up an array of nine string variables although the DIM statement is DIMD$(8) - the reason for this was explained in chapter 2. The names that are defined will be displayed on the screen whenever a record is created, examined or updated and must be free of ambiguity. They should also guide the user to make the correct response and this is why some field names include bracketed characters. Only

line 600 needs explanation. The name ´JOINED´ replaces
the original ´EMPLOYED SINCE´ because that is too long
for the screen format. For the time being, the date of
joining the firm is required in reverse order because
procedures for sorting by date sequence are simpler
when the year digits, (YY), are given first. Later on,
in Self-test 3.3, further work is carried out to
overcome the obvious objection by readers to using two
different date formats in the same record. The reason
why reverse order is not used for line 580 will be
given later.

LISTING 3.1
```
520 DEFPROCdefine_field_names
530 DIMD$(8)
540 D$(0)="EMPLOYEE NO."
550 D$(1)="SURNAME"
560 D$(2)="INITIALS"
570 D$(3)="SEX (M/F)"
580 D$(4)="BORN (DDMMYY)"
590 D$(5)="DEPARTMENT NO."
600 D$(6)="JOINED (YYMMDD)"
610 D$(7)="JOB CODE"
620 D$(8)="SALARY (POUNDS)"
630 ENDPROC
```

PROCdefine_initial_values
Listing 3.2 gives the procedure that sets up another
nine string variable array to hold strings of ´9´ or
´A´ characters. A string of ´9´ characters is used to
emphasise the fact that the required data entry is
numeric. The number of ´9´ characters will indicate
either the maximum length of the numeric string
required for that field or the maximum length that the
field can accept. For example, a date is required as
six digits but ´JOB CODE´ can be one or two digits in
length.
   At this point, readers should note that string
variables cannot be treated in the same way as numeric
variables. For example,

```
A=12
B=34
PRINT A+B
```

will produce the value 46, that is, the arithmetic sum
of 12 and 34.

However

```
A$="12"
B$="34"
PRINT A$+B$
PRINT B$+A$
```

will produce 1234 and 3412 respectively. It is possible to combine alphabetic and numeric strings as in the following example

```
A$="I am"
B$=" 21"
PRINT A$+B$
```

will give ´I am 21´ but

```
A$="I am"
B$=" 21"
C$="1"
PRINT A$+B$+C$
```

will produce ´I am 211´ and not, as might be expected, ´I am 22´. The User Guide deals with this subject more fully.

Of the three alphabetic strings, that in line 370 requires an entry of either ´F´ or ´M´; the other two must have at least one character with a limit of two characters for ´INITIALS´ and of sixteen characters for ´SURNAME´.

LISTING 3.2
```
320 DEFPROCdefine_initial_values
330 DIMI$(8)
340 I$(0)="999"
350 I$(1)="AAAAAAAAAAAAAAAA"
360 I$(2)="AA"
370 I$(3)="A"
380 I$(4)="999999"
390 I$(5)="99"
400 I$(6)="999999"
410 I$(7)="99"
420 I$(8)="99999"
430 ENDPROC
```

PROCinitialise_file
Listing 3.3 is for a procedure to set up an 8 by 19 array which will hold twenty columns, each with nine rows. (Remember that in this example there will be a maximum of twenty records.) There are two nested

FOR...NEXT loops with the inner loop, lines 470 to 490, allocating a string variable, I$(N%), to the same row in each of the twenty columns in turn. The outer loop wiil select each one of the nine rows in turn.

Thus when N%=3, each column will have the string ´A´ allocated to its fourth row. Note that the resident integer variables E% and N% are used to increase the speed of setting up the array and, although speed is not important in this particular part of the program, the adoption of this technique will pay dividends later.

LISTING 3.3

```
440 DEFPROCinitialise_file
450 DIME$(8,19)
460 FOR N%=0 TO 8
470 FOR E%=0 TO 19
480 E$(N%,E%)=I$(N%)
490 NEXT
500 NEXT
510 ENDPROC
```

PROCcreate_record
This is a procedure that calls up another procedure called PROCupdate_attributes which passes a parameter, R%, from the parent procedure. R% must be set to the value zero in the main program and it identifies a particular record position in the file. Note, however, that R% does NOT indicate the order of the contents of the file. For example, employees will be entered on the file as they accept an offer of employment but this will not mean that the file is in alphabetical order. As each record is updated so the value of R% is incremented.

Another integer variable, record%, is incremented after updating the record and this also must be set to value zero in the main program. The purpose of this variable is to keep a running total of the number of records in the file. It might be thought that both the above functions could be carried out by one variable but, as line 180 reveals, the two values are unequal at the end of the procedure. The process of updating a fresh record will continue until an EMPLOYEE NO. entry of ´999´ is made. This will set a variable, file_end, to TRUE and thus satisfy the UNTIL statement in line 170 which then terminates the procedure. Before this is done, however, record% is decremented in line 180. The variable, file_end, must be set to FALSE in the main program.

```
LISTING 3.4
120 DEFPROCcreate_record
130 REPEAT
140 PROCupdate_attributes(R%)
150 record%=record%+1
160 R%=R%+1
170 UNTIL file_end=TRUE
180 record%=record%-1
190 ENDPROC
```

PROCsave_file

The main part of this procedure will deal with the
saving of the file and is based on the routine given in
chapter 1, listing 1.1. Instead of using NUMBER to
indicate the length of the file, record% is used. The
data that is put onto the file is obtained from the
array that was built in the procedure
PROCcreate_record, as described above.

Two local variables, A$ and N$, are defined before
giving information to the user and asking whether or
not the file is to be saved. The affirmative response
can be either ´Y´ or ´y´ but any other key depression
will be taken as a negative response - see line 1890.
The user must give a name to the file if it is to be
saved and then the saving routine, lines 1920 to 1990,
follows. Finally, a message is given to the user by
line 2010. The purpose of PRINT´´, for example, is to
give a three-line spacing between printed statements on
the screen.

```
LISTING 3.5
1780 DEFPROCsave_file
1790 LOCAL A$,N$
1800 PRINTTAB(12,2);"SAVING THE FILE"
1810 PRINTTAB(12,3);"---------------"
1820 PRINT´
1830 PRINT"There are ";record%;" records on the file"
1840 PRINT"that has been created."
1850 PRINT´´
1860 PRINT"Is the file to be saved? (Y/N)",
1870 A$=GET$
1880 PRINT´´
1890 IF A$="Y" OR A$="y" THEN 1900 ELSE 2020
1900 PRINT"Please input the name of the file"
1910 INPUT"that is to be saved "N$
1920 FILE=OPENOUT(N$)
1930 PRINT#FILE,record%
1940 FOR V%=0 TO record%-1
1950 FOR N%=0 TO 8
1960 PRINT#FILE,E$(N%,V%)
1970 NEXT
```

```
1980 NEXT
1990 CLOSE#FILE
2000 PRINT´´
2010 PRINT"The file ";N$;" has been saved"
2020 ENDPROC
```

The Main Program

As will be seen from listing 3.6, this is very short
for the amount of work that is being done and the
reason for this is the extensive use of procedures. The
ordering of the commands in lines 50,60 and 70 is
unimportant but the procedure in line 40 cannot be
placed before that in line 30. Similarly, the procedure
in line 100 must be carried out after that in line 80
but PROCdefine_field_names can be placed anywhere
before line 80. The order which is used, however,
results from the systematic refining process for the
design of the program.

As the program is extended to give more facilities
to the user so the new procedures will be inserted into
the main program. There is, of course, no reason why a
procedure should not be called into use more than once
and this is what takes place within
PROCupdate_attributes.

```
LISTING 3.6
  10 CLS
  20 PROCdefine_field_names
  30 PROCdefine_initial_values
  40 PROCinitialise_file
  50 R%=0
  60 file_end=FALSE
  70 record%=0
  80 PROCcreate_record
  90 CLS
 100 PROCsave_file
 110 END
```

PROCupdate_attributes(R%)

This is the longest procedure used so far, but it is
not as complicated as a cursory glance at listing 3.7
might imply. There are, in fact, nine similar routines
which deal successively with the nine fields of a
record. Each routine starts with a procedure,
PROCdisplay_record(R%), which will display on the
screen a copy of the record numbered R%. This is
followed by two staements which add to the screen
display a request regarding the field with the name
given by D$(number). See for example, lines 690, 700
and 710. Notice the use of TAB statements to maintain
the presentation of the record on the screen.

The next statement will assign to a string variable
such as ´employee_no$´ and ´born$´ the result of
carrying out a function called FNenter_data. Functions
differ from procedures in that they return a value to
the program which uses them, whereas procedures do not.
Certain tests are carried out on the string which is
returned by the function in addition to those that are
performed by the function itself. It is these tests
that constitute the differences between the nine
routines. After the tests, an assignment of the
returned string to the array, E$, is made and this will
cause the string of ´9´ or ´A´ characters that was
inserted by PROCinitialise_file to be replaced by the
data input from the keyboard.

The tests on the returned string will now be
examined. Line 730 will cause the variable file_end to
be set to TRUE if ´999´ is input for EMPLOYEE NO. and
the procedure is then terminated - see lines 730 and
740. Lines 750 to 820 will ensure that if ´5´ is
entered, the record will hold ´005´. Similarly, if ´39´
is entered, this will be stored on the record as ´039´.
This result is obtained by using the LEN command which
counts the number of characters in the string returned
by the function. In line 750 the VAL command will
ensure that EMPLOYEE NO. is at least ´1´.

The next field entry is for SURNAME and the only
test carried out by the procedure is to ensure that at
least one alphabetic character has been entered as the
surname.

Line 1040 tests the returned string to ensure that
only ´F´ or ´M´ is accepted for SEX. Any other letter
will cause a return to the entry routine after a short
beep has been given by the micro - this is produced by
the VDU7 command in line 1050.

The BORN field entry is tested for six numeric
characters and a return to the entry routine will occur
UNTIL the string LENgth is six. This will be satisfied,
as the program presently exists, by entering six zeros
and this is obviously unacceptable. A procedure for
validating a date will be necessary to overcome this
problem and this will be dealt with later.

The next field entry is for DEPARTMENT NO. and the
only test presently included is that a numeric
character is entered; this could be one or two zeros
and these values are not excluded because they will be
used later to determine those staff who are
extra-departmental and to grade them.

The field entry for JOINED is dealt with next and
although the date is requested as ´YYMMDD´ there is no
test to ensure that this request has been complied
with. Examination of the two date entry routines will

reveal that they are identical. Again, future work will overcome this deficiency.

The field entry for JOB is tested only for the existence of one or two numeric characters, including zero. Again, this is a deliberate ploy and will be explained later.

The last tested entry is for SALARY and ensures that the salary input is at least 3500 - see line 1450. The upper limit is set by the string defined in PROCdefine_initial_values.

Finally, the screen displays the full record and a message requesting verification by the user of the details. The response, line 1510, can be ´Y´ or ´y´ and if either of these letters is input, the procedure is terminated. If not, the complete record, in this example of a record creation routine, has to be input again.

Two items that require explanation are in lines 650, 660, 1520 and 1530. The first two are to disable the cursor edit keys and the ESCAPE key respectively and the last two are to reverse these effects. Thus, during data entry these keys have no effect; this is not a complete precaution, however, and further safeguards are included in the data entry routine described later.

```
LISTING 3.7
  640 DEFPROCupdate_attributes(R%)
  650 *FX4,1
  660 *FX229,1
  670 LOCAL A$
  680 CLS
  690 PROCdisplay_record(R%)
  700 PRINTTAB(13,22);"Please input"
  710 PRINTTAB(1,24);D$(0)
  720 employee_no$=FNenter_data(22,23,3,"N")
  730 IF employee_no$="999" THEN file_end=TRUE ELSE 750
  740 GOTO 1520
  750 IF VAL(employee_no$)>=1 THEN 760 ELSE 720
  760 IF LEN(employee_no$)=3 THEN 820
  770 IF LEN(employee_no$)=2 THEN 800
  780 E$(0,R%)="00"+employee_no$
  790 GOTO 830
  800 E$(0,R%)="0"+employee_no$
  810 GOTO 830
  820 E$(0,R%)=employee_no$
  830 CLS
  840 PROCdisplay_record(R%)
  850 PRINTTAB(13,22);"Please input"
  860 PRINTTAB(1,24);D$(1)
  870 REPEAT
  880 surname$=FNenter_data(22,23,16,"S")
```

```
 890 UNTIL NOT NIL
 900 E$(1,R%)=surname$
 910 CLS
 920 PROCdisplay_record(R%)
 930 PRINTTAB(13,22);"Please input"
 940 PRINTTAB(1,24);D$(2)
 950 REPEAT
 960 initials$=FNenter_data(22,23,2,"S")
 970 UNTIL NOT NIL
 980 E$(2,R%)=initials$
 990 CLS
1000 PROCdisplay_record(R%)
1010 PRINTTAB(13,22);"Please input"
1020 PRINTTAB(1,24);D$(3)
1030 sex$=FNenter_data(22,23,1,"S")
1040 IF sex$="M" OR sex$="F" THEN 1070
1050 VDU7
1060 GOTO 1030
1070 E$(3,R%)=sex$
1080 CLS
1090 PROCdisplay_record(R%)
1100 PRINTTAB(13,22);"Please input"
1110 PRINTTAB(1,24);D$(4)
1120 REPEAT
1130 born$=FNenter_data(22,23,6,"N")
1140 UNTIL LEN(born$)=6
1150 E$(4,R%)=born$
1160 CLS
1170 PROCdisplay_record(R%)
1180 PRINTTAB(13,22);"Please input"
1190 PRINTTAB(1,24);D$(5)
1200 REPEAT
1210 dept$=FNenter_data(22,23,2,"N")
1220 UNTIL NOT NIL
1230 E$(5,R%)=dept$
1240 CLS
1250 PROCdisplay_record(R%)
1260 PRINTTAB(13,22);"Please input"
1270 PRINTTAB(1,24);D$(6)
1280 REPEAT
1290 joined$=FNenter_data(22,23,6,"N")
1300 UNTIL LEN(joined$)=6
1310 E$(6,R%)=joined$
1320 CLS
1330 PROCdisplay_record(R%)
1340 PRINTTAB(13,22);"Please input"
1350 PRINTTAB(1,24);D$(7)
1360 REPEAT
1370 job$=FNenter_data(22,23,2,"N")
1380 UNTIL NOT NIL
1390 E$(7,R%)=job$
```

```
1400 CLS
1410 PROCdisplay_record(R%)
1420 PRINTTAB(13,22);"Please input"
1430 PRINTTAB(1,24);D$(8)
1440 salary$=FNenter_data(22,23,5,"N")
1450 IF VAL(salary$)<3500 THEN 1440
1460 E$(8,R%)=salary$
1470 CLS
1480 PROCdisplay_record(R%)
1490 PRINTTAB(6,22);"Are details correct? (Y/N)"
1500 A$=GET$
1510 IF A$="Y" OR A$="y" THEN 1520 ELSE 640
1520 *FX4,0
1530 *FX229,0
1540 ENDPROC
```

FNenter_data(across%,down%,size%,S_N$)

Listing 3.8 is for the data entry routine which is defined as a function. Four parameters are passed to the function by PROCupdate_attributes(R%) and line 720, for example, in listing 3.7 gives a typical occurrence. The first number, 22, is the value of ´across%´ and the second is the value of ´down%´.

In line 1580 of listing 3.8, the two values are used in the TAB statement to position the first character input as a field entry. The purpose of ´STRING$(size%," ")´ is to set the maximum size of the entered string to the value ´size%´. Thus for line 720, the maximum length of the entered string is 3.

The purpose of adding this string to STRING$(size%,CHR$(127)), known as concatenating, is to move the cursor back to the original TAB position. 127 is the code for backspace and delete.

There are three local variables, line 1560, and the first of these is used to hold the input character – see line 1610. In line 1620, if the input character is ´backspace and delete´ then line 1720 is obeyed. This will check if input$ is empty and, if so, make the micro give a short beep and then prepare to accept a further character. If not, the value of the last local variable, length, is decremented to obtain the correct character count. The new value of length is then used to modify the contents of input$, line 1740, before deleting the last character on the screen and then returning to accept a further character – line 1610.

Examining line 1630, if the input character is the code for ´start of line´, produced by pressing the RETURN key, then the next instruction is taken from line 1760. The logical variable NIL can take one of two values, that is 0 and -1, and these values are the same as those given by the functions FALSE and TRUE respectively. Any meaningful name can be given to the logical variable provided that the usual rules for variable names are observed. Thus if NIL has been assigned the value of 0, then NIL is FALSE, or untrue. Conversely, if the value of NIL is -1, then NIL is TRUE.

Some examples of the use of logical variables may be of value in the understanding of the use of NIL in this segment of program. The statement PRINT 7=7 will produce ´-1´ on the screen whereas PRINT 7=8 will produce ´0´. Similarly

```
CORRECT=(7=7):PRINT CORRECT will produce ´-1´ and
CORRECT=(7=8):PRINT CORRECT will produce ´0´
```

Here, the logical variable is called CORRECT and using 7=7 will set it to TRUE but 7=8 is obviously incorrect and will thus set it to FALSE. This variable will now be used to illustrate other features of TRUE and FALSE.

Running the program

```
10 CORRECT=(7=7)
20 PRINT CORRECT
30 IF CORRECT=FALSE THEN 50
40 PRINT "TRUE":GOTO 60
50 PRINT "FALSE"
60 END
```

will produce ´-1´ and ´TRUE´ on the screen. Replacing 7=7 by 7=8 will, as probably expected, produce ´0´ and ´FALSE´. Note that the ´(´ and ´)´ in line 10 are not essential but aid in the comprehension.

Rewriting line 30 as ´IF CORRECT=0 THEN 50´ and RUNning with 7=7 will again produce ´-1´ and ´TRUE´ because FALSE has the value 0. Check that using 7=8 produces ´0´ and ´FALSE´ as required. If line 30 is now rewritten as ´IF CORRECT THEN 50´ and the program RUN with 7=7, an anomaly is produced because the screen displays ´-1´, which is correct, and ´FALSE´ which is incorrect. The reason is that line 30 is interpreted as ´IF CORRECT (=TRUE) THEN 50´ and the screen display is, therefore, correct. Using 7=8 will produce ´0´ and ´TRUE´, as should be expected in these circumstances.

As this format of line 30 is more compact than the previous versions, and therefore more desirable, it is necessary to alter lines 40 and 50 to remove the anomaly. Replacing line 40 with ´PRINT"FALSE":GOTO 60´ and line 50 with PRINT"TRUE" will produce the desired result. Alternatively, altering line 30 to ´IF NOT CORRECT THEN 50´ will give the correct display, but this format is not so compact.

In line 1760, the logical variable NIL will be set to 0 if ´length´ equals 1 or more, that is NIL is FALSE, and set to -1 otherwise. The meaning of line 1760 is thus: NIL is set to TRUE if ´length´ is equal to 0. The value of NIL is tested in some sections of the parent procedure to ensure that a null, that is empty, string is not accepted. Following on, line 1770 passes the result of the function to the parent procedure.

Line 1570 sets the initial value of length to zero and the initial contents of input$ to the null string. In line 1690 the value of length is incremented every time an input character is accepted as correct and thus line 1640 will cause a beep to be produced if an attempt is made to exceed the number of characters set by size%.

The last of the parameters passed to the function, S_N$, is used in lines 1650 to 1670 to prevent the entry of certain keys. Thus in line 1660 only letters will be accepted and in line 1670 only numbers will be accepted. A beep will be produced for unacceptable entries.

Finally, when all validity checks have been satisfied, the input character is added to input$, length is incremented and the character is printed on the screen.

```
LISTING 3.8
1550 DEFFNenter_data(across%,down%,size%,S_N$)
1560 LOCAL char$,length,input$
1570 length=0:input$=""
1580 PRINTTAB(across%,down%);STRING$(size%," ")
     +STRING$(size%,CHR$(127));
1590 GOTO1610
1600 VDU7
1610 char$=GET$
1620 IFchar$=CHR$(127)THEN1720
1630 IFchar$=CHR$(13)THEN1760
1640 IFlength=size%THEN1600
1650 IFS_N$<>"S"THEN1670
1660 IFchar$<CHR$(65) OR char$>CHR$(90)THEN
     1600ELSE1680
1670 IFchar$<CHR$(48) OR char$>CHR$(57)
     THEN1600
1680 input$=input$+char$
1690 length=length+1
1700 PRINTchar$;
1710 GOTO1610
1720 IFinput$=""THEN1600
1730 length=length-1
1740 input$=LEFT$(input$,length)
1750 GOTO1700
```

```
1760 NIL=(length=0)
1770 =input$
```

PROCdisplay_record(R%)

This is a procedure called in PROCupdate_attributes(R%) and it will display on the screen the up to date contents of location R% of the array E$. A heading is given by line 210 for a record called R%+1, the reason for this value being that R% starts at zero but the first record is numbered one.

All the remaining display lines have the format Field Number, Field Name, Field Value and are positioned by the TAB statements.

LISTING 3.9
```
200 DEFPROCdisplay_record(R%)
210 PRINTTAB(8,2);"** EMPLOYEE RECORD ";R%+1;" **"
220 PRINTTAB(1,4);"1";TAB(3,4);D$(0);TAB(22,4);E$(0,R%)
230 PRINTTAB(1,6);"2";TAB(3,6);D$(1);TAB(22,6);E$(1,R%)
240 PRINTTAB(1,8);"3";TAB(3,8);D$(2);TAB(22,8);E$(2,R%)
250 PRINTTAB(1,10);"4";TAB(3,10);D$(3);TAB(22,10);
    E$(3,R%)
260 PRINTTAB(1,12);"5";TAB(3,12);D$(4);TAB(22,12);
    E$(4,R%)
270 PRINTTAB(1,14);"6";TAB(3,14);D$(5);TAB(22,14);
    E$(5,R%)
280 PRINTTAB(1,16);"7";TAB(3,16);D$(6);TAB(22,16);
    E$(6,R%)
290 PRINTTAB(1,18);"8";TAB(3,18);D$(7);TAB(22,18);
    E$(7,R%)
300 PRINTTAB(1,20);"9";TAB(3,20);D$(8);TAB(22,20);
    E$(8,R%)
310 ENDPROC
```

This chapter has covered a number of different techniques used in setting up files but, as mentioned previously, some requirements were left out deliberately. Before dealing with these, it is suggested that the complete program be loaded and RUN. Those readers using the program cassette will notice that program L3 uses the technique of putting more than one statement on a line so as to reduce the number of lines and thus increase operating speed and reduce memory use. This procedure must be carried out with care, however, as some statements cannot be separated by colons and need a different line. The tape version should be used as an example of what can be done.

The following data should be used when the program is executed so that future development work can be checked against the expected results. Remember to use another tape for filing the data, not the program tape. Note that although the symbol "/" is used as a separator for the three parts of the date in the following table, the dates should not be entered with separators.

FIELD NUMBERS								
1	2	3	4	5	6	7	8	9
122	CHARNOCK	DV	M	1/9/36	3	10/1/50	15	8500
61	BISHOPS	A	F	27/8/51	7	19/11/70	11	8950
337	HURRELL	FH	F	11/1/52	3	1/1/75	32	6000
412	MCGEE	JT	M	30/9/54	3	27/3/80	3	5100
3	ADAMS	B	F	14/12/37	2	1/12/51	19	11000
54	SMEE	H	M	27/7/30	12	7/9/45	15	11000
30	ZUBOVIC	RK	F	14/2/56	0	1/7/72	0	26000
185	DEREVE	A	F	2/6/59	3	9/7/74	32	6200
38	KETCHER	DL	F	29/2/48	2	1/7/62	3	5900
397	HUMPHRIES	N	M	18/12/64	7	21/11/80	11	7800
27	YARDLEY	RA	M	31/12/57	7	18/3/77	14	14500
943	YARDLEY	RK	F	19/3/43	12	14/10/70	32	6400
96	SMITH	AW	F	15/5/55	9	7/5/78	3	5350
42	SMITH	AW	M	10/10/50	13	15/12/66	15	6500

PROCcheck_date(date$)

One of the outstanding deficiencies in the program for setting up the file is that no check is made on the validity of entered dates. This is easily overcome by using a procedure that checks whether April, June, September and November have DD entries greater than thirty and whether, with the exception of February, the remaining months have DD entries greater than thirty-one. In the case of February, the DD entry must not be greater than twenty-eight unless the YY entry is for a leap year. The procedure is given in listing 3.10.

LISTING 3.10

```
4000 DEFPROCcheck_date(date$)
4010 date=TRUE
4020 D$=LEFT$(date$,2)
4030 IFD$<"01"THENdate=FALSE:GOTO4130
4040 Y$=RIGHT$(date$,2)
4050 M$=MID$(date$,3,2)
4060 IFM$>"12" OR M$<"01"THENdate=FALSE
     :GOTO4130
4070 IFM$="02"THEN4110
```

```
4080 IFM$="04" OR M$="06" OR M$="09" OR M$="11"
     THEN4100
4090 IFD$<"32"THEN4130ELSE date=FALSE
     :GOTO 4130
4100 IFD$<"31"THEN4130ELSE date=FALSE
     :GOTO 4130
4110 IFD$<"29"THEN4130
4120 IFVAL(Y$)MOD 4=0 AND D$="29"THEN 4130
     ELSE date=FALSE:GOTO4130
4130 ENDPROC
```

Some Comments on the Program

At several points in this chapter, reference has been made to a later explanation of the reason for some particular inclusion or omission of part of the program. The most obvious requirement is that the date-checking procedure given above should be incorporated. Load program L3 and add listing 3.10 starting at, say, line 800, and using the same compacting technique as that used in the program.

Self-test 3.2
The reader should now modify program L3 to include the procedure PROCcheck_date(date$) for use at both points in the program where a date entry is made. When the program has been fully modified, the modified version should be SAVEd - use a different tape from that containing the data file that was created previously.

Self-test 3.3
Obviously, to check that the modification works correctly it should be tested by using it to create a file containing the first two records in the data list given previously. If the modification works, the dates in each record will be presented in the correct order, that is DDMMYY for field 5 and YYMMDD for field 7. This now presents a further problem, however, in that field 7 specifies YYMMDD and if the date is entered in this order, the date checking procedure will, quite correctly, reject the entry.
    The reader should now attempt to modify the program to overcome this problem.

    The JOB CODE entry routine does not exclude the value ´00´. The reason for this is that such a value can be used to indicate, say, an executive or managerial post when a sorting of the file is being carried out.

The character checking routine accepts only upper case or capital letters for names and thus the name McGEE will not be accepted, as readers will have found out when entering the data for the test file. A modification to line 1660, listing 3.7, must be made if lower case letters are to be allowed.

Line 1510 of listing 3.7 checks the response to the question "Are details correct? (Y/N)". However, all responses other than "Y" or "y" are treated as negative. The response checking can be made more informative should this be desired by the user.

A similar situation exists in listing 3.5 in the checking of the response to the question in line 1860. If, owing to inexperience or haste, the key for "T","H" or "U" is pressed instead of "Y" then all the data recorded on the file will be lost. The obvious thing to do in order that such a catastrophe should not occur is to modify line 1890 so that the error is rendered harmless. A suggested modification is given below.

Change 1890 to

```
1890 IF A$="Y" OR A$="y" THEN 1900 ELSE IF
     answer=TRUE AND (A$="N" OR A$="n") THEN 2020
```

Add

```
1845 answer=FALSE
1895 answer=TRUE:PRINT"SAFETY CHECK!!!":PRINT:GOTO1860
```

This modification will ensure that if either the wrong key is pressed or the "N" or "n" key is pressed, the user will be given a chance to either correct the error or to confirm the negative response.

Listing 3.5, for example, contains in lines 1940 to 1960, two integer variables, V% and N%. This procedure, and others, will work correctly if the variables are not integer but as the programs should operate as quickly as possible, all variables should be integer in type.

In listing 3.7, a question is asked of the user in line 1490. If the response by the user is negative, the response check, line 1510, will return control to line 640 and the whole record must be input again. A modification by which the question and response can be given after each data entry is left to the reader to introduce if it is felt necessary. A return to the beginning of the faulty data entry would remove the need to enter the whole record again.

Finally, although the termination of data entry by an input of ´999´ for Employee No. is mentioned in the text, no reminder of this fact is given to the user of the program. It is important that such information is not kept from the user and a modification to line 710, listing 3.7, to include a reminder of the escape mechanism would solve the problem.

4 Sorting Files

As pointed out in chapter 2, a file of data is normally required in a sorted form. An author index in a library would be of little use if the cards were filed randomly. Similarly, a telephone directory would be valueless if all the entries were in telephone number order. Numerical ordering is necessary, of course, in a great many activities - imagine the problems that would be created if householders were allowed to choose their own house numbers! In some cases, however, ordering will be required on data that is a mixture of letters and numbers; lists of Premium Bond winning numbers provide a good example of this.

Assume that the following set of data is a list of addresses with the delivery ordering of street names represented by single letters

$$3C,4A,7B,1C,2D,4C,2B$$

A sorting of this data into an order that would allow easy distribution of mail would give

$$4A,2B,7B,1C,3C,4C,2D$$

A computer sorting procedure would use the fact that the various characters are given weighted codes or values and, for the BBC micro, these are listed on page 486 of the User Guide. This shows that numbers have lower code values than capital letters which, in turn, have lower code values than lower case letters.

The sorting procedures will compare the code values of two characters, and choose the character with, normally, the lowest value and that will give an ascending order both numerically and alphabetically. In the case of mixed characters such as in the example above, the value of the complete identifier, or key, is taken into account. Thus, although 3 is lower than 4, 4A is lower than 3C (and 2B and 2D).

The writing of sorting routines for computers has occupied many software writers for many hours, mostly in attempts to produce more efficient procedures, either from the point of view of sorting speed or of program length. Attempts to meet both criteria in one routine have so far met with little success and the compromise solutions produced can always be faulted from some particular point of view.

Operating speed can always be improved if the routine is written in machine code rather than, say, BASIC but the sorting routine to be described is written in BASIC in order that an easier understanding can be gained by the reader.

The sort routines given in data-processing books are usually based on the Quicksort, the Bubblesort or the Shellsort algorithm, or method. The fact that all are in common use shows that they each have certain attributes that are desirable for particular types of work.

The algorithm used in this book has the attributes that it is fast enough, even when written in BASIC, for most of the envisaged applications, the program does not require a large amount of memory and, in operation, it takes only one record's worth of memory over and above that required for the complete file being sorted. As the sorting proceeds, each record is taken from its incorrect position and then placed in its correct position in the file.

The routine is based on the "Heap Sort" algorithm designed by J.W.J. Williams. An understanding of the way in which the algorithm works will be gained by considering the result of running the program given in listing 4.1 (L4.1). Note that this is a demonstration program only and it is not in a form that could be used as a sorting routine in a data-processing program.

Before analysing the program, it should be LOADed and RUN. In response to the succession of ?´s which then appear on the screen, the following set of data items should be entered, one by one, with RETURN being pressed after each item

Q,W,E,R,T,Y,U,I,O,P

After the last item has been entered, the routine will sort the data by making fourteen comparisons on the ten data items. After each comparison, the set of data is printed together with the two columns identified as S% and E% - these will be explained later. The complete result, apart from the row numbers, will be the same as that which now follows

1	5	10	Q	W	E	R	T	Y	U	I	O	P
2	4	10	Q	W	E	R	T	Y	U	I	O	P
3	3	10	Q	W	E	R	T	Y	U	I	O	P
4	2	10	Q	W	Y	R	T	E	U	I	O	P
5	1	10	Q	W	Y	R	T	E	U	I	O	P
6	1	9	P	W	U	R	T	E	Q	I	O	Y
7	1	8	O	T	U	R	P	E	Q	I	W	Y
8	1	7	I	T	Q	R	P	E	O	U	W	Y
9	1	6	O	R	Q	I	P	E	T	U	W	Y
10	1	5	E	P	Q	I	O	R	T	U	W	Y
11	1	4	O	P	E	I	Q	R	T	U	W	Y
12	1	3	I	O	E	P	Q	R	T	U	W	Y
13	1	2	E	I	O	P	Q	R	T	U	W	Y
14	1	1	E	I	O	P	Q	R	T	U	W	Y

ROW   S%   E%   DATA

Examining the table of results will show that this has the original data in row 1 and the sorted data in row 14. Note that rows 1,2 and 3 are the same and also that row 13 is the same as row 14. Thus there is a total of three rows in which no change of order takes place. It will become apparent later that this duplication of rows (or, in reality, no change of order) is a feature of the particular routine being used.

As a result, like some others, this sorting routine has the disadvantage that there is no reduction in the number of comparisons when the entered data is nearly or completely sorted. Entering the following data will provide evidence of this fact

A,B,C,D,E,F,G,H,I,J

For this data, there are two rows in which there are no changes to the order of the data and readers can be excused for thinking that there should be fourteen rows in which no changes take place. The algorithm is not unique in this respect and some algorithms work very slowly when presented with sorted or nearly sorted data. Their advantage is that they work very fast with randomly filed data.

When the data is in complete reverse order, the number of changes is less than in the above example. Enter the following data

J,I,H,G,F,E,D,C,B,A

Examination of the resulting table shows that there are four rows in which no changes take place. Readers should now appreciate the fact that, regardless of the order of the original data, there will always be fourteen comparisons for ten data items because the number of comparisons is determined by the values of S% and E% which, in turn, depend on the value of T%, the total number of items to be sorted.

The Algorithm

This section deals with the way in which the algorithm works but it should be noted that an understanding of the method is not necessary in order to use it. Readers may, therefore, omit this section with impunity. Listing 4.1 is for the specially adapted demonstration version of the Heap Sort algorithm but it consists of the framework of the procedure that will be used for sorting a file of records.

```
LISTING 4.1
  5 T%=10:REM INPUT 10 STRINGS
 10 DIMA$(T%)
 20 FORI=1TOT%
 30 INPUTN$
 40 A$(I)=N$
 50 NEXT
 60 CLS:PRINT´´´´´
 70 S%=INT(T%/2)+1:E%=T%
 80 IFS%=1THEN100
 90 S%=S%-1:W$=A$(S%):GOTO160
100 W$=A$(E%):A$(E%)=A$(1):E%=E%-1
110 PRINTTAB(1);S%;TAB(4);E%;TAB(8);W$;" ";
120 FORI=2TOT%
130 PRINTA$(I);" ";
140 NEXT:PRINT
150 IFE%<>1THEN200ELSEA$(1)=W$:END
160 PRINTTAB(1);S%;TAB(4);E%;TAB(8);
170 FORI=1TOE%
180 PRINTA$(I);" ";
190 NEXT:PRINT
200 J%=S%
210 I%=J%
220 J%=2*J%
230 IFJ%<E%THEN260
240 IFJ%=E%THEN270
250 IFJ%>E%THEN290
260 IFA$(J%)<A$(J%+1)THENJ%=J%+1
270 IFW$>=A$(J%)THEN290
280 A$(I%)=A$(J%):GOTO210
290 A$(I%)=W$:GOTO80
```

Lines 5 to 50 inclusive set up and load the array, A$, with the data items that are to be sorted. Note that the value of T%, initialised in line 5, dimensions the size of the array, A$, and also determines the number of items that will be accepted by the routine. Line 60 clears the screen and positions the printing of the first display line six lines down the screen. Line 70 initialises the integer variables S% and E%. S% is calculated using the INT command so that the value is always more than half the value of T%. Thus if T% has the value 19, S% will be given by INT(19/2)+1 which is 9+1 or 10. If T% has the value 20, S% has the value of INT(20/2)+1 which is 11.

The second and third columns of the displayed table indicate how the values of S% and E% vary as the sorting of the data progresses.

In line 90, S% will be decremented and the temporary record, W$, is given the value held by the ´S%th´ element in A$ which is the array holding the data items. Line 160 prints the values of S% and E% and then, on the same line, the contents of the array, A$, are printed before returning to the start of the next line.

Line	S%	E%	W$	A$(1)	A$(2)	A$(3)	I%	J%
40				7	2	4		
70	2	3		7	2	4		
90	1		7	7	2	4		
160-190	1	3		7	2	4		
200-220							1	2
260					2	4		3
270			7			4		
290				7				
100		2	4			7		
110	1	2	4		2	7		
200-220							1	2
270			4		2			
290				4				
100		1	2		4			
110	1	1	2		4	7		
150				2	4	7		

To make the understanding of listing 4.1 easier, it will be assumed that a three-element array has been set up with the values 7,2 and 4 as elements A$(1), A$(2) and A$(3) respectively. This size of array is the minimum size that can usefully be demonstrated and takes less time to analyse than the previous ten-element array. Readers will probably realise that the value of S% determines the S(tart) item for comparison and E% is the E(nd) item. E% will not change until S% has been decremented to the value 1.

The values of the variables as the program proceeds are given on the previous page. In order to prevent congestion, column entries are made only when a change in a value occurs.

There now follows a description of the operation of the program in the production of the values given in the table.

1. T% has the value 3 and the result of lines 5 to 50 will be that A$(1)=7, A$(2)=2 and A$(3)=4.

2. In line 70, S% is calculated as INT(3/2)+1 which equals 2 and E% takes the value of T% which equals 3.

3. As S% is not equal to 1, line 90 is the next line to be obeyed.

4. The value of S% becomes 1 and the temporary data store, W$, takes the value of A$(1) which is equal to 7. Line 160 is then the next line to be obeyed.

5. In line 160, the values of S% and E%, that is 1 and 3 respectively, are displayed on the screen and because of the semicolon, no line return occurs.

6. Lines 170 to 190 will then display A$(1), A$(2) and A$(3).

7. Lines 200 to 220 then set up the values of variables I% and J% to 1 and 2 respectively.

8. In lines 230 to 250, the values of J% and E% are compared. At this point in the program, J%=2 and E%=3 and the test in line 230 is thus satisfied.

9. Line 260 is the next line to be obeyed and here a comparison of the values of A$(2) and A$(3) is made. As 2 is less than 4, J% is incremented to a value of 3.

10. Line 270 compares the values of W$ and A$(3), that is 7 and 4 respectively, and as 7 is greater than 4, line 290 is linked to.

11. In line 290, A$(1) takes the value of W$, that is A$(1) is given the value of 7. Note that the

order of the data items is, so far, unchanged but this is quite correct and does not indicate a fault condition.

12. A link back to line 80 follows and as S% is equal to 1, a link to line 100 now results.

13. In line 100, W$ now takes the value of A$(3), A$(2) takes the value of A$(1) and E% is decremented, that is W$=4, A$(3)=7 and E%=2. Note that the largest data item, that is 7, is now in the correct sorted position.

14. In line 110, the values of S%, E% and W$, that is 1,2 and 4, are displayed. Because of the semicolon at the end of the line, further values can be displayed on that line.

15. Line 120 uses the values of I=2 and I=3 to display the values of A$(2) and A$(3). Thus the data items 2 and 7 are displayed. Line 140 contains PRINT which initiates a new display line.

16. In line 150, a check is made on the value of E% and as this is equal to 2, a link is made to line 200 for the second time.

17. Lines 200 to 220 will carry out the process of assigning new values to I% and J% and, because of the value given to T%, that is 3, the value of J% will change to 2 but I% will remain at the previous value of 1.

18. The tests in lines 230 to 250 will result in a link to line 270 because J% and E% now have the same value, that is 2.

19. In line 270, the values of W$=4 and A$(2)=2 are compared. As 4 is greater than 2, a link is made to line 290 and this results in A$(1) taking the value of W$=4. The sequence of the input data items is now 4,2 and 7.

20. In line 80, the value of S%=1 causes a link to line 100.

21. In line 100, W$ takes the value of A$(2)=2, A$(2) takes the value of A$(1)=4 and E% is decremented to the value 1.

22. Line 110 displays the value of S%=1 and E%=1 and
     then the value of W$=2. On the same display line,
     the values of A$(2)=4 and A$(3)=7 are displayed by
     lines 120 to 140.

23. In line 150, the value of E% is compared with the
     value 1 and as E%=1, line 200 will not be linked
     to. Instead, A$(1) takes the value of W$=2 and the
     sort routine ends with the three data items in the
     correct ascending order.

     This explanation of the operation of the program
when   producing   the   table of variables and array
elements should be sufficient to indicate how those
elements are   interchanged when necessary. Readers who
feel that a deeper understanding is essential should
arrange the same data items in different orders and
then produce new tables. There are, in fact, six
different arrangements and these are

2	4	7
2	7	4
4	2	7
4	7	2
7	2	4
7	4	2

     Carrying out such "dry runs", as they are called,
will enable readers to establish that it is the
ordering of the input data that determines the path
that is followed as the program proceeds.

The Sorting Routine

When the Heap Sort algorithm is to be used, one feature
may be an obvious stumbling block, that is the fact
that it can only sort one field - the key, or
identifier, field. The work on sorting that has been
carried out so far has been on single-field records,
that is numbers, but actual records will have several
fields and one of these fields will be selected as the
key field in a particular sorting requirement. This may
be numeric, as in the above example, alphabetic or
alphanumeric but the ordering of the key field will
then determine the ordering of the records to which the
key values apply. Thus, as each pair of key values is

interchanged so must the other fields in those
particular records be interchanged.

This requirement is incorporated in the file-sorting
demonstration program given in listing 4.2 (L4.2). The
program should now be LOADed and LISTed.

```
LISTING 4.2
   10 CLS
   20 PROCdefine_field_names
   30 PROCdefine_initial_values
   40 PROCinitialise_file
   50 PROCretrieve_file
   60 DIMS$(8)
   70 PRINT:INPUT"What is the key field (1-9) ",N%
   80 PROCsort_file(N%)
   90 PROCexamine_record
  100 CLS:PRINT"Any more sort demo's required?":A$=GET$
  110 IFA$="Y" OR A$="y"THEN70ELSE120
  120 END
  130
  140 DEFPROCexamine_record
  150 PRINT:PRINT"There are ";record%;" records in the
      file"
  160 PRINT:INPUT TAB(1,22),"Which record is to be
      examined ",R%
  170 IFR%<1 OR R%>record%THEN210
  180 CLS
  190 PROCdisplay_record(R%-1)
  200 GOTO160
  210 ENDPROC
  220
  230 DEFPROCdisplay_record(R%)
  240 PRINTTAB(8,2);"** EMPLOYEE RECORD ";R%+1;" **"
  250 PRINTTAB(1,4);"1";TAB(3,4);D$(0);TAB(22,4);
      E$(0,R%)
  260 PRINTTAB(1,6);"2";TAB(3,6);D$(1);TAB(22,6);
      E$(1,R%)
  270 PRINTTAB(1,8);"3";TAB(3,8);D$(2);TAB(22,8);
      E$(2,R%)
  280 PRINTTAB(1,10);"4";TAB(3,10);D$(3);TAB(22,10);
      E$(3,R%)
  290 PRINTTAB(1,12);"5";TAB(3,12);D$(4);TAB(22,12);
      E$(4,R%)
  300 PRINTTAB(1,14);"6";TAB(3,14);D$(5);TAB(22,14);
      E$(5,R%)
  310 PRINTTAB(1,16);"7";TAB(3,16);D$(6);TAB(22,16);
      E$(6,R%)
  320 PRINTTAB(1,18);"8";TAB(3,18);D$(7);TAB(22,18);
      E$(7,R%)
  330 PRINTTAB(1,20);"9";TAB(3,20);D$(8);TAB(22,20);
      E$(8,R%)
```

```
340 ENDPROC
350
360 DEFPROCdefine_initial_values
370 DIMI$(8)
380 I$(0)="999"
390 I$(1)="AAAAAAAAAAAAAAAA"
400 I$(2)="AA"
410 I$(3)="A"
420 I$(4)="999999"
430 I$(5)="99"
440 I$(6)="999999"
450 I$(7)="99"
460 I$(8)="99999"
470 ENDPROC
480
490 DEFPROCinitialise_file
500 DIME$(8,19)
510 FORN=0TO8
520 FORE=0TO19
530 E$(N,E)=I$(N)
540 NEXT
550 NEXT
560 ENDPROC
570
580 DEFPROCdefine_field_names
590 DIMD$(8)
600 D$(0)="EMPLOYEE NO."
610 D$(1)="SURNAME"
620 D$(2)="INITIALS"
630 D$(3)="SEX (M/F)"
640 D$(4)="BORN (DDMMYY)"
650 D$(5)="DEPARTMENT NO."
660 D$(6)="JOINED (YYMMDD)"
670 D$(7)="JOB CODE"
680 D$(8)="SALARY (POUNDS)"
690 ENDPROC
700
710 DEFPROCretrieve_file
720 CLS
730 INPUT"Name the file to be retrieved ",N$
740 FILE=OPENIN(N$)
750 INPUT#FILE,record%
760 V=0
770 REPEAT
780 FORN=0TO8
790 INPUT#FILE,E$(N,V)
800 NEXT
810 V=V+1
820 UNTIL EOF#(FILE)
830 CLOSE#FILE
840 ENDPROC
```

```
845
850 DEFPROCsort_file(N%)
860 S%=INT(record%/2)+1:E%=record% :N%=N%-1
870 IF S%=1 THEN 890
880 S%=S%-1:W$=E$(N%,S%-1):FOR F%=0 TO 8:
    S$(F%)=E$(F%,S%-1):NEXT:GOTO 930
890 W$=E$(N%,E%-1):FOR F%=0 TO 8:
    S$(F%)=E$(F%,E%-1):NEXT:
    E$(N%,E%-1)=E$(N%,0):FOR F%=0 TO 8:
    E$(F%,E%-1)=E$(F%,0):NEXT:E%=E%-1
900 IFE%=1THEN910ELSE930
910 FORF%=0TO8:E$(F%,0)=S$(F%)
920 NEXT:GOTO1030
930 J%=S%
940 I%=J%
950 J%=2*J%
960 IFJ%<E%THEN990
970 IFJ%=E%THEN1000
980 IFJ%>E%THEN1020
990 IFE$(N%,J%-1)<E$(N%,J%)THENJ%=J%+1
1000 IFW$>=E$(N%,J%-1)THEN1020
1010 FORF%=0TO8:E$(F%,I%-1)=E$(F%,J%-1):NEXT:GOTO940
1020 FORF%=0TO8:E$(F%,I%-1)=S$(F%):NEXT:GOTO870
1030 ENDPROC
```

Readers will recognise that the majority of listing 4.2 consists of procedures from previous listings. The sort procedure, PROCsort_file(N%), is based on the program given in listing 4.1 but has been amended to incorporate the requirement of interchanging all fields in a pair of records instead of just the pair of key items. The other new procedure, PROCretrieve_file, is used to load into the micro's memory the file of data on which the sorting routine is to be used. Lines 10 to 120 inclusive constitute the main program for this demonstration and line 60 sets up an array, S$, that will hold the record that is to be interchanged during the sorting of the file.

PROCretrieve_file is based on the program given in listing 1.2 but, instead of the program allocating a string for N$, the user is asked to input the name of the file that is to be sorted. "NUMBER" in listing 1.2 is replaced by "record%", the number of records in the file. Lines 770 to 820 inclusive take each record from the file and load it into the N by V array, E$. Note that there is no benefit to be gained from using V% and N% here because the speed of the retrieval procedure is governed by the cassette recorder.

Lines 70 and 80 take the value of the key field, N%, which is input by the user, and use it in the sorting of the file of records according to the selected field

number.   Examination   of   the   sort   routine,
PROCsort_file(N%),   shows that in line 860 the value of
N% is reduced by one because the fields   are   numbered,
in   the   records,   from   zero to eight. N% replaces the
numeric, alphabetic or alphanumeric key that   was   used
in   listing   4.1 but now it has to be selected from the
nine possible keys that form a record.

In line 880, the statement   "W$=E$(N%,S%-1)" and the
FOR...NEXT loop set up a temporary store   in   array   S$
for   the   complete   "S%-1´th"   record.   N% is used in a
similar manner in line 890. Notice the use of colons to
form a composite   statement   as   discussed   previously.
Lines   990   and   1000   make   further   use   of N% in the
multiple testing of key   values   which   this   algorithm
uses.

To   aid   in   the   comparison   of   listing   4.1   and
PROCsort_file(N%), the following cross reference   table
of line numbers may be used

Listing 4.1	PROCsort_file(N%)
70	860
80	870
90	880
100	890
150	900-920
200	930
210	940
220	950
230	960
240	970
250	980
260	990
270	1000
280	1010-1020

As   already   stated,   the differences are connected with
the   requirement   to   interchange   records   instead   of
single fields. The PRINT statements used in listing 4.1
are, of course, no longer necessary.

Summarising,   the   program loads the named file into
memory, sorts the records into the ascending   order   of
the   specified   key field and then presents any desired
record   for   examination   by   the   user   -   line   90.
PROCexamine_record informs   the   user how many records
have been sorted and then allows the user to   select   a
record.   Line   170   ends   the   procedure   if the record
number that is input falls outside the available range.
The selection of records in this   manner   can   continue
until a terminating value such as zero is input.

A return to line 100 will then occur and the user will be asked if any more demonstrations of the sort routine are required. An affirmative answer will allow a further key field to be selected and thus the user can investigate how the sorting routine deals with the different key types.

Analysing the Results

To test the demonstration program, the file of data created as a result of the activity at the end of chapter 3 should be used. The response to the request by the program for the file name to be input should be the name given to that file. Pressing RETURN after the name has been input will generate a flashing cursor. The cassette recorder should now be played so that the file can be retrieved.

When the file has been loaded, the cassette recorder will stop and a request will be made for the user to input the key field number. Using "1" and RETURN will result, after a short time, in messages stating that fourteen records are on the file and asking which record is required for examination. Using "1" and RETURN will produce the display of record 1 which is for employee number 003, the lowest value of this field. Checking the details of the displayed record against the table of data given in Chapter 3 will indicate that the complete record has indeed been selected. Checking the ordering of the records up to, and including, 14 will show that they have been ordered according to ascending employee number.

Selecting record number 15 for display will terminate the examination because there are only fourteen records on the file.

The user will now be presented with a message asking if any more demonstrations of sorting are required. Answering with "Y" or "y" will produce the key field message as before. Using "2" and RETURN will give the file size message and ask for a record selection to be made.

Using "1" and RETURN will display record number 1 which is for ADAMS, the first name in the alphabetic ordering. Working through the records from 1 to 14 will show that the records are in alphabetic order as would be expected. Records 10 and 11 are both for SMITH but the order in which they are presented is not predictable because no further ordering on, for example, INITIALS or any other field has been carried out. Records 12 and 13 present the same problem because they are both for YARDLEY.

Using "0" will terminate the examination and the user will be asked to indicate if there is a further demonstration requirement. The presence of identical key data will cause a problem in field 3 because there are two sets of A, AW and RK initials. Again, the outcome of a sort using field 3 will not be predictable and readers should verify this statement by selecting "3" and pressing RETURN. The problem is more pronounced when a sort using field 4 is carried out.

A sort on field 7 will emphasise a point made earlier about the filing of dates. For field 7, the date entry was treated so that the year figure was placed before the month and day figure. Selecting record 1 will give the record in which field 7 has the value 450907, that is the joining date was September 7th. 1945. A check on the data table will indicate that this record is for the longest serving employee. The employee with the shortest service will be on record 14 and is for the joining date of November 21st. 1980.

A sort on field 5 will show that date of birth, when stored as DDMMYY, will not produce the correct ordering. The oldest employee was born on July 27th. 1930 but record 1 is for a date of birth of September 1st. 1936, stored as 010936. This is treated by the computer as 10936 which is smaller in value than 270730, the number for the date of birth for the oldest employee. In fact, his record is the tenth in the sorted file!

As readers will probably have deduced already, a sort on field 9 will not, for a similar reason, give ascending salary figures. The result of the ordering is 11000, 11000, 14500, 26000, 5100, 5350 and so on up to 8950.

Self-test 4.1
(a)   By comparison of the results of sorting by fields 5 and 7, explain why the sort using field 9 is not in ascending salary order.
(b)   One method of overcoming this problem would be to enter a leading zero for those salary values below #10000. Devise a change to a procedure given in chapter 3 that would remove the need to enter a zero from the keyboard.

In conclusion, a sort of the file on field 6 gives department numbers 12 and 13 before department numbers 2,3,7 and 9. Similarly, a sort using field 8 gives job codes 11,14,15 and 19 before 3 and 32. Both of these results are caused by the same sort of problem as was manifested for fields 5 and 9 and a cure will be obtained by the same method as that given in the answer to part (b) of the previous self-test question.

Self-test 4.2
Hopefully, all readers will have noticed that the sort
program was developed in the text with no mention of
the use of top-down-design which was introduced in
chapter 2 and used in chapter 3 to produce a structured
program. However, readers can see that the program
consists of a main program part which calls up various
procedures and thus it is structured. As mentioned in
this chapter, the majority of the procedures had been
developed in chapter 3.

This self-test will enable readers to check their
ability to use top-down-design by assuming that the
program has still to be developed. The problem should
be analysed and defined and then the solution
successively refined until the level at which
procedures can be written is reached.

5 Searching Files

It is now necessary to deal with the main purpose of data-processing. This is the provision of an item of data that is of interest to the user of a particular filing system. This is not to infer that all the previous work or that which is to be covered in future chapters is not important. Every part complements the whole, but to a lesser or greater degree.

For example, the method to be used to find an item of data, if it exists in a file, will depend on whether or not the data is ordered. A file can be searched even if the data is not ordered but for lengthy files the time becomes excessive. Thus, the previous work on the sorting of files was of importance from the point of view of data-processing efficiency.

The problem is defined as

1. Search an ordered file for required data
2. Tell the user where the data is or give a "not found" message
3. Provide the option of further searching.

It will be necessary to refine level 1, in order to place an ordered file in memory, as follows:-

1.1 Place the required file in memory
1.2 Search for the required data.

Now, level 1.1 has been dealt with previously in chapter 4 when it was found necessary to place a file of data into memory before a sorting of that data could be carried out. Level 1.1 consists of the following four procedures

```
PROCdefine_field_names
PROCdefine_initial_values
PROCinitialise_file
PROCretrieve_file
```

This is a further example of the value of using procedures when building up a complex program in easy stages - the present task of producing a search program will require the writing of only two new procedures and a few commands.

Level 1.2 can be refined as follows

1.2.1 Request search data from user
1.2.2 Search the sorted file for reqired item.

Level 1.2.1 will consist of a set of questions displayed on the screen, the answers to which form parameters that are passed to the search routine. The actual questions cannot be finalised until the search routine has been developed and tested - level 1.2.2.
Level 2 can be refined as follows

2.1 Tell the user which record holds the required item, if it exists in the file or
2.2 Tell the user that the item does not exist
2.3 Tell the user how many records are in the file.

Further refinement is necessary to allow the user to examine the record that holds the item that the search has found. This is catered for by using an existing procedure, PROCexamine_record, and forms level 2.3.1. Reference to chapter 4 will reveal that this procedure calls up another procedure, PROCdisplay_record which has also been dealt with previously.
As with sort routines, the methods used for searching files will depend on a number of factors but the example to be developed will be for a sorted file with possibly 100 or more records. A search routine based on the so-called binary chop method is, therefore, suitable. This method will not cope, however, with duplicated entries such as several employees with the same name as in the set of data given in chapter 3.
It will be necessary, therefore, to call up a procedure to check whether or not the item found in one record exists in one or more other records. This will require a further refinement of level 1.2.2. The complete design is

1.1 PROCdefine_field_names
    PROCdefine_initial_values
    PROCinitialise_file
    PROCretrieve_file
1.2.1 Obtain search data from user
1.2.2.1 PROCsearch_file
1.2.2.2 PROCrepeated_entries
2.1 Inform user which record/s hold required item or
2.2 Inform user that record does not exist
2.3.1 PROCexamine_record
2.3.2 Inform user of number of records in file
3 Ask user about further search requirements

The Binary Chop

This method consists of chopping, or dividing, the sorted file into two, or binary, parts of equal length. A comparison of the value of the record at the middle of the file with the item being searched for will determine if the item is, according to its value, positioned in the lower or upper half of the file. The appropriate half is then selected and a further chop carried out on that half, thus giving two new halves. A comparison is made to select the correct half for the required item and the process of chopping and comparing is repeated until either the item is found at its correct position or a different item is found. In the latter case, the required item does not exist in the file.

An implementation of the algorithm, written in BASIC, is given in listing 5.1.

```
LISTING 5.1
 10 DIMA(100)
 20 CLS
 30 FORN%=1 TO 100
 40 A(N%)=N%
 50 NEXT
 60 A(5)=5.5:A(10)=10.5:A(50)=50.5:A(99)=99.5
 70 PRINT´´:INPUT"What number are you looking
    for ",data%:CLS:IF data%=999THEN220
 80 L%=1:H%=101:up=FALSE:prevM%=0
 90 M%=INT((H%-L%)/2)+1:PRINT´´
100 PRINTTAB(3);"L%=";L%;TAB(13);"M%=";M%;
    TAB(23);"H%=";H%
110 IFM%=prevM%THEN200
120 prevM%=M%
130 IFA(M%)=data%THEN180
140 IFA(M%)<data%THEN160
150 H%=M%:M%=INT((H%-L%)/2)+1:IFup=TRUE
    THEN170ELSE100
160 L%=M%
170 M%=L%+INT(H%-L%)/2:up=TRUE:GOTO100
180 PRINT:PRINT"The search for ";data%;"
    was successful"
190 GOTO70
200 PRINT´:PRINTdata%;" NOT FOUND"
210 GOTO70
220 END
```

Basically, this program sets up a file consisting of the numbers 1 to 100 inclusive in ascending order so that, for example, A(5) holds the value 5, A(98) holds the value 98 and so on - see lines 10, 30, 40 and 50.

To simulate the situation when a file does not contain
an item of data, line 60 allocates new values to
certain elements in the array, A, that holds the file.
The user is then asked to input a number, data%, to be
searched for in the file - line 70.

Line 80 initialises two variables, L% and H%. L%
holds the number of the array element at the lowest end
of the file or its part that is being searched.
Similarly, H% should hold the number of the array
element at the highest end of the file or its part that
is being searched but, for operational reasons, this
value is initialised to a value that is one more than
the file size - 101 in this example.

In line 90, the initial value of M% is calculated
and, in this example, will have the value 51. Line 100
will print the values of L%, M% and H%. The test in
line 110 will fail because the variable, prevM%, was
set to zero in line 80 and thus cannot be equal to M%
which has just been set to 51. The variable, prevM%, is
used by the program to deduce that an item does not
exist in the file and this is done by comparing the
present and previous values of M% - line 110. The
present value of M% is given to prevM% in line 120.

Line 130 tests whether or not the value held in
A(M%) is equal to data% and, if it is, causes the micro
to take its next instruction from line 180 which prints
a success message. It is suggested that the program
given in listing 5.1 is loaded into the micro before
proceeding - use L5.1 on the program cassette.

Once the program is in memory, RUN it and input the
number 51. The response will be

        L%=1   M%=51   H%=101

        The search for 51 was successful

This example indicates how the data for a successful
search is presented. The values 26 and 76 give the
following results.

        L%=1   M%=51   H%=101
        L%=1   M%=26   H%=51

        The search for 26 was successful

        L%=1   M%=51   H%=101
        L%=51   M%=76   H%=101

        The search for 76 was successful

From   these two results, readers will see that after
two binary chops of the file, the   required   items   are
found. This is because 26 and 76 are the middle values,
M%, of the lower and upper halves of the file. For the
value 26, the lines followed in the program are

     70,80,90,100,120,150,100,120,130 and 180

In line 150, the lower half of the file is selected
by giving H% the value of M% which is 51. A new value
of M% is calculated and because line 170 has   not   been
visited,   the   variable   ´up´ has not been set to TRUE.
Thus line 100 is selected rather than 170.

When the value 76 is input, the program   traces   the
following path

     70,80,90,100,120,140,160,170,100,120,130 and 180

In   line 160, the upper half of the file is selected
by giving L% the value of M%. Line 170 provides a   new
value of M% and   sets the variable "up" to TRUE. The
purpose of this is to prevent unnecessary excursions by
the search routine into parts of   the   file   that   have
been   visited   already.   To   see why such prevention is
necessary, LIST the program, after entering 999 as   the
item to be searched for, and delete ":up=TRUE" from
line 170.

When the program is RUN and the value 52   is   input,
the values of M% are

     51,76,13,44,60,9,34,47,53,4,28,40,46,49,51 and 52

This   is   a   total   of sixteen attempts to match the
input item and ten of these attempts   were   for   values
below   the   middle   value   of   the   file, 51, which was
visited twice. Line 170 should now be reinstated or the
program LOADed again and then RUN with 52 as the   input
item.

The   values   of M% are now 51, 76, 63, 57, 54 and 52
which, at six attempts for a match, is   a   considerable
improvement   on   the previous result. In addition, none
of the values are repeated   and   thus   the   routine   is
working   at maximum efficiency since each value is half
the range of values in which the sought-for item lies.

For a file of 100   items,   the   maximum   number   of
binary chops that is required to find an item is seven
but the actual number will depend on   the   position   of
the item in the file as readers will have realised from
the   previous   results. An input of 100 as the required
item will show that seven chops are necessary   to   find
that   value   in   the   file   and   readers will note that

whereas H% does not change, L% takes the previous value
of M% at every unsucccessful chop. Finally, M% is found
as the middle of the range 99 to 101.

The choice of initial value for H% of 101 rather
than 100 may now be apparent to readers but, for
further evidence, readers should alter line 80 to
initialise H% to 100 and then RUN the program to search
for the item 100. The result will be the screen display

L%=1	M%=50	H%=100
L%=50	M%=75	H%=100
L%=75	M%=87	H%=100
L%=87	M%=93	H%=100
L%=93	M%=96	H%=100
L%=96	M%=98	H%=100
L%=98	M%=99	H%=100
L%=99	M%=99	H%=100

100 NOT FOUND

The reason why the routine cannot find the value 100
is that M%=100 cannot be calculated from
99+INT((100-99)/2) as required by line 170. Readers
will also notice that the last two lines of the table
have M% equal to 99. This is the situation that is
tested in line 110 and, as it is satisfied in this case
the routine exits via line 200. Because the test
requires two consecutive values of M% to be equal
before such an exit, the total number of chops is
increased by one - the maximum number for a successful
search is unaffected however.

Reinstating line 80 will allow the following values
to be used to test this claim - 99, 101, 123, 0 and
-35. These values, together with 5, 10 and 50, will all
produce NOT FOUND messages because they are either
outside the file's range or have been replaced with
values that the routine cannot accept - these are
inserted into the file in line 60 of the program.

For a file containing 1000 items, a more likely
real-life situation, the maximum number of chops to
find an item in the file is eleven. To illustrate this,
the program given as listing 5.2 below, L5.2 on the
program cassette, should be entered.

LISTING 5.2

```
10 DIMA(1000):FORN%=1TO1000:A(N%)=N%:NEXT
20 A(1)=1.5
   :A(100)=100.5:A(200)=200.5
   :A(300)=300.5:A(400)=400.5
   :A(600)=600.5:A(1000)=1000.5
```

```
      :A(499)=499.5:A(500)=500.5
      :A(501)=501.5:A(700)=700.5
      :A(800)=800.5:A(900)=900.5
 30 CLS:PRINTTAB(6);"CHOPS";TAB(21);"RESULT:PRINT
 40 FORN%=1TO1000:data%=N%:C%=0
    :L%=1:H%=1001:up=FALSE:prevM%=0
    :M%=INT((H%-L%)/2)+1
 50 C%=C%+1:IFM%=prevM%THEN130
 60 prevM%=M%
 70 IFA(M%)=data%THEN140
 80 IFA(M%)<data%THEN100
 90 H%=M%:M%=INT((H%-L%)/2)+1
    :IFup=TRUE THEN110ELSE50
100 L%=M%
110 M%=L%+INT(H%-L%)/2:up =TRUE:GOTO50
120 GOTO140
130 PRINTTAB(8);C%;TAB(18);data%;" NOT FOUND"
140 NEXT
150 PRINT´:PRINTTAB(6);"AUTOMATIC SEARCH COMPLETED"
    :END
```

When the program is RUN, the screen display will be

CHOPS	RESULT
11	1 NOT FOUND
11	100 NOT FOUND
12	200 NOT FOUND
12	300 NOT FOUND
12	400 NOT FOUND
11	499 NOT FOUND
12	500 NOT FOUND
11	501 NOT FOUND
11	600 NOT FOUND
12	700 NOT FOUND
12	800 NOT FOUND
12	900 NOT FOUND
12	1000 NOT FOUND

           AUTOMATIC SEARCH COMPLETED

   As with the previous program, the numbers that are
not found are the result of allocating non-integer
values to various elements of the array - see line 20.
The original allocation of values to the array elements
is carried out in line 10 and, after printing table
headings of the results - line 30, the routine selects
successive values from 1 to 1000 in ascending order. A
counter, C%, is cleared before the search commences and
this counter will be incremented on every passage
through the routine - line 50.

The main part of the routine is the same as in the previous program but instead of printing the result of a successful search the next value is then searched for - lines 70 and 140. When an unsuccessful search results, the program follows lines 50 and 130 and the NOT FOUND message is printed.

The 1000 searches take a total of less than 2 minutes which is better than eight searches per second, on average. If line 140 is amended to read "140 PRINT N%:NEXT" and then RUN, after first pressing CTRL O to remove the paging mode, the fact that each of the 1000 numbers is being searched for will be illustrated. Finally, the number of chops required for each unsuccessful search never exceeds twelve and thus the claim made in the paragraph before listing 5.2 is seen to be correct.

Sufficient evidence now exists to allow the use of the above binary chop implementation in the search routine for the Employee Records file.

The search routine that is described below will deal correctly with files having unique keys such as Employee No. However, a file that is sorted on surname only will not be searched correctly if multiple surnames exist. Such a situation is built into the set of data for the Employee Records and this will be used to demonstrate the inadequacy of this search routine. An additional procedure to deal with repeated entries will then be described.

The program given below should now be entered - L5.3 on the program cassette. If the cassette is not available, the procedures that are not given in full in the listing can be copied from listing 4.2 or obtained from the procedure library, the creation of which is described at the end of this chapter.

LISTING 5.3

```
   10 CLS
   20 PROCdefine_field_names
   30 PROCdefine_initial_values
   40 PROCinitialise_file
   50 PROCretrieve_file
   65 PRINT"What field is to be used in the search?"
   66 INPUTfield%
   70 PRINT"What is the item to be searched for"
   75 INPUTsearch$
   80 PROCsearch_file(field%,search$)
   90 PROCexamine_record
   95 INPUT"ANY MORE SEARCHES",A$
   96 IF A$="Y" THEN 70
  120 END
  130
```

```
140 DEFPROCexamine_record
210 ENDPROC
220
230 DEFPROCdisplay_record(R%)
340 ENDPROC
350
360 DEFPROCdefine_initial_values
470 ENDPROC
480
490 DEFPROCinitialise_file
560 ENDPROC
570
580 DEFPROCdefine_field_names
690 ENDPROC
700
710 DEFPROCretrieve_file
840 ENDPROC
845
990 DEFPROCsearch_file(field%,search$)
1010 L%=1:H%=record%+1:up=FALSE:prevM%=0
1020 M%=INT((H%-L%)/2)+1
1030 IF M%=prevM%THEN 1110
1040 prevM%=M%:PRINTTAB(8);M%;TAB(12)
     ;E$(field%-1,M%-1)
1050 IFE$(field%-1,M%-1)=search$THEN1120
1060 IFE$(field%-1,M%-1)<search$THEN1080
1070 H%=M%:M%=INT((H%-L%)/2)+1
     :IF up=TRUE THEN 1090 ELSE 1030
1080 L%=M%
1090 M%=L%+INT(H%-L%)/2:up=TRUE:GOTO 1030
1110 PRINTsearch$;" NOT FOUND":GOTO 1130
1120 PRINTsearch$;" found in RECORD NO ";M%
1130 ENDPROC
```

The program is seen to contain a number of commands,
lines 65 to 120 inclusive, which deal with the
questions and responses that correspond to level 1.2.1
in the design established previously. The presentation
of the questions is not up to the standard that will be
required in the final version but is sufficient for the
present purpose which is for development and
demonstration only.

Line 66 requires the input of a variable, field%,
even though the file to be searched will be sorted
already - this is a feature that will be fully used in
the complete file-handling program. Thus, the present
program requires that if a search on field 2 is
required, the file must have been sorted into
alphabetic order using the sort program given in
listing 4.2.

A second parameter, search$, is requested in line 70 and this will be used, with field%, in line 80 when the program enters the file search procedure, lines 990 to 1130 inclusive. As the number of records will be recorded as record%, this value is increased by one to form H% - line 1010. The PRINT statement in line 1040 will give the value of M% and the surname that is given in the record identified by M%. The use of field%-1 and M%-1 as the element identifiers for the array E$ should need no explanation but readers who are confused can refer to the treatment of array dimensioning given in chapter 2.

Lines 1020, 1030 and 1050 to 1090 inclusive are of the same form as lines 90, 110 and 130 to 170 inclusive in listing 5.1. The program should now be RUN using the alphabetically sorted file of Employee Record data previously created.

After responding with the name of that file in answer to the first question and 2 for the answer to the second question, readers should use ADAMS as their response to the third question. The screen should display

```
8    MCGEE
4    DEREVE
2    BISHOPS
1    ADAMS
```

ADAMS found in RECORD NO 1

In addition there will be a message stating that the file holds 14 records and one asking which record is to be examined. An answer of any value from 1 to 14 inclusive will display the chosen record but a response of 0, or of a value higher than 14, will cause the program to take the next instruction from line 95. This will ask if any more searches are required and a response of Y permits the user to initiate a further search.

An input of ZUBOVIC will produce the display

```
8    MCGEE
11   SMITH
13   YARDLEY
14   ZUBOVIC
```

ZUBOVIC found in RECORD NO 14

A search for MCGEE will, as probably expected, give a single-line display - readers should confirm this. A search for SMITH will indicate the failure of this routine to deal with multiple entries - the display is

8   MCGEE
11   SMITH

SMITH found in RECORD NO 11

   Examination of records 10 and 11 will confirm that the surnames are both SMITH but the routine will never find the SMITH in record 10 while the file remains unchanged. The same comments apply to a search for YARDLEY since this name exists in both records 12 and 13.

   Readers may feel that this is not a serious fault but a typical search might be for information on all employees earning a certain salary. A modification to the routine is thus necessary and will be dealt with next.

   Listing 5.4 extends the program given in listing 5.3 by a procedure that is called by PROCsearch_file when a search for an item in a file has been successful. The relevant details are given below, the incomplete procedures being the same as those in listing 5.3. The program is L5.4 on the program cassette.

LISTING 5.4

```
 10 CLS
 20 PROCdefine_field_names
 30 PROCdefine_initial_values
 40 PROCinitialise_file
 50 PROCretrieve_file
 65 PRINT"What field is to be used in the search?"
 66 INPUTfield%
 70 PRINT"What is the item to be searched for"
 75 INPUTsearch$
 80 PROCsearch_file(field%,search$)
 90 PROCexamine_record
 95 INPUT"ANY MORE SEARCHES",A$
 96 IFA$="Y"THEN70
120 END
130
140 DEFPROCexamine_record
210 ENDPROC
220
230 DEFPROCdisplay_record(R%)
340 ENDPROC
350
360 DEFPROCdefine_initial_values
470 ENDPROC
480
```

```
 490 DEFPROCinitialise_file
 560 ENDPROC
 570
 580 DEFPROCdefine_field_names
 690 ENDPROC
 700
 710 DEFPROCretrieve_file
 840 ENDPROC
 845
 990 DEFPROCsearch_file(field%,search$)
1010 L%=1:H%=record%+1:up=FALSE:prevM%=0
1020 M%=INT((H%-L%)/2)+1
1030 IFM%=prevM%THEN1110
1040 prevM%=M%:PRINTTAB(8);M%;TAB(12);E$(field%-1,M%-1)
1050 IFE$(field%-1,M%-1)=search$ THEN1120
1060 IFE$(field%-1,M%-1)<search$ THEN1080
1070 H%=M%:M%=INT((H%-L%)/2)+1
     :IF up=TRUE THEN 1090 ELSE 1030
1080 L%=M%
1090 M%=L%+INT(H%-L%)/2:up =TRUE:GOTO1030
1110 PRINTsearch$;" NOT FOUND":GOTO 1130
1120 PROCrepeated_entries(field%,M%,search$)
1130 ENDPROC
1135
1140 DEFPROCrepeated_entries(field%,M%,search$)
1150 C%=0
1160 IF M%-1=0 OR M%=record%THEN 1300
1162 Z%=M%-1
1165 REPEAT
1166 Z%=Z%-1
1170 UNTILE$(field%-1,Z%)<>search$
1172 B%=Z%+2
1174 REPEAT
1176 Z%=Z%+1:C%=C%+1
1178 UNTILE$(field%-1,Z%)<>search$
1179 IF C%-1=1 THEN 1300
1180 PRINT"There are ";C%-1;" records containing"
1190 PRINTsearch$;", beginning at RECORD NO ";B%
     :GOTO1310
1300 PRINTsearch$;" found at RECORD NO ";M%
1310 ENDPROC
```

The changes made to the search procedure affect lines 1050 and 1120. In line 1050, a successful search links the program to line 1120 which, in turn, calls up the repeated entries procedure, defined in line 1140. An unsuccessful search gives a NOT FOUND message as before.

The parameters that are passed to the procedure include M% - note that there is no need to pass the value M%-1 since this can be quite easily obtained from

M%. Should the sought-for item be located in the first record of the file, the binary chop routine will have tested the second record - see the result of testing listing 5.3 with ADAMS given previously. Thus, if the first record has been identified as holding the required item, the second record cannot also hold it.

Line 1160 uses this fact by testing M%-1=0 and if the result is in the affirmative it means that only the first record holds the required item. The search for ZUBOVIC when testing listing 5.3 indicates that the penultimate record is tested by the routine before finding the sought-for item in the ultimate record. Thus, if the item is in the last record of a file it cannot be in any other record. This fact is also tested in line 1160.

The routine that is used in checking for repeated entries is to test the record "below" that holding the sought-for item and, if it has the same valued entry, test the record "below" that record. The process is repeated until no match of entries is found. The value of the variable Z% is decremented at the beginning of each of these tests and the relevant lines are 1165 to 1170 inclusive. The value of Z% is used as one of the two parameters of the array, E$.

As Z% has been initialised to value M%-1 in line 1162, the actual record number of the first record holding the sought-for item will be given by Z%+2 - line 1172 gives this value to the variable B. The routine described above will, therefore, find the first record that holds the sought-for item and it is now necessary to find the last record that holds this item.

The previous process of moving "down" the file is reversed by incrementing the value of Z% in line 1176 and moving "up" the file until there is again no match of items - line 1178. C%, set to zero in line 1150, is also incremented at each test. If there is only one record containing the sought-for item, this will be established by the test in line 1179 but if the test fails it means that there are repeated entries in the file.

The number of records with repeated entries will be given by C%-1 and the first such record will be given by B%. The program should now be entered, L5.4 on the program cassette, and RUN.

An input of SMITH will give the screen display

        8   MCGEE
       11   SMITH

        There are 2 records containing
        SMITH, beginning at RECORD NO 10

An examination of records 10 and 11 will verify that SMITH is contained in both of them. An input of YARDLEY will test the other repeated entry in the file and will produce the screen display

       8 MCGEE
      11 SMITH
      13 YARDLEY

        There are 2 records containing
        YARDLEY, beginning at RECORD NO 12

When records 12 and 13 are examined, readers will again note that the routine has identified the repeated entries contained in the file.

Self-test 5.1
Readers will probably notice that after the search has been carried out, the screen will display the message "TWhich record is to be examined" in which the letter T before the word "Which" is an obvious error. By examination of listing 5.4, find which line or lines is responsible for the error and decide upon a method by which it can be eliminated.

The final version of the development model of the search routine is given in the following listing - L5.5 on the program cassette.

LISTING 5.5
```
  10 CLS
  20 PROCdefine_field_names
  30 PROCdefine_initial_values
  40 PROCinitialise_file
  50 PROCretrieve_file
  60 PRINT´
  70 PRINTTAB(0,6);"What field is to be used in the
     search":PRINT´
  80 INPUTfield%
  90 CLS:PRINTTAB(1,4);"What item is to be searched
     for":PRINT
 100 INPUTsearch$
 110 PROCsearch_file(field%,search$)
 120 PROCexamine_record
 130 CLS:PRINT´
 140 PRINT"Are any more searches to be carried"
 150 INPUT"out in this field (Y/N)",A$
 160 IFA$="N"ORA$="n"THEN170ELSE90
 170 END
 180
```

```
 190 DEFPROCexamine_record
 200 PRINT´:PRINT"There are";record%;"records in the
     file"
 210 PRINT´:PRINT"Which record is to be examined -
     input"
 220 PRINT" ´0´ for no record examination"
 230 INPUTR%
 240 IF R%<1 OR R%>record% THEN 280
 250 CLS
 260 PROCdisplay_record(R%-1)
 270 GOTO210
 280 ENDPROC
 290
 300 DEFPROCdisplay_record(R%)
 410 ENDPROC
 420
 430 DEFPROCdefine_initial_values
 540 ENDPROC
 550
 560 DEFPROCinitialise_file
 630 ENDPROC
 640
 650 DEFPROCdefine_field_names
 760 ENDPROC
 770
 780 DEFPROCretrieve_file
 910 ENDPROC
 920
 930 DEFPROCsearch_file(field%,search$)
 940 L%=1:H%=record%+1:up=FALSE:prevM%=0
 950 M%=INT((H%-L%)/2)+1
 960 IFM%=prevM%THEN1030
 970 prevM%=M%
 980 IFE$(field%-1,M%-1)=search THEN1040
 990 IFE$(field%-1,M%-1)<search THEN1010
1000 H%=M%:M%=INT((H%-L%)/2)+1
     :IFup=TRUE THEN1020ELSE960
1010 L%=M%
1020 M%=L%+INT(H%-L%)/2:up =TRUE:GOTO960
1030 PRINT´:PRINTsearch$;" NOT FOUND":GOTO1050
1040 PROCrepeated_entries(field%,M%,search$)
1050 ENDPROC
1060
1070 DEFPROCrepeated_entries(field%,M%,search$)
1080 C%=0
1090 IFM%-1=0ORM%=record%+1 THEN1210
1100 Z%=M%-1
1110 REPEAT
1120 Z%=Z%-1
1130 UNTILE$(field%-1,Z%)<>search$
1140 B%=Z%+2
```

```
1150 REPEAT
1160 Z%=Z%+1:C%=C%+1
1170 UNTILE$(field%-1,Z%)<>search$
1180 IFC%-1=1THEN1210
1190 PRINT´:PRINT"There are ";C%-1;" records
     containing"
1200 PRINTsearch$;", beginning at RECORD NO ";B%
     :GOTO1220
1210 PRINT´:PRINTsearch$;" found at RECORD NO ";M%
1220 ENDPROC
```

The program does not contain any parts that alter the routine for searching files, but the screen display has been improved by presenting an uncluttered picture to the user. The relevant lines are 70, 90, 140 and 150 - line 160 allows users to input either "N" or "n" as the response to the question produced by lines 140 and 150.

One question that might be raised by readers is - will the repeated entries procedure deal with more than two repetitions? The question cannot be answered by demonstration until a file with three or more repeated entries has been created. The creation of such a file will be dealt with in chapter 6.

Procedure Library

A number of loose ends need to be tied before further development can be carried out. All the routines that have been produced so far are based on the use of procedures - thus there is a procedure for saving a file, another for displaying a record, another for checking that a date is within the calendar values and so on. A total of fourteen such procedures have been developed to deal with the file-handling requirements that have been dealt with so far. As was explained earlier, the value of procedures is that, once written and proved, they can be used in other parts of the suite of routines that constitute a software package.

An important point to note is that once proved, a procedure should not be altered to suit a new requirement that is practically the same as the original requirement - the chances are that the alteration will affect the operation of the procedure when it is used for its original purpose. It is much safer to modify the procedure to satisfy the new requirement and refer to it by another name. Again, a danger exists in this practice since a software package could then become cluttered with procedures that differ only slightly in some cases.

The solution is a compromise in which a small modification is introduced and then fully tested under both the original and the new requirements. Once this has been done, the new procedure can replace the original and be filed, together with a description of what the procedure does and which routines it has been used with. Chapter 9 will be based on an example of the value of such an approach since it will collect all of the proven routines to form a complete data-processing package.

To form a procedure library, it is necessary to save a copy of a procedure so that when required for use in a routine it can be incorporated without having to key it into the micro. This will save valuable time, both in the keying-in requirements and in the elimination of mistakes that are usually introduced in such operations.

The method advocated here is to isolate a proven procedure from the complete routine by using the DELETE command - page 235 of the User Guide. The RENUMBER command, with no numbers given, will number the procedure from line 10 in increments of 10 and it can then be saved as a program would be, either on cassette or disc. Readers should remember that the names used to define and call the procedures are usually too long to be used as file names when saving and an abbreviated version can be linked to the full name by using a manual cross-reference record.

To use the procedure in a new routine, it only needs to be added to the end of the routine and called whenever it is required. To add it to the end of the routine, the SPOOL command described on page 402 of the User Guide should be used. An important point to note concerns the last line number of the routine - the procedure to be added must be renumbered, after LOADing "SHORT", see page 402, to start with a line number that is greater than the last line number of the routine. In this way, any procedure from the library can be used whenever required.

6 Updating Files

The updating of files will take any one of the
following three forms - it may be the addition of new
records to an existing file provided that there is
sufficient space, it may be the deletion of records
from the file or it may be the changing of part of an
existing record on the file. The three requirements
will be dealt with separately in order of complexity.

Extending a File

The simpler problem to deal with is the addition of
more records to an existing file. This will mean that
the procedure for creating new records must be used,
but that also the existing file must be retrieved.
These two functions are not compatible since records
are normally created from the first position in the
file and the present requirement is to create them from
the next empty position in the existing file.

A further requirement is that the routine must
recognise when the end of the available file space in
memory has been reached. In addition, the possibility
of retrieving a file that is already full must be
catered for because until a file is available for
display on the screen, the user will not know whether
or not any more records can be accepted. Finally, as
always, the user must be aware of what is happening and
appropriate messages must be displayed on the screen.

The above requirements can be expressed using the
top-down-design method dealt with previously

1 Prepare micro to hold file
2 Find out which file is to be extended
3 Retrieve the file
4 Add records to the file
5 Examine records of interest in the file
6 Save the extended file.

The levels can be refined using, where possible, the
procedures already available. Thus level 1 becomes

1.1 PROCdefine_field_names
1.2 PROCdefine_initial_values
1.3 PROCinitialise_file.

Level 3 is basically the file-retrieval procedure but there will be some other refinements apparent later on. Thus, the first refinement is

3.1 PROCretrieve_file.

In a similar manner, levels 4,5 and 6 will consist of

4.1 PROCcreate_record
5.1 PROCexamine_record
6.1 PROCsave_file.

Level 2 will allow the user to make a decision regarding continuation of the file-extending operation and also set up a variable that holds the available file-capacity value. For the purpose of this development, the value of twenty records is being used. Thus, level 2 becomes

2.1 Set the file capacity
2.2 Obtain user requirement.

Level 3 refinements will determine the action to be taken should the retrieved file have no space for more records - if this should be the case, only record examination will be available to the user. In addition, the variables that determine which record is to be created and the variable that allows record creation to be terminated must be initialised. The result is

3.2 If the file is full pass to level 5.1
3.3 Set up record creation variables
3.4 Set up termination variable.

This design is implemented in listing 6.1.

LISTING 6.1
```
  10 CLS
  20 PROCdefine_field_names
  30 PROCdefine_initial_values
  40 PROCinitialise_file
  50 max_file%=20
  60 PRINTTAB(3,6)"Is a file to be extended ?";
  70 A$=GET$:*FX15,1
  80 IF NOT(A$="Y" OR A$="y") THEN180
  90 PROCretrieve_file
 100 IFrecord%=max_file%THEN150
 110 R%=record%:record%=record%+1
 120 file_end=FALSE
 130 PROCcreate_record
```

```
 140 record%=record%-1
 150 PROCexamine_record
 160 CLS
 170 PROCsave_file
 180 END
 190
 200 DEFPROCcreate_record
 210 REPEAT
 220 PROCupdate_attributes(R%)
 230 record%=record%+1
 240 R%=R%+1:IFfile_end=TRUE THEN270
 250 IFR%=max_file%THEN260ELSE270
 260 file_end=TRUE:record%=record%+1
 270 UNTILfile_end=TRUE
 280 record%=record%-1
 290 ENDPROC
 300
 310 DEFPROCexamine_record
 400 ENDPROC
 410
 420 DEFPROCdisplay_record(R%)
 530 ENDPROC
 540
 550 DEFPROCdefine_initial_values
 660 ENDPROC
 670
 680 DEFPROCinitialise_file
 750 ENDPROC
 760
 770 DEFPROCdefine_field_names
 880 ENDPROC
 890
 900 DEFPROCupdate_attributes(R%)
1840 ENDPROC
1850
1860 DEFFNenter_data(across%,down%,size%,S_N$)
2080 =input$
2090
2100 DEFPROCsave_file
2360 ENDPROC
2370
2380 DEFPROCcheck_date(date$)
2510 ENDPROC
2520
2530 DEFPROCretrieve_file
2660 ENDPROC
```

Readers may wonder why the procedure for creating a record has been included in the listing - the reason is that a slight change was required in order to cater for the needs of the record-addition routine. This is in accordance with the philosophy expressed in the latter part of chapter 5. The main part of the routine will be explained before dealing with the need for the change.

Line 50 sets the file-capacity value, max_file%, to 20 but this instruction could be placed anywhere before line 100. The answer to the question produced by line 60 is tested in line 80 using the NOT operator and, unless the response by the user is "Y" or "y", the routine will end. An answer in the affirmative will cause the file to be retrieved. The possibility of an input of "Yes" or "yes" exists and although this will not prevent the program from working, the letters "e" and "s" will remain in the keyboard input buffer. Using "*FX15,1" in line 70 will flush the buffer of unwanted input. Note that no question regarding the file's name is made in this routine because it is incorporated into the file-retrieval procedure.

Line 100 tests whether or not the file is full by comparing the values of "record%" and "max_file%". If the two values match, the file cannot be added to and the routine takes its next instruction from line 150.

Now, R% would normally be set to zero before the record creation-procedure was entered, but "record%", which has been obtained from the file, indicates how many records are on the file. Readers will recall that during record creation, R% is always one less in value than record% because the array E$ starts at element zero. Thus, to select the next empty record position in the file, R% is set to the value of record% and to maintain the relationship between the two variables, record% is then incremented - line 110.

The method by which the record-creation routine terminates is by recognising that the variable, file_end, has been set TRUE. The variable is set in the attribute-update procedure which is called by the record-creation procedure. Thus, before entering the latter procedure, the variable must be set to FALSE - line 120.

The amended record-creation routine, defined from line 200, will call the attribute-update procedure with the parameter R% that was initialised in line 110. At the end of that procedure both record% and R% are incremented - lines 230 and 240. If file_end has not been set TRUE, that is the EMPLOYEE NO. value has not been entered as 999, then line 250 is used. Here, the value of R% is tested against max_file% to see whether or not the file is full. If it is, line 260 is used to set file_end to TRUE and record% is incremented before line 270 is obeyed to terminate the routine. If R% is not equal to max_file%, the routine will link back to line 210.

When file_end is set to TRUE, the routine terminates after incrementing record% and R%, line 240. The incrementing of record% is the feature that necessitated amending the record-creation routine and the result is that the routine is then able to deal with both manual termination, that is an input of 999, and automatic termination due to the file becoming full.

As an illustration of the way in which the routine works, the following "dry run" is produced, starting at line 220 with values of R%=18 and record%=20.

```
220 PROCupdate_attributes(18) - this
    is to create the 19th record
230 record%=20
240 R%=19
250 R% is not equal to max_file%
270 return to line 210
210 repeat routine
220 PROCupdate_attributes(19) - this
    is to create the 20th record.
    999 entered for EMPLOYEE NO - this
    will set file_end to TRUE.
230 record%=21
240 R%=20, but file_end=TRUE and 270
    is the next line therefore
270 no return to line 210 this time
280 record%=20
290 line 140 is next
140 record%=19
```

The value of record% is correctly set for saving the file of 19 records when line 170 is reached by the main part of the program. The manual termination of the procedure has been tested and it is now necessary to test the procedure under automatic termination conditions.

Assume that at the second visit to line 220 in the above dry run, 999 was not entered but the 20th record was created instead. The next part of the dry run would be

```
230 record%=21
240 R%=20
250 R%=max_file% - the next line is 260
260 file_end is set to TRUE and
    record%=22
270 no return to line 210 this time
280 record%=21
290 line 140 is next
140 record%=20
```

Thus, the value of record% is correctly set after the record creation routine has terminated automatically on the file becoming full.

Listing 6.1 should be entered and tested with the data given below and the file of fourteen records that was created with the data given in chapter 3. However, only the first five items are used before entering 999 for EMPLOYEE NO. This will result in nineteen records being on the file, which should be saved at the appropriate point in the routine.

The routine should then be tested again but this time the data file containing nineteen records should be used. After entering the data for the 20th record, the routine will link to the record-examination procedure automatically. The file should then be saved using a name that is different from the name used for the nineteen-record file.

Finally the routine should be tested by using the twenty-record file just created. This time the routine will link to the record-examination procedure without passing through the record-creation procedure. There will be no need to save this file since it has already been saved.

FIELD NUMBERS								
1	2	3	4	5	6	7	8	9
123	SMITH	JW	F	27/12/60	7	1/8/77	11	4900
245	SMITH	J	M	14/1/39	12	11/7/55	15	8000
290	HUMPHRIES	W	F	24/9/64	7	20/10/80	11	7600
789	JONES	A	M	1/9/36	3	14/1/52	14	8300
724	JONES	B	F	29/2/48	4	1/7/62	15	7150
413	ABBAS	C	M	5/4/47	5	1/1/65	32	6200

Amending a Record

The task of amending one or more fields in a record will require a modification of the attribute-update procedure that has already been developed. The modification must allow the normal sequence of field creation in that procedure to be stepped through, field by field, with a change only to those fields that are incorrect. The field that is being offered for amendment must be clearly indicated at the same time as the existing field entry is being displayed.

Considering these criteria, the following first-level design results

1 Prepare the micro to hold the file
2 Find out whether file is to be amended
3 Retrieve the file
4 Select and amend the appropriate record or records
5 Save the amended file.

Using the experience of the previous file-extension routine, levels 1, 3 and 5 can be given in refined form as

1.1 PROCdefine_field_names
1.2 PROCdefine_initial_values
1.3 PROCinitialise_file

3.1 PROCretrieve_file

5.1 PROCsave_file.

Level 2 consists of a question that is required only because this routine is being dealt with in isolation – if it existed as part of a data-handling package, it would not be necessary.

2.1 Print query about file amendment
2.2 Input answer
2.3 If answer is not "yes", end the routine.

Level 4 will contain the new procedure for amending the record or records and the necessary questions and user answers to select those records correctly.

4.1 Display the file size
4.2 Ask user about record to be amended
4.3 Reject erroneous answers
4.4 PROCamend_record
4.5 Give user the opportunity to amend more records
4.6 Return to level 4.2 if required.

Combining the various refinements will provide an illustration of the fact that, once again, this new requirement can be provided with only a minimum of programming effort because it uses a number of existing procedures.

1.1 PROCdefine_field_names
1.2 PROCdefine_initial_values
1.3 PROCinitialise_file
2.1 Print query about file amendment
2.2 Input answer
2.3 If answer is not "yes", link to level 5.2
3.1 PROCretrieve_file

4.1 Display the file size
4.2 Ask user about record to be amended
4.3 Reject erroneous answers
4.4 PROCamend_record
4.5 Give user the opportunity to amend more records
4.6 Return to level 4.2 if required
5.1 PROCsave_file
5.2 End of routine.

There are three procedures that are not listed above even though they are called when the routine is carried out - these are PROCdisplay_record, PROCcheck_date and the function FNenter_data. Readers will recall that these are called when the attribute-update procedure is used and they will be used also in the amendment routine. The changes that are required in the attribute-update procedure can be demonstrated by considering a part of that procedure, that is the SURNAME entry routine. This is given below in the form in which it appears in chapter 3.

```
830 CLS
840 PROCdisplay_record(R%)
850 PRINTTAB(13,22);"Please input"
860 PRINTTAB(1,24);D$(1)
870 REPEAT
880 surname$=FNenter_data(22,23,16,"S")
890 UNTIL NOT NIL
900 E$(1,R%)=surname$
```

There is a control mechanism to ensure that at least one letter is entered as a surname, but once the RETURN key is pressed, there is no way in which the entry can be changed until the end of the record is reached. Even then, the complete record must be entered again. For an amendment, the record will have been created using the data available at the time but it is possible that an entry was either erroneous or incompletely known.

Thus, after line 840 the existing record will be displayed on the screen and lines 850 and 860 can be modified to offer a change of entry opportunity to the user. The item D$(1) consists of the letters that make the word SURNAME and this is displayed at position (1,24). This word can be made to flash so that attention is drawn to it - the way that this is done is to use "CHR$(136)" in a PRINT statement. This is dealt with on page 152 of the USER GUIDE and a possible complete statement for the present requirement is

PRINT CHR$(136);D$(1)

This will affect all the printing on the particular line after the flash has been initiated. The semicolon is not always required as readers can verify by typing PRINT CHR$(136)"BBC" and then pressing RETURN. However, if the line to be printed is a mixture of steady and flashing text, semicolons may be required. Try the following two statements.

        PRINT"Attention is given to ";CHR$(136);"FLASHERS"

        PRINT"Attention is given to "CHR$(136)"FLASHERS"

The statement in line 850 needs to be replaced and a satisfactory composite statement is

        PRINT:PRINT"Do you wish to amend ";CHR$(136);D$(1)

The effect of this will be that the first piece of text will appear on the same line as the flashing word, SURNAME, below the display of the record. An answer will be required and this can be prompted by an INPUT command. The response must be used either to follow the data-entry routine or to pass to the next field. A suitable statement is

INPUT"Y/N",A$:IF A$<>"Y" THEN go to next field entry point

The complete modified version of the surname entry routine is given below.

```
830 CLS
840 PROCdisplay_record(R%)
850 PRINT:PRINT"Do you wish to amend ";CHR$(136);D$(1)
860 PRINT:INPUT"Y/N",A$:IF A$<>"Y" THEN 910
870 REPEAT
880 surname$=FNenter_data(22,23,16,"S")
890 UNTIL NOT NIL
900 E$(1,R%)=surname$
```

Self-test 6.1
Could the statements in lines 850 and 860 be combined as a procedure?

    Using this example, the attribute-update procedure can be modified, identified as PROCamend_record(R%) and incorporated into the procedure library. The complete record-amending program is given below but procedures that have been described previously are not listed fully. The exceptions are PROCretrieve_file and PROCsave_file which have been modified. The modifications and the reason or reasons for their incorporation will be given later.

LISTING 6.2

```
  10 CLS
  20 PROCdefine_field_names
  30 PROCdefine_initial_values
  40 PROCinitialise_file
  50 PRINTTAB(3,6)"Is a record to be amended ?";
  60 A$=GET$
  70 IFNOT(A$="Y"ORA$="y")THEN160
  80 PROCretrieve_file
  90 CLS:PRINTTAB(3,6)"THIS FILE HOLDS ";record%;
     " RECORDS"
 100 PRINT:INPUTTAB(3,8)"Which record is to be
     amended ",N%
 110 IFN%<1ORN%>record%THEN90
 120 PROCamend_record(N%-1)
 130 CLS:INPUTTAB(3,8)"Are more records to be
     amended ",A$
 140 CLS:IF(A$="Y"ORA$="y")THEN100
 150 PROCsave_file
 160 END
 170
 180 DEFPROCdisplay_record(R%)
 290 ENDPROC
 300
 310 DEFPROCdefine_initial_values
 420 ENDPROC
 430
 440 DEFPROCinitialise_file
 510 ENDPROC
 520
 530 DEFPROCdefine_field_names
 640 ENDPROC
 650
 660 DEFPROCamend_record(R%)
 670 *FX4,1
 680 *FX229,1
 690 LOCAL A$
 700 CLS
 710 PROCdisplay_record(R%)
 720 PRINT:PRINT"Do you wish to amend";CHR$(136)
     ;D$(0)
 730 PRINT:INPUT"Y/N",A$:IFA$<>"Y"THEN850
 740 employee_no$=FNenter_data(22,23,3,"N")
 750 IFemployee_no$="999"THEN file_end=TRUE ELSE770
 760 GOTO1580
 770 IFVAL(employee_no$)>=1THEN 780ELSE740
 780 IFLEN(employee_no$)=3THEN840
 790 IFLEN(employee_no$)=2THEN820
```

```
 800 E$(0,R%)="00"+employee_no$
 810 GOTO850
 820 E$(0,R%)="0"+employee_no$
 830 GOTO850
 840 E$(0,R%)=employee_no$
 850 CLS
 860 PROCdisplay_record(R%)
 870 PRINT:PRINT"Do you wish to amend";CHR$(136)
     ;D$(1)
 880 PRINT:INPUT"Y/N",A$:IFA$<>"Y"THEN930
 890 REPEAT
 900 surname$=FNenter_data(22,23,16,"S")
 910 UNTIL NOT NIL
 920 E$(1,R%)=surname$
 930 CLS
 940 PROCdisplay_record(R%)
 950 PRINT:PRINT"Do you wish to amend";CHR$(136)
     ;D$(2)
 960 PRINT:INPUT"Y/N",A$:IFA$<>"Y"THEN1010
 970 REPEAT
 980 initials$=FNenter_data(22,23,2,"S")
 990 UNTIL NOT NIL
1000 E$(2,R%)=initials$
1010 CLS
1020 PROCdisplay_record(R%)
1030 PRINT:PRINT"Do you wish to amend";CHR$(136)
     ;D$(3)
1040 PRINT:INPUT"Y/N",A$:IFA$<>"Y"THEN1100
1050 sex$=FNenter_data(22,23,1,"S")
1060 IF sex$="M" OR sex$="F" THEN 1090
1070 VDU7
1080 GOTO1050
1090 E$(3,R%)=sex$
1100 CLS
1110 PROCdisplay_record(R%)
1120 PRINT:PRINT"Do you wish to amend";CHR$(136)
     ;D$(4)
1130 PRINT:INPUT"Y/N",A$:IFA$<>"Y"THEN1200
1140 REPEAT
1150 born$=FNenter_data(22,23,6,"N")
1160 UNTIL LEN(born$)=6
1170 PROCcheck_date(born$)
1180 IFdate=FALSE THENVDU7:GOTO1140
1190 E$(4,R%)=D$+M$+Y$
1200 CLS
1210 PROCdisplay_record(R%)
1220 PRINT:PRINT"Do you wish to amend";CHR$(136)
     ;D$(5)
1230 PRINT:INPUT"Y/N",A$:IFA$<>"Y"THEN1280
1240 REPEAT
1250 dept$=FNenter_data(22,23,2,"N")
```

```
1260 UNTIL NOT NIL
1270 E$(5,R%)=dept$
1280 CLS
1290 PROCdisplay_record(R%)
1300 PRINT:PRINT"Do you wish to amend";CHR$(136)
     ;D$(6)
1310 PRINT:INPUT"Y/N",A$:IFA$<>"Y"THEN1380
1320 REPEAT
1330 joined$=FNenter_data(22,23,6,"N")
1340 UNTIL LEN(joined$)=6
1350 PROCcheck_date(joined$)
1360 IFdate=FALSE THENVDU7:GOTO1320
1370 E$(6,R%)=Y$+M$+D$
1380 CLS
1390 PROCdisplay_record(R%)
1400 PRINT:PRINT"Do you wish to amend";CHR$(136)
     ;D$(7)
1410 PRINT:INPUT"Y/N",A$:IFA$<>"Y"THEN1460
1420 REPEAT
1430 job$=FNenter_data(22,23,2,"N")
1440 UNTIL NOT NIL
1450 E$(7,R%)=job$
1460 CLS
1470 PROCdisplay_record(R%)
1480 PRINT:PRINT"Do you wish to amend";CHR$(136)
     ;D$(8)
1490 PRINT:INPUT"Y/N",A$:IFA$<>"Y"THEN1530
1500 salary$=FNenter_data(22,23,5,"N")
1510 IF VAL(salary$)<3500 THEN 1500
1520 E$(8,R%)=salary$
1530 CLS
1540 PROCdisplay_record(R%)
1550 PRINTTAB(6,22);"Are details correct? (Y/N)"
1560 A$=GET$
1570 IF A$="Y" OR A$="y" THEN 1580ELSE 660
1580 *FX4,0
1590 *FX229,0
1600 ENDPROC
1610
1620 DEFFNenter_data(across%,down%,size%,S_N$)
1840 =input$
1850
1860 DEFPROCsave_file
1870 LOCAL A$,N$
1880 PRINTTAB(12,2);"SAVING THE FILE"
1890 PRINTTAB(12,3);"---------------"
1900 PRINT´
1910 PRINT"There are ";record%;" records on the file"
1920 PRINT"that has been created."
1930 PRINT´´
1940 PRINT"Is the file to be saved?(Y/N) ",
```

```
1950 INPUTA$
1960 IF NOT(A$="Y" OR A$="y" OR A$="N" OR A$="n")
     THEN1940
1970 PRINT´´
1980 IFA$="Y" OR A$="y"THEN2010
1990 PRINT"SAFETY CHECK!!!":PRINT:PRINT"INPUT
     ´Y´ OR ´y´ FOR SAVING THE FILE"
2000 INPUTA$:IF NOT(A$="Y" OR A$="y")THEN2130
2010 PRINT"Please input the name of the file"
2020 INPUT"that is to be saved "N$
2030 FILE=OPENOUT(N$)
2040 PRINT#FILE,record%
2050 FORV%=0TOrecord%-1
2060 FORN%=0TO8
2070 PRINT#FILE,E$(N%,V%)
2080 NEXT
2090 NEXT
2100 CLOSE#FILE
2110 PRINT´´
2120 PRINT"The file ";N$;" has been saved"
2130 ENDPROC
2140
2150 DEFPROCcheck_date(date$)
2280 ENDPROC
2290
2300 DEFPROCretrieve_file
2310 CLS
2320 INPUTTAB(3,6)"What file is to be retrieved ",N$
2330 IFN$=""THEN2320
2340 FILE=OPENIN(N$)
2350 INPUT#FILE,record%
2360 V%=0
2370 REPEAT
2380 FORN%=0TO8
2390 INPUT#FILE,E$(N%,V%)
2400 NEXT
2410 V%=V%+1
2420 UNTIL EOF#(FILE)
2430 CLOSE#FILE
2440 ENDPROC
```

As can be seen from the listing, the record-amending
procedure is the largest part of the routine and this
should indicate to readers that some method of
incorporating it into the attribute-update procedure is
desirable in order to save memory space. Readers will
remember that with a fixed amount of memory available,
any space used for program must be at the expense of
file space. Having made that point, however, it is not
necessary to pursue the matter further at this stage.

Lines 50 to 70 inclusive deal with the escape route
for users that was mentioned earlier - this is
necessary because the routine is not yet part of a
complete package. After retrieving the file, line 80,
the value of record% is given to the user in line 90
and, should record identity numbers outside the file
range be input, the program links back to line 90. Line
100 makes the assumption that the user knows the number
of the record that is to be amended. This is, of
course, quite likely because either a search will have
been carried out previously or a printout of relevant
records will be available.

Accepting the risk of repetition, the record
identity number is always one more than the actual
number of the record in the file and this is why N% is
used in line 100 but N%-1 is used in line 120. A return
to line 100 is made for an affirmative answer to the
question in line 130 or else the amended file can be
saved.

The original file saving procedure was not
sufficiently foolproof and it was possible merely to
press RETURN without entering "Y" or "y" and thus lose
all the records on that file. Line 1960 ensures that
the program will link back to line 1940 unless upper or
lower case versions of either "Y" or "N" are input at
line 1950. Line 1980 deals with the affirmative
response by the user, but users giving a negative
response are offered a further chance to either change
their response or confirm the original one - this is
dealt with in lines 1990 and 2000.

The other change to the procedure concerns lines
2050, 2060 and 2070 in which the numeric variables V
and N have been replaced by V% and N% respectively.

As mentioned earlier, the file-retrieval procedure
has been altered also. Line 2330 ensures that the user
response to the question in line 2320 is not the null
string - a definite character must be input. A further
change concerns the replacement of the variables V and
N by V% and N% respectively - lines 2360, 2380, 2390
and 2410.

Listing 6.2 (L6.2) should now be entered and RUN
using the data files that have been created as a result
of the work in previous chapters. Readers should
remember that saving amended files with the names of
the original files will erase the pre-amendment data
and so different names must be used if all versions are
required to be kept.

When running the routine, it should be noted that
lines 70, 140 and the lines in PROCamend_record(R%)
that accept user responses, for example 730, 880 etc.,
only test for an input of "Y" or "y" and any other

input will be interpreted as a negative response.
Readers should be aware that the method may be unsafe
in certain circumstances - see the previous comments
about the changes to the saving and retrieval
procedures.

Removing a Record

This part of the file-updating work has been left until
last because it is possibly the most difficult of the
three parts to implement as a concept although the
concept is, in itself, very simple. Imagine that a
queue has formed at a bus stop, in a well-behaved
manner with everyone taking the correct place at the
end of the line. This corresponds to an ordered file of
records of the sort that has been considered so far. In
this case, however, the ordering is chronological as
opposed to alphabetic or numeric ordering. A passing
car stops and the driver invites one of the persons in
the queue to join him in the car. This corresponds to
the removal of a record from the file.
   The bus queue example can be extended because when
the person leaves the queue, any persons behind will
move along one place to fill the gap that has been
left. In the record-removal situation, all the records
"behind" the gap that has been created will move along,
in order, to fill the gap. This is the method that will
be incorporated as a procedure for record removal.
   The top down design for the routine is

1 Prepare the micro to hold a file
2 Find out if a file is to be reduced
3 Retrieve the file
4 Examine the records
5 Remove the record(s) from the file
6 Save the remaing records.

   The usual second level of refinement will give

1.1 PROCdefine_field_names
1.2 PROCdefine_initial_values
1.3 PROCinitialise_file
3.1 PROCretrieve_file
4.1 PROCexamine_record
6.1 PROCsave_file.

   Level 2 will, as discussed in the previous section,
provide an escape route in case of a change of
intention on the part of the user. The second level

refinement will give

2.1 Ask the user if a record is to be removed
2.2 Input the answer
2.3 If answer is negative, link to the end of the routine.

Level 5 is refined to cater for both the record-removal procedure and the questioning of the user regarding further record removals.

5.1 PROCremove_record(R%)
5.2 Find out about further record removals

Further refinement of level 5.2 is possible to give

5.2.1 Ask user if another record is to be removed
5.2.2 Input user response
5.2.3 Link back to level 5.1 if answer is "yes".

The final result of the refining process is

1.1 PROCdefine_field_names
1.2 PROCdefine_initial_values
1.3 PROCinitialise_file
2.1 Ask the user if a record is to be removed
2.2 Input the answer
2.3 If answer is negative, link to level 7
3.1 PROCretrieve_file
4.1 PROCexamine_record
5.1 PROCremove_record(R%)
5.2.1 Ask user if another record is to be removed
5.2.2 Input user response
5.2.3 Link back to level 5.1 if answer is "yes"
6.1 PROCsave_file
7 End.

The implementation of the record-removal concept is fairly easy if it is remembered that a record is identified by the value of R% that is equal to zero for the first record. In addition, each field in a record is identified by a combination of R% and the field number. The number of records in the file is given by "record%" and, when a record is removed from the file, record% must be decremented. Thus, knowing the value of R% for the record that is to be removed allows the record that is "behind" to be given the same value of R%. This has the effect of removing the required record from the file. Of course, the procedure must be applied, in turn, to all the remaining records in the file so that the original ordering of the file is not altered.

The resulting procedure is given in listing 6.3.

```
LISTING 6.3
  10 CLS
  20 PROCdefine_field_names
  30 PROCdefine_initial_values
  40 PROCinitialise_file
  50 PRINTTAB(3,6)"Is a record to be removed ?";
  60 A$=GET$
  70 IFNOT(A$="Y"ORA$="y")THEN150
  80 PROCretrieve_file
  90 PROCexamine_record
 100 CLS:PROCremove_record(R%)
 110 CLS:PRINTTAB(3,6)"Are any more records to be
     removed ?";
 120 A$=GET$
 130 IFA$="Y"ORA$="y"THEN100
 140 CLS:PROCsave_file
 150 END
 160
 170 DEFPROCexamine_record
 260 ENDPROC
 270
 280 DEFPROCdisplay_record(R%)
 390 ENDPROC
 400
 410 DEFPROCdefine_initial_values
 520 ENDPROC
 530
 540 DEFPROCinitialise_file
 610 ENDPROC
 620
 630 DEFPROCdefine_field_names
 740 ENDPROC
 750
 760 DEFPROCremove_record(R%)
 770 PRINTTAB(3,6)"Which record is to be removed ";
 780 INPUTR%:IFR%<1ORR%>record%THEN770
 790 FORE%=R%-1TOrecord%-2
 800 FORN%=0TO8
 810 E$(N%,E%)=E$(N%,E%+1)
 820 NEXT:NEXT
 830 record%=record%-1
 840 ENDPROC
 850
 860 DEFPROCretrieve_file
1000 ENDPROC
1010
1020 DEFPROCsave_file
1290 ENDPROC
```

Readers will have realised that the order of presentation of procedures within a routine is unimportant because it is the name that is recognised, not the position within the routine.

Examination of lines 770 to 830 inclusive indicates that the procedure is both compact and straightforward. A check that the value of R%, for the record that is to be removed, lies inside the file's range is carried out in line 780. The outer of the two nested FOR...NEXT loops, line 790, uses R%-1 as its starting value and record%-2 as its terminating value. A little thought will convince readers that these values are correct. It is felt that enough discussion about the values of R% has taken place already but some explanation of the choice of terminating value is in order.

Consider that the file holds ten records and that one record is to be removed. If a count from the beginning to the end of the file is to be carried out, the counter could use the values of record% from one to ten. It could also use the values of R% from zero to nine or record%-1 because they are the same. At the end of the record-removal procedure, the number of records in the file will be nine or record%-2. Thus for the removal of a record from any position in the file, the upper limit will be record%-2.

Line 800 defines the limits of the inner FOR...NEXT loop in accordance with the dimensioning of the array that holds the file. Thus lines 790 to 820 inclusive cause the rejected record to be removed by successively moving all the records "behind" it along one place. Finally, line 830 decrements record% so that the removal of a record from the file is completed in all respects.

Listing 6.3 should now be entered and tested with the previously created files. No attempt should be made at this stage, however, to remove the last record in any file. Readers will observe that line 90 allows the user to make an examination of the file in order that the numbers of records that are to be removed can be verified before a mistake is made. During examination, the input of a record number that is outside the file's range will terminate the procedure - this is, of course, the usual response.

Self-test 6.2
(a)   If a value that is outside the file's range is
      input during the actual record-removal part of
      the routine, the original number remains on
      display when the user is requested to input again
      - this is controlled by line 770. This is not

desirable and readers are asked to formulate a correction to the error.

b)   If an attempt is made to remove the last record in a file, an error message is displayed by the micro to the effect that a subscript error exists in line 810. The reason is that, for the last record only, there is no record to be moved along to take its place when it is removed. The subscript referred to is the value E%+1 which is outside the file's range in the case of the last record. It could be argued that the probability of wanting to remove the last record is one in "record%", that is one divided by record%, which will be low for a large file. This is not a valid argument, however, and readers are asked to consider how the problem could be overcome without affecting other procedures.

7 Printing from Files

A common requirement will be to obtain a printed copy of one or more records that are contained in a file. Appendix II gives an overview of the various types of printer that are available for use with the BBC micro. However, because there is such a wide choice, there are several ways of achieving the same printing format for a document when using different printers. It would be a difficult task, therefore, to produce routines for all the printers that exist at the time of writing and are likely to exist in the future. For this reason, and also because some readers will not initially have access to a printer, a printing routine that works with any printer is required.

A General-purpose Printing Routine

The code for a particular printed character will be standard in most cases and so the output of letter "A" from the micro will cause the same letter to be printed by most printers. Some printers provide a choice of character sets to suit differing languages and thus the code for a particular letter or symbol, although presented correctly on the screen, may result in the wrong character being printed on paper. In the experience of the writer, however, all printers will correctly interpret the codes for letters, numbers, punctuation marks, space and the key marked "return" on the BBC micro.

The usual problem that is met when printing is the use of the same code for the hash symbol, "#", in the USA character set and the sterling symbol, "£", in the UK character set. It is expected that the majority of readers will be printing from the UK character set and using the hash symbol only for programming and then there will be no problem because the correct code will be SAVEd when storing programs.

It is this fact that allows a successful all-printer output routine to be developed. The method is based on the availability in BBC BASIC of a "space" statement – see page 354 of the User Guide. The statement includes

a number that tells the printer to move along the paper
without printing anything, that is to print spaces. It
is used with a PRINT statement and so will have an
effect on the screen display. Thus, the routine can be
tested by readers even if a printer is not available.

A demonstration routine will be developed before
employing the method with records on the files that
readers   have   already   created.   An   easy   method of
producing columns of results is looked at in listing
7.1.

LISTING 7.1
```
 10 DIMN$(10)
 20 DIMN(10)
 30 FORI=1TO10
 40 READN$(I),N(I)
 50 NEXT
 60 FORI=1TO10
 70 PRINTN$(I),N(I)
 80 NEXT
 90 DATA ABLE,123.789,BAKER,0.89,
    CHARLIE,123456.01,DOG,3.0000034,
    EASY,1.2345,FOX,.8,GEORGE,3456,
    HOW,12.89,ITEM,7890000,JIG,.3456789
100 END
```

This is a simple routine that READs ten pairs of data
items from a DATA statement and places the first of the
pair into array N$ and the second of the pair into
array N. This part of the routine is given in lines 30,
40, 50 and 90 with the arrays being dimensioned in
lines 10 and 20. The remaining part of the routine, in
lines · 60 to 80 inclusive, will print ten rows of two
data items each consisting of a name and a number.   The
output will be the same as in the table that follows.

ABLE	123.789
BAKER	0.89
CHARLIE	123456.01
DOG	3.0000034
EASY	1.2345
FOX	0.8
GEORGE	3456
HOW	12.89
ITEM	7890000
JIG	0.3456789

This result is produced by the separation of N$(I) and
N(I) by a comma in line 70. This type of formatting is

described on page 324 of the User Guide and is acceptable if right-justification of the second column is desired. However, if the spacing between the two columns is to be different from that given in the example, this method is unusable. This is because the comma separator makes each new column start ten printing positions from the previous column. In fact, there are really eleven printing positions between columns because a position is reserved for a minus sign should one be required. This feature can be tested by loading listing 7.1 and running it.

If a parallel printer is available, pressing CTRL B before typing RUN will switch the printer on and the result will be displayed on the screen and printed on the paper. CTRL C wil switch the printer off again. If a serial printer is being used, it will be necessary to key in *FX5,2 before CTRL B is used. This is because the BBC micro defaults to a parallel printer mode when switched on - further details are given on pages 404-8 and page 423 of the User Guide.

Now use the edit keys to change the DATA statement so that the number after "CHARLIE" is "-123456.01". RUN the program again to check that although a minus sign appears, the position of the last character in the third row remains unchanged, thus illustrating that ten positions separate each column produced by using a comma. If a semicolon is used as a separator in the PRINT statement, there will be no separation between the data items.

When a ten-position separation is not acceptable, the usual procedure is to use TAB in the PRINT statement - see page 360 of the User Guide. Now this method will produce the desired column spacing on the screen but it is unlikely that an acceptable printed output will result because the code for TAB will not be interpreted correctly. Some printers have a tabulate facility but this has to be initiated by sending the correct codes from the micro.

Listing 7.2 uses the SPC statement introduced earlier to overcome this problem.

LISTING 7.2

```
 10 DIMN$(10)
 20 DIMN(10)
 30 FORI=1TO10
 40 READN$(I)
 50 READN(I)
 60 NEXT
 70 FORI=1TO10
 80 PRINTSPC(5);N$(I);
```

```
 90  Y$=STR$(N(I))
100  X=20-LEN(N$(I))-LEN(Y$)
110  PRINTSPC(X);N(I)
120  NEXT
130  DATA ABLE,123.789,BAKER,0.89,
     CHARLIE,123456.01,DOG,3.0000034,
     EASY,1.2345,FOX,.8,GEORGE,3456,
     HOW,12.89,ITEM,7890000,JIG,.3456789
140  END
```

In line 80, the first data item, N$(I), is displayed on
the screen 5 spaces in from the left-hand edge of the
screen. The semicolon at the end of the statement will
ensure that the next character group to be displayed
will be on the same line as the first data item. This
group will be the second data item which is printed
after "X" spaces have been "printed" - line 110. The
value of X is calculated using the number of characters
in N$(I) and in N(I). The two quantities are produced
by using the LEN function in line 100 and subtracting
them from twenty. The variable, Y$, is used in line 100
to prevent syntax errors but the value of this string
variable has to be produced from a numeric variable
using the STR$ function - line 90.

Thus the total distance from the beginning of the
first data item to the end of the second data item is
twenty printing positions and loading the program and
RUNning it will give the same display as the previous
routine did. The difference between the two routines
lies in the fact that this total distance can be
changed to suit whatever requirements exist. Readers
should experiment by changing the value given as twenty
in line 100.

The second column in the previous two examples was
right-justified and a particular requirement may be for
a left-justified column. This means that the first data
item's length must be subtracted from say, twenty, and
the result will be the number of spaces that are to be
printed before the second data item is printed. The
problem is, in fact, much simpler than that solved in
listing 7.2 and the solution is given in listing 7.3.

LISTING 7.3
```
10  DIMN$(10)
20  DIMN(10)
30  FORI=1TO10
40  READN$(I)
50  READN(I)
60  NEXT
70  FORI=1TO10
```

```
 80 PRINTSPC(5);N$(I);
 90 X=20-LEN(N$(I))
100 PRINTSPC(X);N(I)
110 NEXT
120 DATAABLE,123.789,BAKER,0.89,
    CHARLIE,123456.01,DOG,3.0000034,
    EASY,1.2345,FOX,.8,GEORGE,3456,
    HOW,12.89,ITEM,7890000,JIG,.3456789
130 END
```

There is no need to form the length of the numeric
variable, N(I), in this program because
left-justification will require printing to start at
the beginning of the first character of the second data
item. Thus line 90 forms "X" which is the result of
subtracting the length of N$(I) from twenty. This value
is then used to print the correct number of spaces in
line 100. Readers should now input the program given in
listing 7.3 and RUN it. After first testing it using
the value twenty given in line 90 of the listing, other
values should be used to demonstrate that full control
of the printing position of the second column is
provided.

There is likely to be a requirement to present
printed numerical data with the decimal points aligned
instead of the random positioning produced in the
previous examples. There are various ways of achieving
this sort of result but, in order to use the space
statement as before, it is necessary to take into
account the position of the decimal point in relation
to the beginning of the number. When this has been
done, the problem is easily solved.

A string value for the number, N(I), is required as
in listing 7.2 but this time it is only the whole or
integer part of the number that is of interest. The
integer part of N(I) can be extracted by using the
INTeger function - page 282 of the User Guide. The
value for the length of the integer part of the number
is then given by

$$LEN(STR\$(INT(N(I))))$$

The use of the nested brackets aids understanding of
what the statement is being used for although, with the
exception of the inner pair, they are not always
essential for the three separate functions to be
carried out correctly. The inner function, INT, is
carried out first and will extract the whole number
part of N(I). Next, the STR$ function is performed and
forms the equivalent string representation of the
integer part of the number. Finally, the LEN function

will count how many digits were extracted by the function INT. The complete program is given below.

```
LISTING 7.4
 10 DIMN$(10)
 20 DIMN(10)
 30 FORI=1TO10
 40 READN$(I):READN(I)
 50 NEXT
 60 FORI=1TO10
 70 PRINTSPC(5);N$(I);
 80 Y$=STR$(INT(N(I)))
 90 X=20-LEN(N$(I))-LEN(Y$)
100 PRINTSPC(X);N(I)
110 NEXT
120 DATAABLE,123.789,BAKER,0.89,
    CHARLIE,123456.01,DOG,3.0000034,
    EASY,1.2345,FOX,.8,GEORGE,3456,
    HOW,12.89,ITEM,7890000,JIG,.3456789
130 END
```

In this program, the composite instruction given before the listing is split into two separate statements - lines 80 and 90. Listing 7.4, as given above, should be entered and RUN to verify that the display is as now illustrated.

```
ABLE           123.789
BAKER            0.89
CHARLIE        123456.01
DOG                3.0000034
EASY             1.2345
FOX              0.8
GEORGE         3456
HOW             12.89
ITEM         7890000
JIG              0.3456789
```

Again, readers should vary the value given as twenty in line 90, to check that full control of positioning is still available. Readers should also check that changing lines 80 and 90 to the form given below does not affect the output format.

```
80 Y$=STR$INTN(I)
90 X=20-LENN$(I)-LENY$
```

In concluding this introductory work on printing data, it must be repeated that other methods do exist and that each one may be efficient with a given printer but possibly less efficient or even unusable on another printer. It is essential, therefore, that users have access to a method that can be used on their printer and then, when sufficient familiarity has been gained, the method advocated by the manufacturer of that printer can be adopted if desired.

Printing from Data Files

The use of the SPC statement will now be extended to cover the requirement of printing records from data files. The usual top-down-design method will be used and the introduction of modified or new procedures will be kept to a minimum. A little thought will reveal that a printing requirement will normally follow a file-search operation and this indicates that the routine developed in chapter 5 could be extended to include a printing option. The resulting routine should be able to cater for a user requirement of printing a number of individually selected records or of printing a sequence of records starting and finishing at selected records.

The top-down-design developed for the search routine will be extended to cover the printing requirement and the procedure is

1. Search an ordered file for required data
2. Tell the user where the data is or give a "not found" message
3. Provide the option of printing one or more records
4. Provide the option of further searches

There is no need to refine levels 1, 2 and 4 because they have already been dealt with in chapter 5. The refinement of level 3 is

3.1 Offer option of printing records
3.2 If option not taken up, link to level 4
3.3 Offer choice of single-record or multiple-record printing
3.4 Provide required printing
3.5 Offer option of further printing
3.6 If option taken up, link to level 3.3

3.3.1.1 Question user regarding readiness of printer
3.3.1.2 If answer is negative, link to 3.3.1.1
3.3.1.3 Offer option of single-record printing
3.3.1.4 If option not taken up, link to level 3.3.2.1
3.3.1.5 Request data on record to be printed
3.3.1.6 Use record-printing procedure
3.3.1.7 Offer option of further printing of single record

3.3.1.8 If option taken up, link to level 3.3.1.5
3.3.2.1 Offer option of multiple-record printing
3.3.2.2 If option not taken up, link to level 4
3.3.2.3 Request data on first and last records of
sequence to be printed
3.3.2.4 Repeat use of record-printing procedure
3.3.2.5 Until last record of sequence is printed

3.4.1 Prepare screen for display of printed item
3.4.2 Enable printer to accept data
3.4.3 Repeat printing of a field, using the SPC
statement, until all the fields are printed
3.4.4 Disenable printer.

Level 3.4.3 cannot be refined until the problem has
been defined a little more clearly. It has already been
stated that certain key depressions on the keyboard of
the micro will either produce an incorrect printed
character or no character at all. One such key is that
marked "TAB" which is used, readers will recall, when
formatting the screen display in the record-display
procedure. Thus the record-display procedure is
unusable because it contains TAB statements.

It is therefore necessary to present for printing
each of the data items for a field, using a loop
structure within the procedure, instead of calling up
the record-display procedure that has been used for
screen displays so far. Does this mean that
PROCdisplay_record(R%) has to be changed? A little
thought will reveal that this is not necessary because,
in this case, the printed record and the screen display
serve different purposes.

The screen display is subject to the constraints
imposed by the size of the screen whereas the printed
output can be formatted to suit the requirements of
users who should not be made to suffer the consequences
of limited screen measurements. Certain information is
presented on the screen during the various file
handling-operations that is of little or no interest to
other users of those records. More importantly, certain
information might be contained on a record that is not
for general use. Date of birth and salary details are
examples of information that should be revealed only to
certain types of user - accounts department staff, for
example.

Taking the above comments into account, the example
of printing from a record will use only the fields that
are listed below. It is not necessary to print a record
number and, in fact, to do so might be misleading
because this is a value that will most likely change
whenever a file-update or file-sort operation is
carried out.

EMPLOYEE NO.
SURNAME
DEPARTMENT NO.
JOB CODE

For this example, no other selection of fields will be available although this requirement is obviously one that will need to be catered for eventually. Taking these features into account at this stage will allow for future extension of the facilities when the need arises. The immediate consequence of this decision is that the present refinement of level 3 is insufficient since information regarding the fields to be printed is not conveyed to the printing routine.

The problem can be overcome, when necessary, by further refinement of levels 3.3.1 and 3.3.2 to enable users to select the fields appropriate to a particular need. This feature may, as discussed previously, require some type of privacy or access control so that only authorised personnel are allowed access to certain information.

Level 3.4.3 can now be refined to include these features.

3.4.3.1 Access array holding information on fields to be printed
3.4.3.2 Repeat use of array element to print desired field
3.4.3.3 Until last array element dealt with

3.4.3.2.1 Print leading spaces
3.4.3.2.2 Print field name using array element and record identifier
3.4.3.2.3 Print intermediate spaces
3.4.3.2.4 Print field value using array element and record identifier

The result of using selectable field numbers is that the sequence of fields on the printed output can also be controlled by the user. The routine that results from the refinement of the design is given in listing 7.5.

```
LISTING 7.5
  10 CLS
  20 PROCdefine_field_names
  30 PROCdefine_initial_values
  40 PROCinitialise_file
  50 PROCretrieve_file
  60 DIMF(8)
  70 PRINT´
```

```
 80 PRINTTAB(0,6);"What field is to be used in the
    search":PRINT´
 90 INPUTfield%
100 CLS:PRINTTAB(1,4);"What item is to be searched
    for":PRINT
110 INPUTsearch$
120 PROCsearch_file(field%,search$)
130 PROCexamine_record
140 CLS:PRINT´
150 INPUTTAB(0,6)"Is a printout required (Y/N)",A$
160 IFNOT(A$="Y"ORA$="y")THEN410
170 INPUTTAB(0,9)"Is printer ready for printing
    (Y/N)",A$
180 IFNOT(A$="Y"ORA$="y")THEN170
190 PRINTTAB(0,12)"Is a printout of a single"
200 INPUTTAB(0,13)"record required (Y/N)",A$
210 IFNOT(A$="Y"ORA$="y")THEN290
220 F(0)=1:F(1)=4:F(2)=2:F(3)=5:F(4)=9:F(5)=7:F(6)=3
    :F(7)=6:F(8)=8
230 CLS:PRINT´´:PRINTTAB(0,6)"Please input the number
    of the"
240 PRINTTAB(0,7)"record that is to be printed"
250 INPUTN%:R%=N%-1
260 PROCprint_record(R%)
270 PRINTTAB(1,22)"Are any more single records to be
    printed (Y/N)"
280 INPUTA$:IFA$="Y"ORA$="y"THEN230
290 CLS:PRINTTAB(0,6)"Is a sequence of records"
300 INPUTTAB(0,7)"to be printed (Y/N)",A$
310 IFNOT(A$="Y"ORA$="y")THEN410
320 F(0)=1:F(1)=2:F(2)=6:F(3)=8
330 CLS:INPUTTAB(0,6)"The first record in the sequence
    is ",F%
340 INPUTTAB(0,9)"and the last record in the sequence
    is ",L%
350 FORR%=F%-1TOL%-1
360 PROCprint_record(R%)
370 NEXT
380 PRINTTAB(0,22)"Are any more sequences to be
    printed"
390 INPUTA$
400 IFA$="Y"ORA$="y"THEN330
410 CLS:PRINT´
420 PRINTTAB(0,6)"Are any more searches to be carried"
430 INPUTTAB(0,7)"out in this field (Y/N)",A$
440 IFNOT(A$="Y"ORA$="y")THEN450ELSE100
450 END
460
470 DEFPROCexamine_record
560 ENDPROC
570
```

```
 580 DEFPROCdisplay_record(R%)
 690 ENDPROC
 700
 710 DEFPROCdefine_initial_values
 820 ENDPROC
 830
 840 DEFPROCinitialise_file
 910 ENDPROC
 920
 930 DEFPROCdefine_field_names
1040 ENDPROC
1050
1060 DEFPROCretrieve_file
1190 ENDPROC
1200
1210 DEFPROCsearch_file(field%,search$)
1330 ENDPROC
1340
1350 DEFPROCrepeated_entries(field%,M%,search$)
1500 ENDPROC
1510
1520 DEFPROCprint_record(R%)
1530 CLS:VDU2:PRINT´´
1540 FORN%=1TO9
1550 X%=F(N%-1)
1560 IFX%=0THEN1620
1570 X%=X%-1
1580 PRINTSPC(2);D$(X%);
1590 X=30-LEN(D$(X%))-LEN(E$(X%,R%))
1600 PRINTSPC(X);
1610 PRINTE$(X%,R%)
1620 NEXT
1630 VDU3
1640 ENDPROC
```

Lines 140 to 400 inclusive deal with the dialogue
between the micro and the user when a printing of one
or more records is required. A choice of one or more
single-record printing operations or the printing of a
range of sequential records is offered in line 190.
Line 220 allocates field number values to the array F
that is DIMensioned in line 60. The purpose of the
array is to provide information to the record-printing
routine regarding the fields that are to be printed. In
line 220, all fields are nominated for printing but not
in the same order as they appear in the record display
used when searching, sorting and updating files. This
is to demonstrate how selective printing of data can be
obtained. A further demonstration of this feature is
given in line 320 where only four fields are selected.

After specifying the record that is to be printed, in lines 230 to 250 inclusive, the record-printing routine is entered. The option of more single-record printing is then given to the user. A negative response will result in the option of printing a record sequence being given in line 290 and if this is not taken up, an offer of further searching is made. A positive response will, after nominating fields in line 320, result in the user being asked to state the range of the sequence in lines 330 and 340. The two values that are input are used, after necessary modification, as the limits for the FOR...NEXT loop in lines 350, 360 and 370.

The option of further record-sequence printing is given in line 380 and if the response is negative, a further search option is presented. An answer in the affirmative will enable further printing of single records to be made if desired. Record-sequence printing can then be obtained as before and the offers of further printing will not terminate until a negative answer is given to the questions in lines 380 and 420.

Referring now to the printing procedure, defined from line 1520, lines 1530 and 1630 contain VDU statements. These are defined, on page 378 of the User Guide, as enabling and disenabling the printer respectively. This means that an easy means of testing the printing routine can be provided, for users not having access to a printer, by simply deleting the VDU2 statement from line 1530.

There is a maximum of nine fields that can be printed from records in the EMPLOYEE file and this value is used to set up the FOR...NEXT loop in line 1540. When array F was DIMensioned in line 60, all elements were initialised to zero – see page 237 of the User Guide. Thus the allocation of four values to the array in line 320 will leave the last five elements in the array still containing zero. The first zero that is obtained from array F by the statement in line 1550 will cause the test in line 1560 to be satisfied and the procedure will terminate by taking the next instruction from line 1620. Readers should note that an exit from the procedure via line 1630 instead of line 1620 is incorrect because the FOR...NEXT loop will not be completed and an error situation will be created.

The reason why line 1570 is included is to take account of the fact that the arrays used for holding field names and field values are numbered from zero. The value of X% is then used to obtain the correct field name and field value, lines 1580 and 1610 respectively, and to calculate the correct number of spaces between these two items in line 1590. As the value 30 is used in this line, the result will be a

total line length of thirty characters including field
name and field value. In addition, two spaces are
printed before the thirty characters are printed - line
1580. Readers are reminded that the field names used in
the printing procedure are those defined in
PROCdefine_field_names but there is no reason why other
names should not be used if desired. In such a case,
the names should be defined and held in an array that
is accessible from the printing procedure.

The program given in listing 7.5 should be entered
and tested with the EMPLOYEE files. The program
cassette number for this routine is L7.5 but readers
not having access to the cassette can key in the
program and add the necessary procedures from the
library.

This printing routine contains a number of features
that should be dealt with before it is incorporated
into a data-handling package. Some of them are of a
cosmetic nature only and do not impair the operation of
the routine but others could lead to problems. The
major areas that should receive attention are indicated
in the following self-test questions in which readers
are expected to be able to prcvide solutions to
overcome the problem areas indicated.

Self-test 7.1
If readers remove the VDU2 statement from line 1530 and
then insert it before the remaining statements in that
line, the result of printing a number of records will
be different from that expected. Try to state what the
result will be when the modified routine is used for
printing.

Self-test 7.2
If the VDU2 statement is inserted sfter the two
remaining statements in line 1530, the result is again
different from that expected. From the solution to
self-test 7.1 readers should be able to deduce the
effect of this insertion on the printed output.

Self-test 7.3
If the response to the requests in lines 330 and 340 is
a pair of numbers in which the first is larger than the
second, the result will be that only the first number
is used to obtain a printed output. Explain the reason
for this behaviour and devise a modification that will
indicate to the user that an input error has been
perpetrated.

Self-test 7.4
If a sequence of printed records is requested, a set of
four fields will be printed for each record. Should
single record printing be obtained next, while still in
the same RUN, and then a repeat of the initial sequence
is requested, the results will differ from those
obtained previously. What modification to the routine
should be made in order that this result cannot occur?

Self-test 7.5
In the previous question, a possible outcome of the
program fault is a labour-relation problem. By RUNning
the routine in the sequence detailed, deduce why such a
situation could occur.

Self-test 7.6
Although the number of records contained in a file is
given as a result from a search of a file, there is
nothing to prevent a user of the record-printing
routine from requesting a printed copy of a
non-existent record. A modification to the routine is
required and readers should test their solution on a
duplicate of the program, just in case the modification
has serious repercussions on the original program.

Self-test 7.7
This last question was referred to previously when
discussing likely future requirements for the routine.
What modifications are necessary in order that users
can select which fields are to be printed? Incorporate
the modification to the duplicate program and test it.

8 The Use of Floppy Discs

The development work on the file handling routines has been on the assumption that a cassette recorder was being used to store both program and data. The addition of routines to satisfy the emerging requirements of the program was at the expense of memory that had been available for holding the file. By design, the sample file had a maximum of twenty records and so no memory-shortage problems emerged. It should be noted, however, that the complete program, containing all the procedures, has not so far been resident in memory and thus a possible shortage of memory was not revealed to the user.

The problem would have arisen, however, when the complete file-handling package was used to create a file in memory. The quantity of records that could be created would not have been satisfactory for most filing requirements and, although the file could have been saved and retrieved as small-length sub-files, this method would have presented problems when sorting and searching. As will be remembered from previous discussions, the capability for fast manipulation of data depends on the file contents being accessed rapidly and this is not possible with files held on cassette.

Thus, an alternative form of file storage outside the micro's memory is required. That requirement can be met by using a floppy disc system so that the file of data can be held on the disc and individual records can be retrieved and dealt with as necessary. The program for controlling the data-handling routines will be held in the micro's memory and a record that is being created or updated will be in temporary residence in memory.

Using a disc for storing files of records will introduce a new problem, however, since the retrieval of single records from the file will require that each record consists of exactly the same number of characters. If this is not the case, any record that is retrieved from the file and amended in such a way that more characters are used will, when inserted back into the file, cause the next record to be partly overwritten. This is because there is no procedure for moving files along to make room for an enlarged record. The records that have been created for the EMPLOYEE file are of differing lengths but readers will recall that, on initialising the file, each field was allocated a certain number of "A" or "9" characters. Thus, an initialised record, that is a record that has yet to be created, will represent the maximum size that a record can take and when a record has been created, it must contain padding-out characters to ensure that all fields are of the maximum length.

Setting-up a Descriptor File

This fact will be used in the transferring of the existing procedures to a disc-based environment. Before a file of records is stored on disc, certain details about the file must be placed in a descriptor file on the same disc. This procedure will allow an empty file consisting of initialised records to be placed on the disc and will permit the main program to make preparations to receive and deal with records from that file. The procedures for defining field names and initial values will be used in a demonstration of a routine for setting up a descriptor file. The routine is given in listing 8.1.

```
LISTING 8.1
 10 ONERRORREPORT:CLOSE#0:END
 20 record_detail$="EMPLOY1"
 30 PROCdefine_initial_values
 40 PROCdefine_field_names
 50 PROCsave(record_detail$)
 60 CLOSE#0
 70 END
 80
 90 DEFPROCsave(record_detail$)
100 field%=9
110 FILE=OPENOUT(record_detail$)
120 PRINT#FILE,field%
130 FORfield=0TOfield%-1
140 PRINT#FILE,D$(field),LEN(I$(field))
150 NEXT
160 CLOSE#FILE
170 PRINT"EMPLOYEE record details saved"
180 ENDPROC
190
200 DEFPROCdefine_field_names
210 DIMD$(8)
220 D$(0)="EMPLOYEE NO."
```

```
230 D$(1)="SURNAME"
240 D$(2)="INITIALS"
250 D$(3)="SEX (M/F)"
260 D$(4)="BORN (DDMMYY)"
270 D$(5)="DEPARTMENT NO."
280 D$(6)="JOINED (YYMMDD)"
290 D$(7)="JOB CODE"
300 D$(8)="SALARY (POUNDS)"
310 ENDPROC
320
330 DEFPROCdefine_initial_values
340 DIMI$(8)
350 I$(0)="999"
360 I$(1)="AAAAAAAAAAAAAAAA"
370 I$(2)="AA"
380 I$(3)="A"
390 I$(4)="999999"
400 I$(5)="99"
410 I$(6)="999999"
420 I$(7)="99"
430 I$(8)="99999"
440 ENDPROC
```

Of the three procedures contained in the routine, two
are taken from the procedure library and are used here
to provide a source of data to be used by the third
procedure in line 140. Lines 30 and 40 call these two
procedures to set up the arrays E$ and I$. Line 20
defines the name of the file that is to be used to hold
the description of the records in the EMPLOYEE file and
line 50 calls the procedure that saves the record
details on the file.

The Trapping of Errors
Line 10 has not been used before because the
possibility of creating a problem was less likely when
using a cassette file. When using disc systems it is
possible to have five channels open for reading or
writing at any one time and thus the chances of error
are increased. If an error occurs after a file has been
opened, the program will abort and leave the file open.
This will create problems because that file cannot be
accessed until certain procedures have been carried out
to close the file. It is much easier to avoid the
problem by trapping the error and taking action to
prevent the file being left open.
     A method is given in line 10 which uses the ON ERROR
statement - this is described on page 308 of the User
Guide. If an error occurs, the micro will REPORT the
situation to the user by printing the message that is

appropriate to the error - see page 338 of the User Guide. CLOSE#0 will then close all the files that are open when the error occurs and, finally, the routine ends.

If no errors occur, the files will be closed in line 60 before the routine ends. The procedure for saving the record details, lines 90 to 180 inclusive, uses a value "field%" to indicate how many fields have been used in a record. This information is then printed on the file in line 120 and this is followed by entering a FOR...NEXT loop that is controlled by the value of field%. In the loop, two data items are printed on the file. The first item is D$(field) and thus the file will be given the appropriate name from the field-name array - see line 140. The second item is the quantity of "A" or "9" characters that the field can hold.

After closing the file in line 160, a message will be printed on the screen to inform the user that the descriptor file has been created on the disc. Closing all the files in line 60 seems to be superfluous but if the routine ends with files still open, problems will result and it is a wise precaution to close all files in this manner before ending the routine.

The program should now be entered in the normal manner but if this means loading from the program cassette, the disc mode of operation must be selected, using "*DISC" and RETURN, before inserting a formatted disc and then RUNning the program. After a few seconds, the screen will display the message given in line 170 to indicate the completion of the routine.

To check the successful saving of the descriptor file, a routine to retrieve the file from disc will be required. In fact, the same routine can be used in the complete data-handling program to prepare for the various routines to be carried out. A routine that is suitable for this file is given in listing 8.2

```
LISTING 8.2
 10 ONERRORREPORT:CLOSE#0:END
 20 CLS
 30 PRINT''''
 40 record_detail$="EMPLOY1"
 50 PROCload(record_detail$)
 60 CLOSE#0
 70 END
 80 DEFPROCload(record_detail$)
 90 FILE=OPENIN(record_detail$)
100 INPUT#FILE,field%
110 FORfield=0TOfield%-1
120 INPUT#FILE,N$,L%
```

```
130  PRINTTAB(5)N$;TAB(25)L%
140  NEXT
150  CLOSE#FILE
160  PRINT´´´:PRINT"RECORD DETAILS RETRIEVED"
170  ENDPROC
```

Line 40 refers to the name used in the routine given in
listing 8.1 and this will ensure that the descriptor
file-retrieval program accesses the correct file. The
procedure referred to in line 50 uses the value of
field% that is obtained from the file, line 100, to
control the FOR...NEXT loop in lines 110 to 140
inclusive. For each value of field%, two items, N$ and
L%, are retrieved from the file - line 120. The values
are then displayed on the screen using TAB statements.
Finally, after closing the file and printing the
message given in line 160, the routine returns to line
60 to close all the files.

When the program has been entered, the disc
containing the descriptor file, EMPLOY1, should be
placed in the disc drive unit. Then enter RUN and wait
for the message to be displayed. Two columns will be
displayed, one giving the field names and the other
giving the corresponding field lengths. These values
can be used to calculate the total record length but
another method will be demonstrated before considering
this matter further.

In general, the array-defining procedures used in
listing 8.1 will not be available because they were
developed especially for the cassette-based
file-handling routines. Instead, users will create the
descriptor file directly from the record description
that results from consideration of the file
requirements. In the simplest method, the required
field names, characters and lengths will be embedded in
the descriptor file-saving routine as DATA statements.
The use of such a method will give the routine that
appears in listing 8.3.

LISTING 8.3
```
 10  ONERRORREPORT:CLOSE#0:END
 20  record_detail$="EMPLOY2"
 30  PROCsave(record_detail$)
 40  CLOSE#0
 50  END
 60  DEFPROCsave(record_detail$)
 70  FILE=OPENOUT(record_detail$)
 80  READfield%
 90  PRINT#FILE,field%
100  FORfield=0TOfield%-1
110  READname$,char$
```

```
120 PRINT#FILE,name$,char$
130 NEXT
140 CLOSE#FILE
150 PRINT"EMPLOYEE record details saved"
160 ENDPROC
170 DATA 9,
        EMPLOYEE NO.,999,
        SURNAME,AAAAAAAAAAAAAAAA,
        INITIALS,AA,
        SEX (M/F),A,
        BORN (DDMMYY),999999,
        DEPARTMENT NO.,99,
        JOINED (YYMMDD),999999,
        JOB CODE,99,
        SALARY(POUNDS),99999
```

The DATA statement in line 170 normally would be written as a continuous string of data items that are separated by commas. The format used here serves to remind readers of the contents of the nine fields used in the EMPLOYEE records. Thus line 80 will READ the value of field% as 9 and then use that value to control the remaining READing and PRINTing operations - lines 100 to 130 inclusive. For each loop, the two items "name$" and "char$" are obtained from the DATA statement and transferred to the descriptor file under the same names. Apart from the use of the DATA statement, the routine is similar to that in listing 8.1.

The use of the DATA statement, readers should remember, is a result of the absence of the field name and initial value arrays but these will be required by the data-handling routine when records are being created. Thus, one function that must be performed by the descriptor file routine is to create the two arrays. This requirement is covered in the routine given in listing 8.4 below.

```
LISTING 8.4
 10 ONERRORREPORT:CLOSE#0:END
 20 CLS
 30 PRINT´´´´
 40 record_detail$="EMPLOY2"
 50 PROCload(record_detail$)
 60 CLOSE#0
 70 END
 80 DEFPROCload(record_detail$)
 90 FILE=OPENIN(record_detail$)
100 INPUT#FILE,field%
110 DIMD$(field%-1)
120 DIMI$(field%-1)
```

```
130 FORfield=0TOfield%-1
140 INPUT#FILE,name$,char$
150 D$(field)=name$
160 I$(field)=char$
170 PRINTTAB(2)D$(field);TAB(22)I$(field)
180 NEXT
190 CLOSE#FILE
200 PRINT´´´:PRINT"RECORD DETAILS RETRIEVED"
210 ENDPROCR
```

This routine refers, in line 40, to the file named EMPLOY2 that was created when the routine in listing 8.3 was RUN. It is necessary to obtain the value of field%, line 100, before the two arrays D$ and I$ can be dimensioned in lines 110 and 120. The value is then used, as previously, to control the FOR...NEXT loop that obtains the data items "name$" and "char$" from the file, line 140. The same value of field% is then used, lines 150 and 160, to set up the two arrays, D$ and I$. As a check that the arrays have been correctly set up, line 170 produces a screen display of each pair of entries as they are created.

After loading the routine, using "*DISC" and then inserting the disc that holds the descriptor file, EMPLOY2, the routine should be RUN and its operation verified. Two columns will be displayed, one for the field names and the other for the "A" or "9" character strings that are used to indicate to users what the field type and size for each field is. Thus the two arrays that were required by the previous cassette-based routines have now been produced from the descriptor file, EMPLOY2.

Obtaining the Total Record Length
The total record length that was mentioned previously as being necessary for the ordered or random retrieval of records from the record-holding file will now be dealt with. The method used by the BBC micro to retrieve records in this manner is to use the PTR# statement - see page 330 of the User Guide. Further reference is made to page 328 and here, another page of the User Guide is referred to. Readers who are no better informed about this statement after reading the User Guide should find the following explanation of value. The present requirement is to use the field data items to construct a record-holding file in which each record contains strings of "A" or "9" characters. The use of the phrase "strings" is correct because, in line 120 of listing 8.3 that was how the field data items were classified. Reading page 330 again will indicate the action to be taken now.

In the first paragraph, the following statement is made; "each string takes up the number of letters in the string plus 2". The solution to the problem of finding the total record length is, therefore, to count the number of letters in each field, add them together and then add the result of multiplying the number of fields by two. In the records that are to be filed in this example, the sum of the field string lengths is given by

$$12+3+7+16+8+2+9+1+13+6+14+2+15+6+8+2+15+5=144$$

There are nine fields and thus a figure of 9 times 2 must be added to give the total record length of 144+18, that is 162. The string of figures given above is obtained from listings 3.1 and 3.2.

A suitable routine to carry out this calculation is given in listing 8.5.

LISTING 8.5
```
  10 ONERRORREPORT:CLOSE#0:END
  20 record_detail$="EMPLOY2"
  30 PROCload(record_detail$)
  40 total_record_length=0
  50 FORfield=0TOfield%-1
  60 total_record_length=LEN(D$(field))+LEN(I$(field))
     +total_record_length
  70 NEXT
  80 total_record_length=2*field%+total_record_length
  90 PRINT:PRINT"total_record_length = ";
     total_record_length
 100 CLOSE#0
 110 END
 120 DEFPROCload(record_detail$)
 130 CLS:PRINT´´´
 140 FILE=OPENIN(record_detail$)
 150 INPUT#FILE,field%
 160 DIMD$(field%-1)
 170 DIMI$(field%-1)
 180 FORfield=0TOfield%-1
 190 INPUT#FILE,name$,char$
 200 D$(field)=name$
 210 I$(field)=char$
 220 PRINTTAB(2)D$(field);TAB(22)I$(field)
 230 NEXT
 240 CLOSE#FILE
 250 PRINT´´´:PRINT"RECORD DETAILS RETRIEVED"
 260 ENDPROC
```

The routine must have access to the arrays A$ and I$ and as these are set up using the procedure given in listing 8.4, this procedure is used again. The main part of the routine, after calling the retrieval procedure, is to initialise a variable for the total field length value, line 40, and then to add to this value the numbers obtained as each field length is counted - line 60. The calculation is completed by adding twice the value of field% to the previous total in line 80. Verification of the correct results by readers is enabled by line 90 which displays the final value for the total record length together with the array contents that are used in the calculation. The final version of the routine will not, of course, require such screen displays.

Self-test 8.1
The total record length was calculated so that PTR# could be used to select records from the file in either an ordered or a random fashion. If the calculated value is used, a large proportion of the available file space on the disc will be wasted.
(a) Consider the data that was used in the calculation and then deduce why wastage will occur.
(b) Rewrite one of the statements in listing 8.5 so that more space is available for filing EMPLOYEE records on the disc.

Creating the Initialised File
Enough information is now available to allow the initial empty file to be created on the disc. A slight modification to the method of identifying records will be required for any routine using PTR#, standing for "pointer", because one format of such statements is PTR#(channel)=number in which "number" is calculated to give the start of a record. Page 330 of the User Guide gives other examples of the use of the statement but whichever one is used, the record selected will depend on a value that is saved with the record on the file. The records on the cassette-based system were identified according to their position in a sequential file that was held in an array. The retrieval of such records was via the appropriate array element number. In the disc-based system, a record is identified by its position in the sequential file according to a calculation that uses the record length.
    The first record has a pointer value of zero and thus, if the record has a length of, say, 100 characters, the seventh record will start at the six-hundredth character in the file. Readers will now appreciate why each record has to be the same length because, if the length varies, the result of multiplying the record number by a variable length will

not usually give the start of a record. It should be noted that because the pointer value starts at zero, the actual record number will have to be decremented before the record can be retrieved. This is not, of course, a feature that is new to readers of this book.

Retrieving Records from the File

The routine that is given below uses the pointer value, calculated as described above, to set up the empty file, EMPFIL2 which stands for EMPloyeeFILe2. As a demonstration of using a pointer for record retrieval from a disc file, an additional segment of program will allow users to select records from the file and display their contents.

LISTING 8.6

```
 10 ONERRORREPORT:CLOSE#0:END
 20 record_detail$="EMPLOY2"
 30 R%=999
 40 PROCload(record_detail$)
 50 total_record_length=0
 60 FORfield=0TOfield%-1
 70 total_record_length=LEN(I$(field))
    +total_record_length
 80 NEXT
 90 total_record_length=2*field%+total_record_length+
    LENSTR$(R%)+2
100 PRINT"total_record_length = ";total_record_length
110 record_detail$="EMPFIL2"
120 PROCsave_initial_file(record_detail$)
130 PRINT"INITIALISED FILE SAVED"
140 record_detail$="EMPFIL2"
150 FILE=OPENIN(record_detail$)
160 DIMF$(field%-1)
170 INPUT"WHICH RECORD"R%
180 PTR#FILE=(R%-1)*total_record_length
190 INPUT#FILE,R%
200 PRINTR%
210 FORfield=0TOfield%-1
220 INPUT#FILE,char$
230 F$(field)=char$
240 PRINTF$(field)
250 NEXT
260 PRINT´´:INPUT"ANY MORE "A$
270 IFA$<>"Y"THEN280ELSE170
280 CLOSE#0
290 END
300 DEFPROCload(record_detail$)
310 CLS:PRINT´´´´
320 FILE=OPENIN(record_detail$)
330 INPUT#FILE,field%
```

```
340 DIMD$(field%-1)
350 DIMI$(field%-1)
360 FORfield=0TOfield%-1
370 INPUT#FILE,name$,char$
380 D$(field)=name$
390 I$(field)=char$
400 PRINTTAB(2)D$(field);TAB(22)I$(field)
410 NEXT
420 CLOSE#FILE
430 PRINT´´´:PRINT"RECORD DETAILS RETRIEVED"
440 ENDPROC
450 DEFPROCsave_initial_file(record_detail$)
460 FILE=OPENOUT(record_detail$)
470 FORR%=0TO19
480 PRINT#FILE,R%
490 FORfield=0TOfield%-1
500 PRINT#FILE,I$(field)
510 NEXT
520 NEXT
530 CLOSE#FILE
540 ENDPROC
```

Lines 450 to 540 cover the procedure that sets up the
empty file with twenty records, see line 470, each
identified by a unique record number, R%. The maximum
size of this number is given as "999" in line 30 so
that the correct maximum record length can be
calculated in lines 60 to 90 inclusive. When the
program is RUN, the total record length value will be
printed by line 100. After printing the value of R%,
the contents of array, I$, are selected and printed on
the file. I$ contains the initial field values
consisting of strings of "A" and "9" characters and so
all records will be the same, as is required. Note that
R% is incremented from zero - line 470.

On completion of this procedure, the routine
continues from line 140 after printing a message in
line 130. Line 140 is a repeat of line 110 and is not
actually necessary in this example but is included to
allow the routine to be changed into a procedure in
which any file can be examined. After opening the file,
an array is dimensioned in line 160 to the size
field%-1. This array will hold the retrieved field data
items that are obtained using lines 210 to 250
inclusive. Before this is done, however, the user is
asked to indicate the record that is to be examined -
line 170.

Line 180 carries out the calculation to select the
correct starting point for the required record. Thus,
if the user inputs a value of "1", the calculated value
is zero because R%-1 is zero and the record with a

pointer value of zero, that is the first record, will be selected. The first item in a record is its number and this is obtained and printed on the screen by lines 190 and 200. As each field is obtained from the file, the array, F$, is loaded with it and it is also printed on the screen.

Lines 260 and 270 allow the user to obtain more records for examination or to terminate the routine. Evidence that twenty records have been initialised can be obtained by responding with the value 21 to the question, "WHICH RECORD". The routine should now be loaded into the micro and tested.

Now that records can be retrieved from the file, it is possible to consider the addition of the procedures that were developed for the cassette-based system. Readers will appreciate that there is little possibility of incorporating those procedures without modification, but their design was such as to require, in the main, only slight changes. The last listing was intended to demonstrate a principle but, although the method produced the required results, it was not sufficiently developed to incorporate into a file-handling package.

Displaying a Record

Readers will recollect that a procedure for displaying a record was developed for the previous system and, as it produced satisfactory results, it follows that incorporation into the new system is desirable. It is incorporated into a modification of listing 8.6 that appears below as listing 8.7

LISTING 8.7

```
 10 ONERRORREPORT:CLOSE#0:END
 20 record_detail$="EMPLOY2"
 30 R%=999
 40 total_record_length=FNlength(record_detail$,R%)
 50 DIME$(field%-1)
 60 record_detail$="EMPFIL2"
 70 PROCsave_initial_file(record_detail$)
 80 CLS:PROCload_record(record_detail$,field%,
    total_record_length)
 90 CLS
100 PROCdisplay_record(R%)
110 INPUTTAB(1,22)"ANY MORE "A$
120 IFA$<>"Y"THEN130ELSE80
130 CLOSE#0
140 END
150 DEFPROCload(record_detail$)
160 CLS:PRINT´´´´
170 FILE=OPENIN(record_detail$)
```

```
180 INPUT#FILE,field%
190 DIMD$(field%-1)
200 DIMI$(field%-1)
210 FORfield=0TOfield%-1
220 INPUT#FILE,name$,char$
230 D$(field)=name$
240 I$(field)=char$
250 NEXT
260 CLOSE#FILE
270 ENDPROC
280 DEFPROCsave_initial_file(record_detail$)
290 FILE=OPENOUT(record_detail$)
300 FORR%=0TO19
310 PRINT#FILE,R%
320 FORfield=0TOfield%-1
330 PRINT#FILE,I$(field)
340 NEXT
350 NEXT
360 CLOSE#FILE
370 ENDPROC
380 DEFFNlength(record_detail$,R%)
390 PROCload(record_detail$)
400 total_record_length=0
410 FORfield=0TOfield%-1
420 total_record_length=LENI$(field)+
    total_record_length
430 NEXT
440 total_record_length=2*field%+
    total_record_length+LENSTR$(R%)+2
450 =total_record_length
460 DEFPROCdisplay_record(R%)
470 PRINTTAB(8,2);"** EMPLOYEE RECORD ";R%+1;" **"
480 PRINTTAB(1,4);"1";TAB(3,4);D$(0);TAB(22,4);E$(0)
490 PRINTTAB(1,6);"2";TAB(3,6);D$(1);TAB(22,6);E$(1)
500 PRINTTAB(1,8);"3";TAB(3,8);D$(2);TAB(22,8);E$(2)
510 PRINTTAB(1,10);"4";TAB(3,10);D$(3);TAB(22,10);E$(3)
520 PRINTTAB(1,12);"5";TAB(3,12);D$(4);TAB(22,12);E$(4)
530 PRINTTAB(1,14);"6";TAB(3,14);D$(5);TAB(22,14);E$(5)
540 PRINTTAB(1,16);"7";TAB(3,16);D$(6);TAB(22,16);E$(6)
550 PRINTTAB(1,18);"8";TAB(3,18);D$(7);TAB(22,18);E$(7)
560 PRINTTAB(1,20);"9";TAB(3,20);D$(8);TAB(22,20);E$(8)
570 ENDPROC
580 DEFPROCload_record(record_detail$,
    field%,total_record_length)
590 FILE=OPENIN(record_detail$)
600 INPUTTAB(1,24)"WHICH RECORD IS TO BE DISPLAYED "R%
610 PTR#FILE=(R%-1)*total_record_length
620 INPUT#FILE,R%
630 FORfield=0TOfield%-1
640 INPUT#FILE,char$
650 E$(field)=char$
```

```
660 NEXT
670 CLOSE#FILE
680 ENDPROC
```

This is a long listing because, although it is based on the previous listing, some changes have been made in order to remove certain features that are no longer necessary. For example, there is no need to inform the user how long the record is and thus line 100 is removed from listing 8.6. Similarly, line 130 is not needed and so, by removal of screen display that is no longer required, the information that is displayed will have more impact. New procedures to replace lines 40 to 90 and lines 150 to 270 have been introduced, these being called FNlength() and PROCload_record() respectively. The brackets indicate that parameters will be passed from the main program to the function or procedure.

The display-record procedure required only one change from the original form, that is the replacement of the double parameter for E$ because there is no array holding the complete file in this system. Thus, instead of line 530 reading, after the last semicolon, E$(0,R%) it now reads E$(0) because R% has no meaning in the present context.

When the program has been loaded, using items from the procedure library that is being built up (unless readers are using the program cassette), it should be RUN and tested. It will work in the same way as the previous listing but with the improvements described above. In particular, the record display indicates that a move towards the performance of the cassette system has been made. The next step is to incorporate a means of putting employee data onto the file and this will be based on the use of the attributes-update procedure that has been developed already. The modified procedures are incorporated into the following listing which allows data to be input and checked for validity as before. In addition, the new requirement for fields to be the same length by padding with spaces has been taken care of.

LISTING 8.8

```
10 ONERRORREPORT:CLOSE#0:END
20 record_detail$="EMPLOY2"
30 R%=999
40 total_record_length=FNlength(record_detail$,R%)
50 DIME$(field%-1)
60 record_detail$="EMPFIL2"
70 PROCsave_initial_file(record_detail$)
80 R%=1
```

```
 90 file_end=FALSE
100 record%=0
110 max_file%=20
120 CLS:PROCload_record(record_detail$,
    field%,total_record_length,R%)
130 CLS
140 R%=0
150 PROCcreate_record
160 CLOSE#0
170 END
180 DEFPROCload(record_detail$)
190 CLS
200 FILE=OPENIN(record_detail$)
210 INPUT#FILE,field%
220 DIMD$(field%-1)
230 DIMI$(field%-1)
240 FORfield=0TOfield%-1
250 INPUT#FILE,name$,char$
260 D$(field)=name$
270 I$(field)=char$
280 NEXT
290 CLOSE#FILE
300 ENDPROC
310 DEFPROCsave_initial_file(record_detail$)
320 FILE=OPENOUT(record_detail$)
330 FORR%=0TO19
340 PRINT#FILE,R%
350 FORfield=0TOfield%-1
360 PRINT#FILE,I$(field)
370 NEXT
380 NEXT
390 CLOSE#FILE
400 ENDPROC
410 DEFFNlength(record_detail$,R%)
420 PROCload(record_detail$)
430 total_record_length=0
440 FORfield=0TOfield%-1
450 total_record_length=LENI$(field)+
    total_record_length
460 NEXT
470 total_record_length=2*field%+
    total_record_length+LENSTR$(R%)+2
480 =total_record_length
490 DEFPROCdisplay_record(R%)
500 PRINTTAB(8,2);"** EMPLCYEE RECORD ";R%+1;" **"
510 PRINTTAB(1,4);"1";TAB(3,4);D$(0);TAB(22,4);E$(0)
520 PRINTTAB(1,6);"2";TAB(3,6);D$(1);TAB(22,6);E$(1)
530 PRINTTAB(1,8);"3";TAB(3,8);D$(2);TAB(22,8);E$(2)
540 PRINTTAB(1,10);"4";TAB(3,10);D$(3);TAB(22,10);
    E$(3)
550 PRINTTAB(1,12);"5";TAB(3,12);D$(4);TAB(22,12);
    E$(4)
```

```
 560 PRINTTAB(1,14);"6";TAB(3,14);D$(5);TAB(22,14);
     E$(5)
 570 PRINTTAB(1,16);"7";TAB(3,16);D$(6);TAB(22,16);
     E$(6)
 580 PRINTTAB(1,18);"8";TAB(3,18);D$(7);TAB(22,18);
     E$(7)
 590 PRINTTAB(1,20);"9";TAB(3,20);D$(8);TAB(22,20);
     E$(8)
 600 ENDPROC
 610 DEFPROCload_record(record_detail$,
     field%,total_record_length,R%)
 620 FILE=OPENIN(record_detail$)
 630 PTR#FILE=(R%-1)*total_record_length
 640 INPUT#FILE,R%
 650 FORfield=0TOfield%-1
 660 INPUT#FILE,char$
 670 E$(field)=char$
 680 NEXT
 690 CLOSE#FILE
 700 ENDPROC
 710 DEFPROCupdate_attributes(R%)
 720 *FX4,1
 730 *FX229,1
 740 LOCAL A$
 750 CLS
 760 PROCdisplay_record(R%)
 770 PRINTTAB(13,22);"Please input"
 780 PRINTTAB(1,24);D$(0)
 790 employee_no$=FNenter_data(22,23,3,"N")
 800 IFemployee_no$="999"THENfile_end=
     TRUE ELSE820
 810 GOTO1740
 820 IFVAL(employee_no$)>=1THEN830ELSE790
 830 IFLEN(employee_no$)=3THEN890
 840 IFLEN(employee_no$)=2THEN870
 850 E$(0)="00"+employee_no$
 860 GOTO900
 870 E$(0)="0"+employee_no$
 880 GOTO900
 890 E$(0)=employee_no$
 900 CLS
 910 PROCdisplay_record(R%)
 920 PRINTTAB(13,22);"Please input"
 930 PRINTTAB(1,24);D$(1)
 940 REPEAT
 950 surname$=FNenter_data(22,23,16,"S")
 960 UNTIL NOT NIL
 970 REPEAT
 980 surname$=surname$+" "
 990 UNTILLENsurname$=16
1000 E$(1)=surname$
1010 CLS
```

```
1020 PROCdisplay_record(R%)
1030 PRINTTAB(13,22);"Please input"
1040 PRINTTAB(1,24);D$(2)
1050 REPEAT
1060 initials$=FNenter_data(22,23,2,"S")
1070 UNTIL NOT NIL
1080 IFLENinitials$=2THEN1100
1090 initials$=" "+initials$
1100 E$(2)=initials$
1110 CLS
1120 PROCdisplay_record(R%)
1130 PRINTTAB(13,22);"Please input"
1140 PRINTTAB(1,24);D$(3)
1150 sex$=FNenter_data(22,23,1,"S")
1160 IF sex$="M" OR sex$="F" THEN 1190
1170 VDU7
1180 GOTO1150
1190 E$(3)=sex$
1200 CLS
1210 PROCdisplay_record(R%)
1220 PRINTTAB(13,22);"Please input"
1230 PRINTTAB(1,24);D$(4)
1240 REPEAT
1250 born$=FNenter_data(22,23,6,"N")
1260 UNTIL LEN(born$)=6
1270 PROCcheck_date(born$)
1280 IFdate=FALSE THENVDU7:GOTO1240
1290 E$(4)=D$+M$+Y$
1300 CLS
1310 PROCdisplay_record(R%)
1320 PRINTTAB(13,22);"Please input"
1330 PRINTTAB(1,24);D$(5)
1340 REPEAT
1350 dept$=FNenter_data(22,23,2,"N")
1360 UNTIL NOT NIL
1370 IFLENdept$=2THEN1390
1380 dept$=" "+dept$
1390 E$(5)=dept$
1400 CLS
1410 PROCdisplay_record(R%)
1420 PRINTTAB(13,22);"Please input"
1430 PRINTTAB(1,24);D$(6)
1440 REPEAT
1450 joined$=FNenter_data(22,23,6,"N")
1460 UNTIL LEN(joined$)=6
1470 PROCcheck_date(joined$)
1480 IFdate=FALSE THENVDU7:GOTO1440
1490 E$(6)=Y$+M$+D$
1500 CLS
1510 PROCdisplay_record(R%)
1520 PRINTTAB(13,22);"Please input"
1530 PRINTTAB(1,24);D$(7)
```

```
1540 REPEAT
1550 job$=FNenter_data(22,23,2,"N")
1560 UNTIL NOT NIL
1570 IFLENjob$=2THEN1590
1580 job$=" "+job$
1590 E$(7)=job$
1600 CLS
1610 PROCdisplay_record(R%)
1620 PRINTTAB(13,22);"Please input"
1630 PRINTTAB(1,24);D$(8)
1640 salary$=FNenter_data(22,23,5,"N")
1650 IF VAL(salary$)<3500 THEN 1640
1660 IFLENsalary$=5THEN1680
1670 salary$=" "+salary$
1680 E$(8)=salary$
1690 CLS
1700 PROCdisplay_record(R%)
1710 PRINTTAB(6,22);"Are details correct?(Y/N)"
1720 A$=GET$
1730 IF A$="Y" OR A$="y" THEN 1740 ELSE 710
1740 *FX4,0
1750 *FX229,0
1760 ENDPROC
1770 DEFFNenter_data(across%,down%,size%,S_N$)
1780 LOCAL char$,length,input$
1790 length=0:input$=""
1800 PRINTTAB(across%,down%);STRING$(size%,
     " ")+STRING$(size%,CHR$(127));
1810 GOTO1830
1820 VDU7
1830 char$=GET$
1840 IFchar$=CHR$(127)THEN1940
1850 IF char$=CHR$(13) THEN 1980
1860 IFlength=size%THEN1820
1870 IF S_N$<>"S" THEN 1890
1880 IFchar$<CHR$(65)ORchar$>CHR$(90) THEN1820ELSE1900
1890 IF char$<CHR$(48) OR char$>CHR$(57) THEN 1820
1900 input$=input$+char$
1910 length=length+1
1920 PRINTchar$;
1930 GOTO 1830
1940 IFinput$=""THEN1820
1950 length=length-1
1960 input$=LEFT$(input$,length)
1970 GOTO1920
1980 NIL=(length=0)
1990 =input$
2000 DEFPROCcreate_record
2010 REPEAT
2020 PROCupdate_attributes(R%)
2030 record%=record%+1
2040 R%=R%+1:IFfile_end=TRUE THEN2070
```

```
2050 IFR%=max_file%THEN2060ELSE2070
2060 file_end=TRUE:record%=record%+1
2070 UNTILfile_end=TRUE
2080 record%=record%-1
2090 ENDPROC
2100 DEFPROCcheck_date(date$)
2110 date=TRUE
2120 D$=LEFT$(date$,2)
2130 IFD$<"01"THENdate=FALSE:GOTO2230
2140 Y$=RIGHT$(date$,2)
2150 M$=MID$(date$,3,2)
2160 IFM$>"12"ORM$<"01"THENdate=FALSE:GOTO2230
2170 IFM$="02"THEN2210
2180 IFM$="04"ORM$="06"ORM$="09"ORM$="11"THEN2200
2190 IFD$<"32"THEN2230ELSEdate=FALSE:GOTO2230
2200 IFD$<"31"THEN2230ELSEdate=FALSE:GOTO2230
2210 IFD$<"29"THEN2230
2220 IFVAL(Y$)MOD 4=0 AND D$="29"THEN2230
     ELSEdate=FALSE:GOTO2230
2230 ENDPROC
```

This is a long listing because of the inclusion of the
attribute-update procedure that, as mentioned before,
has had to be modified. In addition, the procedures
that are associated with that procedure are also
included in order that the routine can be tested. The
extra procedures are

```
PROCcheck_date(date$)
PROCcreate_record
FNenterdata(across%,down%,size%,S_N$)
```

These three procedures have been incorporated without
modification from their previous form.
    To deal with the modifications that are required to
the update procedure, each field entry point must be
examined in turn. Lines 790 to 900 inclusive are
concerned with the entry for EMPLOYEE NO. This already
meets the requirements for a fixed field length by the
insertion of leading zeros to make a three-digit
number. The SURNAME entry routine will need
modification because the length of surnames is not
fixed. A REPEAT-UNTIL loop is entered to add spaces,
given by " ", to the end of the name until a total of
sixteen characters are in the field.
    In line 1080, a check is made on the LENgth of
"initial$" and if it is not two characters long, an
extra space is inserted before the string in line 1090.
There is no need to modify the "sex$" entry routine
because the entry is already checked for being either
"F" or "M". A similar situation exists for the two date

entries because these are checked by an existing procedure. The remaining entry routines, that is "dept$", "job$" and "salary$", each require a maximum of one space to be inserted.

Line 610 contains a modification so that the parameter, R%, can be passed to it and, in addition, the message regarding the record to be displayed has been removed. This is to enable successive records to be obtained from the file for updating although this facility has not been included at this stage. Line 120 is changed to reflect this feature. Lines 80 to 110 are included to meet the requirements of the new procedures and the reason why line 80 seems to be contradicted by line 140 is to meet the following routine differences. If line 120 is entered with R%=0, the procedure in line 610 will decrement this value to produce a pointer value of (minus one times the record length) - this causes a problem and has to be avoided. Later on, in line 140, R% is set to zero so that line 2020 obtains the first record in the file. This anomaly is removed in a future development.

The routine should now be tested to verify that each successive record can be updated and that entering "999" will, as before, terminate the entry routine. Because the routine is not yet complete, the records will not be saved on the file and, as only one record-retrieval operation is carried out, a record presented for updating will carry the previous entries - this is a feature that will be taken care of in the next development.

Saving a Record

The following procedure has been developed to deal with the requirement of saving a record as soon as it has been verified as correct. The verification is included in the attribute-update procedure and requires a change to a screen message. The record-saving procedure is

```
2240 DEFPROCsave_record(R%)
2250 FILE=OPENIN(record_detail$)
2260 PTR#FILE=(R%-1)*total_record_length
2270 PRINT#FILE,R%
2280 FORfield=0TOfield%-1
2290 PRINT#FILE,E$(field)
2300 NEXT
2310 CLOSE#FILE
2320 ENDPROC
```

Readers are reminded that the details must be saved in exactly the same format as was defined at the beginning of this chapter. To use this procedure, listing 8.8

should be entered and then the procedure should be keyed in. This is because it is not contained on the program cassette. In addition, the following modifications need to be made to the program in memory

1. Delete line 80
2. Line 120 is renumbered as line 149
3. Change - 150 PROCcreate_record:IFfile_end=TRUE THEN 160
4. Add - 151 PROCsave_record(R%)
5. Add - 152 CLS:PRINTTAB(2,4)"Record ";R%;" saved"
6. Add - 153 INPUTTAB(2,8)"More record creation (Y/N) " A$
7. Add - 154 IFA$="Y"ORA$="y"THEN149
8. Change - 630 PTR#FILE=R%*total_record_length
9. Change - 1710 PRINTTAB(6,22)"Can details be saved? (Y/N)"
10. Delete line 2010
11. Delete line 2070
12. Change - 2040 R%=R%+1:IFfile_end=TRUE THEN2080
13. Change - 2050 IFR%=max_file%THEN2060ELSE2080

The change detailed in item 8 overcomes the problem that was highlighted in an earlier paragraph concerning the value of R%. The remaining changes tidy up the routine and should not present any problems of understanding to the reader. The modified version of listing 8.8 should be tested by keying in the first two items of employee data that were given in chapter 3. When the first item has been entered and verified, the disc drive will start and then stop after a few seconds. The screen will state that record 1 has been saved and ask if more records are to be created. Giving a "Y" reply will activate the disc drive again and, when it stops after a few seconds, the screen will display the initialised fields for record 2. Entering the data for record 2 and verifying it will again display a message. If "N" is entered in response to the question, the routine will terminate.

The two records have been entered but there is, at present, no routine to retrieve records from file. If line 70 is deleted from the listing, by typing "70" and then pressing RETURN", the routine can be RUN again and when record 1 is displayed, it will contain the first data item that was entered. If further data is now entered for record 1 and saved, a response of "Y" to the screen question will cause the second data item that was entered to be displayed. Confirmation that the entered data has been correctly saved is thus given. The reason why line 70 has to be deleted is to prevent the normal initialisation of the file.

The Use of OPENIN

An important point to note in connection with saving records is the use of OPENIN in line 2250. In line 320, which is part of the procedure for saving the initial file details, the keyword OPENOUT was used. Page 313 of the User Guide states that if this keyword is used with a disc system and a file with the same name exists on the disc, it will be deleted. Note that the word "file" describes what has been referred in this chapter as a record. Thus, every record that is saved on a file of records will cause the deletion of the previous record and the only record on the file at the end of the saving routine will be the last record that was saved. For this reason, the keyword OPENIN must be used for both saving and retrieving records - see the last line of page 311 of the User Guide. In addition, readers should be aware of the important note concerning OPENIN that is given at the end of this chapter.

The Sorting of Records

It is now necessary to consider how records that are held on disc can be sorted and, as before, the maximum use of existing cassette-based procedures will be made. A sorting procedure that uses the Heap Sort algorithm has been developed and this has been converted into a disc version in the routine that now follows. In this routine, only those procedures that are different from those in listing 8.8 are given in full together with the "main" program.

LISTING 8.9

```
 10 ON ERROR REPORT:CLOSE#0:END
 20 record_detail$="EMPLOY2"
 30 R%=999
 40 total_record_length=FNlength(record_detail$,R%)
 50 DIME$(field%-1):DIMS$(8):DIME1$(8):DIME2$(8)
 60 record_detail$="EMPFILE"
 70 PROCcount_lengths
 80 CLS:PRINTTAB(2,4)"The file";record_detail$;" has
    a"
 90 PRINTTAB(2,6)"capacity of";max_file%;" records"
100 PRINTTAB(2,8)"and holds ";record%;" records."
110 INPUTTAB(2,10)"Is a record examination required "
    A$
120 IFA$<>"Y"THEN140
130 PROCexamine_record(R%)
140 CLS:PRINTTAB(2,12)"What field is the file"
150 INPUTTAB(2,14)"to be sorted on (1-9) "N%
160 CLS:PRINTTAB(2,12)"THE FILE IS BEING SORTED"
170 PROCsort_file(N%)
180 VDU7:CLS:PRINTTAB(2,12)"THE FILE HAS BEEN SORTED"
```

```
190 PRINTTAB(2,14)"Is a record examination"
200 INPUTTAB(2,16)"required (Y/N) "A$
210 IFA$<>"Y"THEN230
220 CLS:PROCexamine_record(R%)
230 CLOSE#0
240 END
245
250 DEFPROCload(record_detail$)
370 ENDPROC
375
380 DEFFNlength(record_detail$,R%)
450 =total_record_length
455
460 DEFPROCdisplay_record(R%)
570 ENDPROC
575
580 DEFPROCload_record(record_detail$,
    field%,total_record_length,R%)
670 ENDPROC
675
680 DEFPROCexamine_record(R%)
750 ENDPROC
755
760 DEFPROCsort_file(N%)
770 S%=INT(record%/2)+1:E%=record%:N%=N%-1
780 IF S%=1 THEN 800
790 S%=S%-1:R%=S%-1:PROCload_record(record_detail$,
    field%,total_record_length,R%):W$=E$(N%):
    FOR F%=0 TO 8:S$(F%)=E$(F%):NEXT:GOTC 840
800 R%=E%-1:PROCload_record(record_detail$,field%,
    total_record_length,R%):FOR F%=0 TO 8:
    S$(F%)=E$(F%):NEXT:W$=S$(N%):R%=0:
    PROCload_record(record_detail$,
    field%,total_record_length,R%):R%=E%:
    PROCsave_record(R%):E%=E%-1
810 IF E%=1 THEN 820 ELSE 840
820 R%=1:FOR F%=0 TO 8:E$(F%)=S$(F%):NEXT:
    PROCsave_record(R%)
830 GOTO 950
840 J%=S%
850 I%=J%
860 J%=2*J%
870 IF J%<E%THEN900
880 IFJ%=E%THEN920
890 IF J%>E% THEN 940
900 R%=J%-1:PROCload_record(record_detail$,field%,
    total_record_length,R%):FOR F%=0 TO 8:
    E1$(F%)=E$(F%):NEXT:R%=J%:
    PROCload_record(record_detail$,
    field%,total_record_length,R%):FOR F%=0 TO 8:
    E2$(F%)=E$(F%):NEXT
```

```
 910 IFE1$(N%)<E2$(N%)THENJ%=J%+1
 920 R%=J%-1:PROCload_record(record_detail$,field%,
     total_record_length,R%):FOR F%=0 TO 8:
     E1$(F%)=E$(F%):NEXT:IF W$>=E1$(N%) THEN 940
 930 R%=I%:PROCsave_record(R%):GOTO850
 940 R%=I%:FOR F%=0 TO 8:E$(F%)=S$(F%):
     NEXT:PROCsave_record(R%):GOTO780
 950 ENDPROC
 955
 960 DEFPROCsave_record(R%)
1040 ENDPROC
1050 DEFPROCcount_lengths
1060 record%=0:R%=0
1070 FILE=OPENIN(record_detail$)
1080 REPEAT
1090 PTR#FILE=(R%)*total_record_length+5
1100 INPUT#FILE,employee_no$
1110 record%=record%+1:R%=R%+1
1120 UNTILemployee_no$="999"
1130 record%=record%-1
1140 R%=0:max_file%=0
1150 REPEAT
1160 PTR#FILE=(R%)*total_record_length
1170 INPUT#FILE
1180 R%=R%+1:max_file%=max_file%+1
1190 UNTIL EOF#(FILE)
1200 max_file%=max_file%-1
1210 CLOSE#FILE
1220 ENDPROC
```

The reader will notice that two new procedures are included in this routine for sorting a file. One has no origins in the cassette-based system because there was no need for the information that this procedure provides. The procedure for counting lengths, defined from line 1050, computes the number of records on the file that is being sorted and identifies the result as "record%". This variable was used previously but was stored with the file when it was transferred from memory. With a disc system, it should not be stored with the file because the file has a fixed format to enable "pointing" to take place and it would, therefore, have to be stored with each record and thus waste storage space. Conversely, the variable cannot be stored with the file details because they remain constant.

The variable, record%, is required in the sorting procedure but the other variable, although used in procedures that have been developed previously, is used only for information purposes in the printed message in line 90. The value of record% is obtained, after

initialisation in line 1060, by incrementing it in line
1110 for every record that does not have the value of
"999" for employee_no$. Note that to obtain this value
from the file, the value of PTR#file is increased by 5
for every record. This value results from its position
in the file, that is five characters in from the
beginning of each record including the allowance for
the room taken by R%. Readers will recall that this
amount of room was allocated to allow the record format
to be established.

When 999 is detected in line 1120, the value of
record% is reduced by one because incrementing took
place before the value of 999 was obtained. When
record% is incremented, the value of R% is also
increased by one so that, on REPEATing the routine, the
next record will be obtained from the file. The next
part of the procedure deals with the calculation of the
file length, max_file%.

The sequential incrementing of R% is used again but
this time the termination of the routine takes place
when the end of the file is detected in line 1190. In
this case, however, there is no value required from the
file and, as a result, line 1170 could be left out. On
detecting the terminating condition, line 1190, the
value of max_file% is reduced by one. The initial
message, lines 80, 90 and 100, will thus give the user
the full information about the file size.

Line 50 deals with the extra arrays that are used by
the sorting procedure. Examination of the file contents
is offered both before and after sorting has taken
place - lines 110 and 190. As can be seen, the main
program is almost entirely devoted to messages for the
user and one is particularly important. This is because
the difference in time required for sorting disc files
as compared with memory files might lead the user to
suspect that the routine was faulty. Thus line 160
provides a reassuring message and, after the file has
been sorted, a confirmatory message and a beep will be
produced - line 180.

The sorting procedure, defined from line 760, uses
the same format as the cassette-based system but takes
into account the fact that to look at the key field,
the complete record has to be obtained from the disc
and placed in memory. For comparison purposes, two
records have to be placed in memory and this explains
why arrays were dimensioned in line 50. The arrays E$
and S$ were used before but E1$ and E2$ are used to
hold records for comparison. The use of FOR...NEXT
loops in lines 790, 800, 820, 900, 920 and 940 is to
transfer data, field by field, between arrays. The two
procedures for reading from or writing to disc have

been dealt with previously and care has to be taken with their use in order that the correct value of R% is used. The record-saving procedure decrements the value given to it - line 980 - but the procedure for loading a record uses the actual value of R% - line 600.

Apart from these minor points, the sorting procedure does not need any further explanation. To use it, the program should be placed in memory after first creating an employee file of fourteen records using the program given in listing 8.8. At this stage, there is no user input for the file name and this has to be inserted into the program at line 60 before the program is RUN. The name must, of course, match the name used when creating the employee file.

When the program is tested, a message states that fourteen records exist on a file that has a capacity of twenty records and has the name that was used in line 60. If record examination is required, the disc drive will run for a few seconds before the selected record is displayed. As indicated at the bottom of the display, examination is terminated by an input of zero for the record number. Note that should a number greater than the value of "max_file%" be used, the routine will end without any sorting being carried out.

Selection of the key field is then requested and when the field number has been input, the disc drive will operate for about two minutes while the file is being sorted. During this time a message will be displayed and at the end of the sorting procedure the message will change to indicate that fact to the user. The disc drive will operate continuously during this time as data is being transferred between the memory and the disc. Examination selection is offered after the sort to allow verification of the correct sorting of the data.

Readers should carry out a sort on fields 3, 6, 8 and 9 to verify the fact that the insertion of spaces for formatting reasons has produced an added bonus. This is the fact that whereas the cassette-based sort procedure did not sort on these fields successfully, the disc-based system carries out a correct sort. Thus the salary figures can now be sorted in ascending value and the initials will be sorted on single initials first and then the double initials. The departmental and job codes will be dealt with in a similar manner.

Searching a File

The next requirement in the conversion to disc filing is a procedure for searching a file for a particular item. Again, the existing procedures will be modified, where possible, to reduce the development work involved

but   as with the sorting procedure, the conversion does
entail a certain amount of new programming. The program
given in listing 8.9 will be extended by the   addition
of   new messages and the modified version of the search
routine. Two new procedures have been included to cater
for the differences between the two filing systems   and
these,   together   with   any   other additions to listing
8.9, are given in full in listing 8.10.

LISTING 8.10

```
 10 ONERRORREPORT:CLOSE#0:END
 20 record_detail$="EMPLOY2"
 30 R%=999
 40 total_record_length=FNlength(record_detail$,R%)
 50 DIME$(field%-1):DIMS$(8):DIME1$(8):DIME2$(8)
 60 record_detail$="EMPFILE"
 70 PROCcount_lengths
 80 CLS:PRINTTAB(2,4)"The file ";record_detail$;
    "has a"
 90 PRINTTAB(2,6)"capacity of ";max_file%;" records"
100 PRINTTAB(2,8)"and holds ";record%;" records."
110 INPUTTAB(2,10)"Is a record examination required "
    A$
120 IFA$<>"Y"THEN131
130 PROCexamine_record(R%)
131 CLS:PRINTTAB(2,12)"Is the file to be sorted"
132 INPUTTAB(2,14)"before the search (Y/N) "A$
133 IFA$<>"Y"THEN181
140 CLS:PRINTTAB(2,12)"What field is the file"
150 INPUTTAB(2,14)"to be sorted on (1-9) "N%
152 IFN%<1ORN%>9THEN154ELSE160
154 VDU7:GOTO150
160 CLS:PRINTTAB(2,12)"THE FILE IS BEING SORTED"
170 PROCsort_file(N%)
180 VDU7:CLS:PRINTTAB(2,12)"THE FILE HAS BEEN SORTED"
181 PRINTTAB(2,16)"What field is to be used in"
182 INPUTTAB(2,18)"the search (1-9) "N%
183 IFN%<1ORN%>9THEN184ELSE185
184 VDU7:GOTO182
185 PRINTTAB(2,20)"What item is to be"
186 INPUTTAB(2,22)"searched for"search$:
    PROCpack_string(N%,search$)
187 CLS:PRINTTAB(2,12)"The item    ";search$;
188 PRINTTAB(2,14)"is being searched
    for"
189 PROCsearch_file(N%,Search$)
190 PRINTTAB(2,16)"Is a record examination"
200 INPUTTAB(2,18)"required (Y/N) "A$
210 IFA$<>"Y"THEN230
220 CLS:PROCexamine_record(R%)
230 CLOSE#0
240 END
```

```
 245
 250 DEFPROCload(record_detail$)
 370 ENDPROC
 375
 380 DEFFNlength(record_detail$,R%)
 450 =total_record_length
 455
 460 DEFPROCdisplay_record(R%)
 570 ENDPROC
 575
 580 DEFPROCload_record(record_detail$,field%,
     total_record_length,R%)
 670 ENDPROC
 675
 680 DEFPROCexamine_record(R%)
 750 ENDPROC
 755
 760 DEFPROCsort_file(N%)
 950 ENDPROC
 955
 960 DEFPROCsave_record(R%)
1040 ENDPROC
1045
1050 DEFPROCcount_lengths
1220 ENDPROC
1225
1230 DEFPROCsearch_file(N%,Search$)
1240 L%=1:H%=record%+1:up=FALSE:prevM%=0
1241 IFN%=1THENA%=5
1242 IFN%=2THENA%=10
1243 IFN%=3THENA%=28
1244 IFN%=4THENA%=32
1245 IFN%=5THENA%=35
1246 IFN%=6THENA%=43
1247 IFN%=7THENA%=47
1248 IFN%=8THENA%=55
1249 IFN%=9THENA%=59
1250 M%=INT((H%-L%)/2)+1
1260 IFM%=prevM%THEN1330
1270 prevM%=M%
1275 R%=M%-1:PROCload_field(A%,R%)
1280 IFfield$=Search$THEN1340
1290 IFfield$<Search$THEN1310
1300 H%=M%:M%=INT((H%-L%)/2)+1:IFup=TRUE THEN
     1320ELSE1260
1310 L%=M%
1320 M%=L%+INT(H%-L%)/2:up =TRUE:GOTO1260
1330 CLS:PRINTTAB(2,12)search$;" NOT FOUND":
     GOTO1350
1340 PROCrepeated_entries(A%,M%,Search$)
1350 ENDPROC
1355
```

```
1360 DEFPROCrepeated_entries(A%,M%,Search$)
1370 C%=0
1380 IFM%-1=0ORM%=record%+1THEN1500
1390 Z%=M%-1
1400 REPEAT
1410 Z%=Z%-1:IFZ%<0THEN1430
1415 R%=Z%:PROCload_field(A%,R%)
1420 UNTILfield$<>Search$
1430 B%=Z%+2
1440 REPEAT
1450 Z%=Z%+1:C%=C%+1
1455 R%=Z%:PROCload_field(A%,R%)
1460 UNTILfield$<>Search$
1470 IFC%-1=1THEN1500
1480 CLS:PRINTTAB(2,12)"There are ";C%-1;
     " records containing"
1490 PRINTTAB(2,14)search$;", beginning at
     RECORD NO ";B%:GOTO1510
1500 CLS:PRINTTAB(2,12)search$;" found
     at RECORD NO ";M%
1510 ENDPROC
1515
1520 DEFPROCload_field(A%,R%)
1530 FILE=OPENIN(record_detail$)
1540 PTR#FILE=R%*total_record_length+A%
1550 INPUT#FILE,field$
1560 CLOSE#FILE
1570 ENDPROC
1575
1580 DEFPROCpack_string(N%,search$)
1590 IFN%=1THEN1700
1600 IFN%=2THEN1760
1610 IFN%=3THEN1810
1620 IFN%=4THEN1880
1630 IFN%=5THEN1680
1640 IFN%=6THEN1810
1650 IFN%=7THEN1680
1660 IFN%=8THEN1810
1670 IFN%=9THEN1850
1680 DIMSearch$(6)
1690 GOTO1880
1700 DIMSearch$(3)
1710 IFLENsearch$=3THEN1880
1720 REPEAT
1730 search$="0"+search$
1740 UNTILLENsearch$=3
1750 GOTO1880
1760 DIMSearch$(16)
1770 REPEAT
1780 search$=search$+" "
1790 UNTILLENsearch$=16
```

```
1800 GOTO1880
1810 DIMSearch$(2)
1820 IFLENsearch$=2THEN1880
1830 search$=" "+search$
1840 GOTO1880
1850 DIMSearch$(5)
1860 IFLENsearch$=5THEN1880
1870 search$=" "+search$
1880 Search$=search$
1890 ENDPROC
```

The program up to line 1220 contains the same procedures as in listing 8.9 and so these have not been repeated in full.

All other additions to the previous listing that have been necessitated by incorporating the search procedure have been given line numbers that are not multiples of ten. Thus, lines 132, 154, 186, etc. are required as a result of adding the search facility. The first set, lines 131 to 134, allow a file to be sorted before a search is carried out and the second set will reject any input that calls for a sort field value outside the available range given in the input message - line 150. The last set of additions includes the same control feature and, in both cases, an audible indication of error is given by using the VDU7 statement.

The statements in lines 185 to 188 prepare the routine for the actual search procedure that is entered in line 189. The user is requested, in lines 185 and 186, to indicate the particular string that is required and when the string is entered, the routine calls a procedure that is made necessary because a disc system is being used. The random access file-handling procedure requires that all the records have the same format and this is achieved by packing some of the strings with spaces so that all entries for a certain field have the same length. As a result, when searching for a particular string, the search string must have the same length as that used by the field in question. The procedure that is defined from line 1580 deals with this requirement.

The field number N%, input by the user, is used to select the appropriate action in the packing procedure. For example, if the value of N% is "2", the string will be for a surname. This is stored as a 16-character string and thus the surname must be packed with spaces to give a total length of sixteen characters - lines 1760 to 1800 inclusive. Spaces or zeros may be required according to the field in question but in the case of field number four, the "sex" entry, a routine is used

when entering the original data to reject all
characters except "F" or "M". Thus no packing is
required but the string variable, "search$", input by
the user must be assigned to the string variable
"Search$" used in the search procedure. Note that the
two variables are not the same because they do not have
the same first letter.

The entries for the date values are treated in a
similar manner, see line 1680, but in this case the
entry is stored in the array that has to be dimensioned
beforehand whereas the single-letter sex entry did not
require an array. There is no general-purpose packing
routine that can be used here because each string must
be treated in a different manner.

The file-searching procedure, defined from line
1230, uses the same method as in the cassette-based
system but certain changes were necessitated in order
that the disc file could be accessed. To select a
particular field in a record, the value of PTR must be
adjusted by adding the appropriate amount to that of
the beginning of the record. This value is identified
as A% and is assigned in lines 1241 to 1249 inclusive.
The value that is assigned will be controlled by the
value of N%, the field selected by the user. The value
of A% is used whenever a record is interrogated, that
is in lines 1275, 1415 and 1455, by being added to the
PTR value - see line 1540. Before calling the field
loading procedure, the value of R% is assigned in the
same lines. The remaining parts of the search and
repeated entry procedures are as described for the
cassette based system. In the field-loading procedure,
defined from line 1520, only one data item is obtained
and this is given the name "field$". In the search
procedure, this item is compared with the variable,
Search$, in lines 1280, 1290, 1420 and 1460.

When the routine is tested, the previously created
file of fourteen employee records can be searched for
any item provided that the search field matches the
field on which the file has been sorted. Obviously, the
search procedure will not work if the file is not
sorted on the same field because it uses the binary
chop method - see chapter 5. The time taken to search
the fourteen-record file will be longer than if the
file is held in memory but this is the result of the
need to start up the disc drive before the data can be
extracted from it.

Adding Records to a File

The next part of the conversion to a disc-based system
deals with the need to extend a file by adding more
records to it. As explained in chapter 6, the solution

is basically to set R% to the value of the next empty
record in the file instead of to zero, as is the case
when creating a file initially. The user must be given
the opportunity to examine the file after being told
how many records exist on the file already and, if the
file cannot be extended this fact must be stated also.
Examination after extending the file must be offered
and, as · each new record is added to the file, the
record number must be displayed so that the user can
decide whether or not to create a new file to hold the
remaining data.

 All of these features are incorporated into the main
program which is given below.

```
 10 ON ERROR REPORT:CLOSE#0:END
 20 record_detail$="EMPLOY2"
 30 R%=999
 40 total_record_length=FNlength(record_detail$,R%)
 50 DIME$(field%-1):file_end=FALSE
 60 record_detail$="EMPFILE"
 70 PROCcount_lengths
 80 CLS:PRINTTAB(2,4)"The file";record_detail$;" has a"
 90 PRINTTAB(2,6)"capacity of";max_file%;" records"
100 PRINTTAB(2,8)"and holds ";record%;" records."
110 INPUTTAB(2,10)"Is a record examination required "A$
120 IFA$<>"Y"THEN140
130 PROCexamine_record(R%)
140 CLS:INPUTTAB(2,12)"Is the file to be extended "A$
150 IFA$<>"Y"THEN280
160 IFrecord%<>max_file%THEN180
170 PRINTTAB(2,12)"SORRY - FILE";record_detail$;
    " IS FULL":GOTO270
180 R%=record%
190 CLS:PROCload_record(record_detail$,field%,
    total_record_length,R%)
200 PROCcreate_record:IFfile_end=TRUE THEN250
210 PROCsave_record(R%)
220 CLS:PRINTTAB(2,12)"Record No. ";R%;
    " has been saved."
230 INPUTTAB(2,16)"Are more records to be created "A$
240 IFA$="Y"ORA$="y"THEN190
250 CLS:INPUTTAB(2,10)"Is a record examination
    required "A$
260 IFA$<>"Y"THEN280
270 PROCexamine_record(R%)
280 CLOSE#0
290 END
```

As can be seen, all of the requirements detailed above
are provided by this program. Line 140 allows the user
to select the extension option and if this is taken up,

a check on the values of the two variables "record%"
and "max_file%" is made. If they are equal, then no
more records can be added to the file and the message
in line 170 is displayed. If the file is not full, the
value of record% is given to the next empty record –
remember that these two variables always differ by one.
The normal procedure for record creation is then
followed and, after saving the new record in line 210,
the option of creating further records is given in line
230. A final opportunity to examine the file contents
is given in line 250 before the files are CLOSEd in
line 280.

The method of record addition is thus seen to be
quite simple and the complete routine is given in
listing 8.11. As usual, only the new procedures or the
changes to existing procedures that continuing
development have made necessary are given in full.

```
LISTING 8.11
  10 ON ERROR REPORT:CLOSE#0:END
  20 record_detail$="EMPLOY2"
  30 R%=999
  40 total_record_length=FNlength(record_detail$,R%)
  50 DIME$(field%-1):file_end=FALSE
  60 record_detail$="EMPFILE"
  70 PROCcount_lengths
  80 CLS:PRINTTAB(2,4)"The file";record_detail$;
     " has a"
  90 PRINTTAB(2,6)"capacity of";max_file%;" records"
 100 PRINTTAB(2,8)"and holds ";record%;" records."
 110 INPUTTAB(2,10)"Is a record examination
     required "A$
 120 IFA$<>"Y"THEN140
 130 PROCexamine_record(R%)
 140 CLS:INPUTTAB(2,12)"Is the file to be
     extended "A$
 150 IFA$<>"Y"THEN280
 160 IFrecord%<>max_file%THEN180
 170 PRINTTAB(2,12)"SORRY - FILE";record_detail$;
     " IS FULL":GOTO270
 180 R%=record%
 190 CLS:PROCload_record(record_detail$,
     field%,total_record_length,R%)
 200 PROCcreate_record:IFfile_end=TRUE THEN250
 210 PROCsave_record(R%)
 220 CLS:PRINTTAB(2,12)"Record No. ";R%;
     " has been saved."
 230 INPUTTAB(2,16)"Are more records to be created "A$
 240 IFA$="Y"ORA$="y"THEN190
 250 CLS:INPUTTAB(2,10)"Is a record examination
     required "A$
```

```
 260 IFA$<>"Y"THEN280
 270 PROCexamine_record(R%)
 280 CLOSE#0
 290 END
 295
 300 DEFPROCload(record_detail$)
 420 ENDPROC
 425
 430 DEFFNlength(record_detail$,R%)
 500 =total_record_length
 505
 510 DEFPROCdisplay_record(R%)
 620 ENDPROC
 625
 630 DEFPROCload_record(record_detail$,
     field%,total_record_length,R%)
 720 ENDPROC
 725
 730 DEFPROCupdate_attributes(R%)
1780 ENDPROC
1785
1790 DEFFNenter_data(across%,down%,size%,S_N$)
2010 =input$
2015
2020 DEFPROCcreate_record
2090 ENDPROC
2095
2100 DEFPROCcheck_date(date$)
2230 ENDPROC
2235
2240 DEFPROCsave_record(R%)
2320 ENDPROC
2325
2330 DEFPROCexamine_record(R%)
2400 ENDPROC
2405
2410 DEFPROCcount_lengths
2420 R%=0:max_file%=0
2430 FILE=OPENIN(record_detail$)
2440 REPEAT
2450 PTR#FILE=(R%)*total_record_length
2460 INPUT#FILE
2470 R%=R%+1:max_file%=max_file%+1
2480 UNTIL EOF#(FILE)
2490 max_file%=max_file%-1
2500 record%=0:R%=0
2510 REPEAT
2520 PTR#FILE=(R%)*total_record_length+5
2530 INPUT#FILE,employee_no$
2540 record%=record%+1:R%=R%+1
2550 IF(record%=max_file%ANDemployee_no$="999")
     THEN2590
```

```
2560 IF(record%=max_file%ANDemployee_no$<>"999")
     THEN2570ELSE2580
2570 record%=max_file%:GOTO2600
2580 UNTILemployee_no$="999"
2590 record%=record%-1
2600 CLOSE#FILE
2610 ENDPROC
```

As readers will notice, the only change to an existing procedure concerns the record and file-size counting procedure that was used satisfactorily in the sorting routine. To understand why the change was necessary, readers should carry out the following work.

The existing file of fourteen records should be extended, using this routine, to nineteen records. A copy of the file should then be made on another disc using the *COPY command described in the disc manual. (It is important to note that all files should be duplicated as and when they are produced in case problems arise during development work.) The extended file should now be sorted using the previous program and this will take about 3 minutes. Checking the file after sorting will demonstrate the correct working of the routine.

Using either of the two nineteen-record files, the last record should now be added. When the routine is RUN, the "size" message will inform the user that there are 19 records on a 20-record capacity file. This is, of course, the correct situation and adding the last file will alter this situation to 20 records. The routine can then be RUN again to allow checking of the file for correct record size. If the file-extension option is chosen, however, the "FILE FULL" message will be displayed.

The file should be copied to give a backup version and then used with the sorting routine. This time, however, there will be an error message because the counting procedure, as used in the sorting routine, will not cope with the situation that arises when the terminating value of "999" for employee$ has been replaced by "413" for the last record entry - see line 1120 of listing 8.10. One method of overcoming the problem is to use the value of max_file% in a comparison with the value of record%. Readers will note, however, that the value of max_file% is not calculated until the second part of the counting procedure.

Thus, the procedure has to be changed to provide the value of max_file% before the number of records is calculated. However, the repositioning of the

statements will not solve the problem fully. When the
file is counted, three possible situations can be
identified as follows. The file can be full, the file
can have exactly one free record space or the file can
have more than one free record space. The first case is
detected by line 2560 and the value of max_file% is
assigned to record% before the procedure ends after the
file has been closed. The second case is detected by
line 2550 and record% is adjusted, in line 2530, to be
one less than max_file% before the procedure ends. The
final situation will not involve lines 2550 and 2560
because the value of record% will not be equal to
max_file%. Thus the statement in line 2580 will be used
to terminate the count by recognising when employee$
has the value of "999".

The modified version of the count procedure should
now be incorporated into the sorting routine given in
listing 8.10 so that the twenty-record file can be
sorted.

Amending the Records in a File

The next requirement is that it must be possible to
amend the existing records in a file. Readers will
recall that in the cassette-based version this feature
was achieved by a modification to the attribute-update
procedure and, of course, the necessary changes in the
questions displayed on the screen. Two changes are
required to the existing record-amendment procedure as
a result of the conversion to disc. One concerns the
need to pack the field lengths to a standard size for
record formatting and the other is the direct
consequence of using the array E$ for holding a single
record while it is processed in memory.

Incorporating these changes will give the routine
identified as listing 8.12 and this is detailed below.
Those lines that are different from the cassette-based
version are listed in two sets. The first set comprises
the lines that were altered to cater for the use of the
array E$ and consists of 1620, 1640, 1660, 1770, 1870,
1960, 2060, 2160, 2260, 2360 and 2450. The second set
is for the lines that cater for the packing requirement
and consists of 1740 to 1760, 1850 to 1860, 2140 to
2150, 2340 to 2350 and 2430 to 2440. Readers will
recall that those fields that were of fixed length in
the cassette-based version do not require packing.

After entering the routine, readers should verify
that individual fields of a record can be changed. In
particular, the file should be extended to twenty
records, sorted on, say, field 2 and then amended. This
will provide a check on the compatibility of the
various routines.

```
LISTING 8.12
  10 ON ERROR REPORT:CLOSE#0:END
  20 record_detail$="EMPLOY2"
  30 R%=999
  40 total_record_length=
     FNlength(record_detail$,R%)
  50 DIME$(field%-1):file_end=FALSE
  60 record_detail$="EMPFILE"
  70 PROCcount_lengths
  80 CLS:PRINTTAB(2,4)"The file ";record_detail$;
     " has a"
  90 PRINTTAB(2,6)"capacity of";max_file%;" records"
 100 PRINTTAB(2,8)"and holds ";record%;" records."
 110 INPUTTAB(2,10)"Is a record examination required "
     A$
 120 IFA$<>"Y"THEN140
 130 PROCexamine_record(R%)
 140 CLS:INPUTTAB(2,12)"Is a record to be amended "A$
 150 IFA$<>"Y"THEN280
 160 CLS:INPUTTAB(2,12)"Which record is to be amended "
     N%
 170 IFN%<1ORN%>record%THEN80
 180 R%=N%-1
 190 CLS:PROCload_record(record_detail$,field%,
     total_record_length,R%)
 200 PROCamend_record(R%):R%=R%+1
 210 PROCsave_record(R%)
 220 CLS:PRINTTAB(2,12)"Record No. ";R%;" has
     been amended."
 230 INPUTTAB(2,16)"Are more records to be amended "A$
 240 IFA$="Y"ORA$="y"THEN160
 250 CLS:INPUTTAB(2,10)"Is a record examination
     required "A$
 260 IFA$<>"Y"THEN280
 270 PROCexamine_record(R%)
 280 CLOSE#0
 290 END
 295
 300 DEFPROCload(record_detail$)
 420 ENDPROC
 425
 430 DEFFNlength(record_detail$,R%)
 500 =total_record_length
 505
 510 DEFPROCdisplay_record(R%)
 620 ENDPROC
 625
 630 DEFPROCload_record(record_detail$,field%,
     total_record_length,R%)
 720 ENDPROC
 725
```

```
 730 DEFFNenter_data(across%,down%,size%,S_N$)
 950 =input$
 955
 960 DEFPROCcheck_date(date$)
1180 ENDPROC
1185
1190 DEFPROCexamine_record(R%)
1260 ENDPROC
1265
1270 DEFPROCcount_lengths
1470 ENDPROC
1475
1480 DEFPROCamend_record(R%)
1490 *FX4,1
1500 *FX229,1
1510 LOCAL A$
1520 CLS
1530 PROCdisplay_record(R%)
1540 PRINT:PRINT"Do you wish to amend ";CHR$(136);
     D$(0)
1550 PRINT:INPUT"Y/N",A$:IFA$<>"Y"THEN1670
1560 employee_no$=FNenter_data(22,23,3,"N")
1570 IFemployee_no$="999"THENfile_end=TRUE ELSE1590
1580 GOTO2510
1590 IFVAL(employee_no$)>=1THEN1600ELSE1560
1600 IFLEN(employee_no$)=3THEN1660
1610 IFLEN(employee_no$)=2THEN1640
1620 E$(0)="00"+employee_no$
1630 GOTO1670
1640 E$(0)="0"+employee_no$
1650 GOTO1670
1660 E$(0)=employee_no$
1670 CLS
1680 PROCdisplay_record(R%)
1690 PRINT:PRINT"Do you wish to amend ";CHR$(136);
     D$(1)
1700 PRINT:INPUT"Y/N",A$:IFA$<>"Y"THEN1780
1710 REPEAT
1720 surname$=FNenter_data(22,23,16,"S")
1730 UNTIL NOT NIL
1740 REPEAT
1750 surname$=surname$+" "
1760 UNTILLENsurname$=16
1770 E$(1)=surname$
1780 CLS
1790 PROCdisplay_record(R%)
1800 PRINT:PRINT"Do you wish to amend ";CHR$(136);
     D$(2)
1810 PRINT:INPUT"Y/N",A$:IFA$<>"Y"THEN1880
1820 REPEAT
1830 initials$=FNenter_data(22,23,2,"S")
```

```
1840 UNTIL NOT NIL
1850 IFLENinitials$=2THEN1870
1860 initials$=" "+initials$
1870 E$(2)=initials$
1880 CLS
1890 PROCdisplay_record(R%)
1900 PRINT:PRINT"Do you wish to amend ";CHR$(136);
     D$(3)
1910 PRINT:INPUT"Y/N ",A$:IFA$<>"Y"THEN1970
1920 sex$=FNenter_data(22,23,1,"S")
1930 IF sex$="M" OR sex$="F" THEN 1960
1940 VDU7
1950 GOTO1920
1960 E$(3)=sex$
1970 CLS
1980 PROCdisplay_record(R%)
1990 PRINT:PRINT"Do you wish to amend ";CHR$(136);
     D$(4)
2000 PRINT:INPUT"Y/N",A$:IFA$<>"Y"THEN2070
2010 REPEAT
2020 born$=FNenter_data(22,23,6,"N")
2030 UNTIL LEN(born$)=6
2040 PROCcheck_date(born$)
2050 IFdate=FALSE THENVDU7:GOTO2010
2060 E$(4)=D$+M$+Y$
2070 CLS
2080 PROCdisplay_record(R%)
2090 PRINT:PRINT"Do you wish to amend ";CHR$(136);
     D$(5)
2100 PRINT:INPUT"Y/N ",A$:IFA$<>"Y"THEN2170
2110 REPEAT
2120 dept$=FNenter_data(22,23,2,"N")
2130 UNTIL NOT NIL
2140 IFLENdept$=2THEN2160
2150 dept$=" "+dept$
2160 E$(5)=dept$
2170 CLS
2180 PROCdisplay_record(R%)
2190 PRINT:PRINT"Do you wish to amend ";CHR$(136);
     D$(6)
2200 PRINT:INPUT"Y/N",A$:IFA$<>"Y"THEN2270
2210 REPEAT
2220 joined$=FNenter_data(22,23,6,"N")
2230 UNTIL LEN(joined$)=6
2240 PROCcheck_date(joined$)
2250 IFdate=FALSE THENVDU7:GOTO2210
2260 E$(6)=Y$+M$+D$
2270 CLS
2280 PROCdisplay_record(R%)
2290 PRINT:PRINT"Do you wish to amend ";CHR$(136);
     D$(7)
```

```
2300 PRINT:INPUT"Y/N",A$:IFA$<>"Y"THEN2370
2310 REPEAT
2320 job$=FNenter_data(22,23,2,"N")
2330 UNTIL NOT NIL
2340 IFLENjob$=2THEN2360
2350 job$=" "+job$
2360 E$(7)=job$
2370 CLS
2380 PROCdisplay_record(R%)
2390 PRINT:PRINT"Do you wish to amend ";CHR$(136);
     D$(8)
2400 PRINT:INPUT"Y/N",A$:IFA$<>"Y"THEN2460
2410 salary$=FNenter_data(22,23,5,"N")
2420 IF VAL(salary$)<3500 THEN 2410
2430 IFLENsalary$=5THEN2450
2440 salary$=" "+salary$
2450 E$(8)=salary$
2460 CLS
2470 PROCdisplay_record(R%)
2480 PRINTTAB(6,22);"Are details correct? (Y/N)"
2490 A$=GET$
2500 IF A$="Y" OR A$="y" THEN 2510 ELSE 1480
2510 *FX4,0
2520 *FX229,0
2530 ENDPROC
```

Removing a Record from a File

The remaining requirement for the disc-based versions of the routines is the removal of a record from a file. Basically, this is simply a question of writing the next ascending order record in the file in the place of the redundant record. All the "higher" records in the file are then moved "down" one place to reposition them in the correct sequence. The last record in the original file must be replaced by a dummy record like those used in the initialised file, that is strings of 9 or A characters. Finally, the value of record% must be decreased by one. The obvious messages and the usual examination options must, of course, be given to the user. The final result is given in listing 8.13.

```
LISTING 8.13
  10 ONERRORREPORT:CLOSE#0:END
  20 record_detail$="EMPLOY2"
  30 R%=999
  40 total_record_length=FNlength(record_detail$,R%)
  50 DIME$(field%-1)
  60 record_detail$="EMPFILE"
  70 PROCcount_lengths
  80 CLS:PRINTTAB(2,4)"The file ";record_detail$;
     " has a"
```

```
  90 PRINTTAB(2,6)"capacity of ";max_file%;" records"
 100 PRINTTAB(2,8)"and holds ";record%;" records."
 110 INPUTTAB(2,10)"Is a record examination
     required "A$
 120 IFA$<>"Y"THEN140
 130 PROCexamine_record(R%)
 140 CLS:INPUTTAB(2,12)"Is a record to be removed "A$
 150 IFA$<>"Y"THEN270
 160 CLS:INPUTTAB(2,12)"Which record is to be
     removed "N%
 170 IFN%<1ORN%>record%THEN80
 180 R%=N%
 190 CLS:PRINTTAB(2,12)"THE RECORD IS BEING REMOVED"
 200 PROCremove_record(R%)
 210 CLS:PRINTTAB(2,12)"Record No. ";R%;" has been
     removed."
 220 INPUTTAB(2,16)"Are more records to be removed "A$
 230 IFA$="Y"ORA$="y"THEN160
 240 CLS:INPUTTAB(2,10)"Is a record examination
     required "A$
 250 IFA$<>"Y"THEN270
 260 PROCexamine_record(R%)
 270 CLOSE#0
 280 END
 285
 290 DEFPROCload(record_detail$)
 410 ENDPROC
 415
 420 DEFFNlength(record_detail$,R%)
 490 =total_record_length
 495
 500 DEFPROCdisplay_record(R%)
 610 ENDPROC
 615
 620 DEFPROCload_record(record_detail$,field%,
     total_record_length,R%)
 710 ENDPROC
 715
 720 DEFPROCsave_record(R%)
 800 ENDPROC
 805
 810 DEFPROCexamine_record(R%)
 880 ENDPROC
 885
 890 DEFPROCcount_lengths
1090 ENDPROC
1095
1100 DEFPROCremove_record(R%)
1110 FORR%=N%TOrecord%-1
1120 PROCload_record(record_detail$,field%,
     total_record_length,R%)
```

```
1130 PROCsave_record(R%)
1140 NEXT
1150 PROCdummy_record
1160 R%=record%
1170 PROCsave_record(R%)
1180 record%=record%-1
1190 ENDPROC
1195
1200 DEFPROCdummy_record
1210 FORfield=0TOfield%-1
1220 E$(field)=I$(field)
1230 NEXT
1240 ENDPROC
```

Readers will notice that only two new procedures are required to achieve the desired result. If the file had at least one dummy record at all times, the FOR...NEXT loop in line 1110 could use record% as the terminator instead of record%-1. There would always be a dummy record after the last genuine record that could be moved "down" to take the place of that last record. Such a possibility cannot be relied on, however, and so the routine must allow for the worst-case condition, that is that a dummy record will not be available in the file.

The terminator value of record%-1 will move all the genuine records in the file to their final position but leave a copy of the last record in its original position. Thus, saving a dummy record at the record position given by R%=record% will achieve the required result. What is still required is the placing of the dummy record details in the array that is used by the record-saving procedure. This is the array E$ and the dummy record details are held in array I$ and so a procedure that will load E$ with the contents of I$ is given in lines 1200 to 1240 inclusive. Readers should be familiar enough with the various statements and commands to have no difficulty in understanding how the procedures work.

A copy of the twenty-record file should be used for testing the routine because the removal procedure is irreversible and a backup copy will remove the need to insert deleted records again. When RUN, users will be presented with the usual file status message and this will be followed by the option of examination of the file. After this, the selection of the record-removal option will be followed by a message of assurance because the time taken to remove a record is directly related to its position in the file. For the twenty-record file, removal of record number one will take about 30 seconds and then the option of further removals is given. If several records are to be removed from a file, time will be saved if the removal is in descending record order.

The Different Meanings of OPENIN

Before leaving the subject of using floppy discs, readers should note that two versions of BASIC are in use with the BBC micro. These are known, not surprisingly, as BASIC I and BASIC II and which version is used in a particular computer depends, mainly, on when it was purchased. The important differences, as far as this topic is concerned, are connected with the "OPEN" commands used in the file procedures of this book.

In BASIC I, OPENIN will open a file for input to the computer and also for output from the computer whereas OPENOUT is used only for output from the computer. In BASIC II, however, OPENIN will open a file purely for input to the computer and, in addition, uses a code value that has no meaning in BASIC I. Thus, programs written for computers that use BASIC II will not work with those that use BASIC I if the keyword OPENIN is used. The keyword in BASIC II that has the same code value as OPENIN in BASIC I is OPENUP. Thus, for compatibility between BASIC I and BASIC II computers, BASIC I programs must use OPENIN and BASIC II programs must use OPENUP.

When this is done, programs written for BASIC I computers will work on BASIC II computers and, similarly, BASIC II programs will work on BASIC I computers. The programs developed in this book use OPENIN, and OPENOUT only when it is considered safe to do so, and will thus work on both BASIC I and BASIC II computers. As explained above, the keyword OPENIN can be used instead of OPENOUT and readers are encouraged to do this if in doubt about the consequences of using OPENOUT.

9 A Sample File Handler

This chapter draws together all of the previous work, particularly that of chapter 8, in order to produce a complete file handling package. For purposes of continuity, the previous employee record details and the same record format have been used for development and testing. Although it is unlikely that the package will represent a complete solution to an actual file-handling requirement, the features that are included in the package are typical of those found in commercially available software.

Disc Drive Equipment
The majority of the procedures that were developed in chapter 8 have been incorporated without change but, inevitably, some minor changes have had to be introduced in order that sufficient flexibility for users is provided. As is stated in the introductory message to users, a double disc drive system is required by the package because this reflects the most likely situation that will exist in practice. Readers who wish to develop a package that uses only one disc drive will find that the necessary changes are quite simple to understand and incorporate. The sample package was developed on a 100 Kbyte disc system and accommodates 999 records of the type used in the development. Readers who develop systems with more fields, each containing an increased number of characters, will probably find that this figure is not achievable unless disc systems with larger capacities are used.

The Provision of a Menu
The usual arrangement for this type of package is that a menu is presented on the screen so that users can choose a particular option. On completion of the option, users are returned to the menu so that a further choice can be made. As usual, great importance has been placed on giving information to the user whenever an operation that takes a long time is being carried out. There are two such operations in the

package and users could be excused for concluding that something had gone wrong if the only signs of activity were a blank screen and the noise of the disc rotation mechanism. Thus, a message is displayed to inform the user of what is happening and a short "beep" sounds when the operation has finished.

The menu contents are fairly standard and, with one exception, reflect the various procedures that have been developed. The single exception is an option to enable the file handling routine to terminate in a controlled manner. When the package is RUN, the user is required to enter the date of use. On terminating the use of the package, that date is recorded on the disc as the last date of use. Thus, a controlled termination helps to keep the filing system well organised. Pressing the ESCAPE key at any time will allow the user to end the proceedings but this method of termination will not provide the user with information on the last date of use and should be considered as an emergency act only.

Key-pressing Dangers

The pressing of keys during disc operations is, of course, something to be avoided under all circumstances if the corruption of data is not to take place. In this package, ample information is given about the disc operations that are taking place and it might be considered that sufficient precautions have been taken. Readers who believe in the belt and braces approach can use the command *FX201,1 to turn the keyboard off just before writing to files and *FX201,0 immediately after writing is complete to turn it on again. A word of warning here - the BREAK key is **not** affected by these FX commands and pressing it at any time while the package is being RUN could have disastrous consequences on the data files. One way of alleviating the results of such action is to "redefine" the BREAK key by adding the statement

        4 *KEY 10 CLOSE#0:END|M

This will close the files correctly but without waiting for the disc operation to be completed. Thus data corruption is quite likely and the only real safeguard is to cultivate the habit of keeping well clear of the BREAK key during filing operations.

Returning now to the file-handling package, the list of available options is given below.

1. CREATE A FILE
2. SORT A FILE
3. SEARCH A FILE
4. PRINT A RECORD
5. ADD A RECORD
6. AMEND A RECORD
7. DELETE A RECORD
8. END

Each of the options, apart from 8, has been developed in chapter 8 as a disc-based procedure but that for creating a file has been extended to allow the "creation" and "last access" dates to be presented to the user. This information is obtained from the user by the main program which is detailed in listing 9.1.

LISTING 9.1
```
 10 REM A FILE HANDLING PROGRAM
 20 CLS:dim_D_I=FALSE:dim_E=FALSE:sort=FALSE:
    search=FALSE:print1=FALSE:print2=FALSE
 30 ON ERROR REPORT:CLOSE#0:END
 40 PRINTTAB(2,5)"THIS FILE HANDLING PROGRAM IS BASED"
 50 PRINTTAB(2,7)"ON THE USE OF A DOUBLE DISC DRIVE."
 60 PRINTTAB(2,9)"THE PROGRAM DISC SHOULD BE PLACED"
 70 PRINTTAB(2,11)"IN DRIVE 0 AND THE FILE DISC"
 80 PRINTTAB(2,13)"IN DRIVE 1 - PLEASE PRESS ´ESCAPE´"
 90 PRINTTAB(2,15)"AND CORRECT IF NOT SO."
100 PRINTTAB(2,17)"PLEASE ENTER TODAY´S DATE, USING"
110 PRINTTAB(2,19)"THE FORMAT - DDMMYY."
120 PRINTTAB(8,22)"THE DATE IS ?"
130 REPEAT
140 date$=FNenter_data(22,22,6,"N")
150 UNTIL LEN(date$)=6
160 PROCcheck_date(date$)
170 IFdate=FALSE VDU7:GOTO130
180 *DRIVE 1
190 PROCmenu
200 ONC%GOTO210,220,230,240,250,260,270,280
210 PROCcreate_file:GOTO190
220 PROCsort_the_file:GOTO190
230 PROCsearch_file:GOTO190
240 print1=TRUE:PROCsearch_file:GOTO190
250 PROCadd_record:GOTO190
260 PROCamend_file:GOTO190
270 PROCdelete_record:GOTO190
280 PROCend
290 END
```

Several status indicators are used in the various procedures. These have to be initialised before use and

this is done in line 20. The purpose of the indicators
will be explained as they are met in the procedures.
The error handling routine in line 30, as explained
before, is an essential safeguard to prevent the
possibility of one or more files being left in an
opened state and it should be incorporated into any
development work that is being carried out by readers.
Lines 40 to 90 inclusive display a message that
indicates the correct disc placings and the necessary
remedial action. In lines 100 to 170 inclusive, the
date is requested and validated using two previously
developed routines - FNenter and PROCcheck_date. If
validation of the date fails, the user is returned to
line 130 after a beep has sounded.

A new command, *DRIVE 1, is introduced in line 180
and its purpose is to change the disc reading and
writing operations from the current default disc drive
unit, Drive 0, to the second drive on a double system.
The details of the file and the file itself are
contained on the disc that is in Drive 1. If readers
develop a package that uses only one disc drive, this
command would need to be replaced by a message asking
that the file disc be put into the drive unit in place
of the program disc. Completion of this operation would
have to be indicated to the program before the routine
was continued and a suitable method is given in line
980.

The menu procedure referred to in line 190 is dealt
with in listing 9.2 but basically it requires an input
of a number to indicate the user´s choice. The number
that is accepted by the procedure will be used in line
200 to direct the program to one of the lines 210 to
280 inclusive. The direction is achieved by the use of
the "ON" command in line 200 and should a user enter
the number "3" when in PROCmenu, the third of the line
numbers given in line 200, that is 230, will be
selected. On completion of the procedure that was
selected, the program will link back to the menu using
the GOTO 190 statement.

One of the selected lines, 240, contains a statement
to set the indicator "print1" to the TRUE state. This
indicator is used to extend the search procedure to
include a printing procedure. This will be explained
further when dealing with the print option.

Listing 9.2 deals with the menu display routine and
the validation of the option number.

LISTING 9.2

```
300 DEFPROCmenu
310 CLS
320 PRINTTAB(8,3)"FILE HANDLING PROGRAM"
330 PRINTTAB(16,5)"MENU"
```

```
340 PRINTTAB(3,6)"------------------------------"
350 PRINTTAB(8,7)"1";TAB(13,7)"CREATE A FILE"
360 PRINTTAB(8,9)"2";TAB(13,9)"SORT A FILE"
370 PRINTTAB(8,11)"3";TAB(13,11)"SEARCH A FILE"
380 PRINTTAB(8,13)"4";TAB(13,13)"PRINT A RECORD"
390 PRINTTAB(8,15)"5";TAB(13,15)"ADD A RECORD"
400 PRINTTAB(8,17)"6";TAB(13,17)"AMEND A RECORD"
410 PRINTTAB(8,19)"7";TAB(13,19)"DELETE A RECORD"
420 PRINTTAB(8,21)"8";TAB(13,21)"END"
430 PRINTTAB(3,22)"------------------------------"
440 INPUTTAB(6,24)"PLEASE INPUT YOUR CHOICE "C%
450 IFC%<1ORC%>8THENVDU7:GOTO310
460 ENDPROC
```

As can be seen, the procedure makes considerable use of
TAB statements to achieve the display format. Line   450
checks   that   the   value of C% does not lie outside the
option range.

Using Directory Names
Option 1 requires a procedure that   differs   from   that
developed   in   chapter   8. The details of the file will
remain unchanged but   the   contents   of   the   file   may
change   at   every   accessing of the file. In chapter 8,
the two sets of data   were   referred   to   by   different
names   and this is a feature to be avoided. A method of
using the same name   for   both   sets   of   data   without
creating   disc-filing   problems   is   thus   required. As
readers can find out by experiment, using a   file   name
that   has already been used will result in the previous
file of that name being overwritten by the new file.
   The disc-filing system used by the BBC micro   allows
files of the same name to be created on a disc provided
that   the   files   are   in different directories on that
disc. The default directory, that is the directory that
files will be   put   into   unless   the   system   is   told
otherwise,   is   identified   by the prefix, "$". Thus, a
number of different files can be used with a single
disc if they have different directory names and this is
the   way that both the file details and the actual file
can have the same name.   The   routine   is   included   in
listing 9.3.

```
LISTING 9.3
470 DEFPROCcreate_file
480 CLS
490 PRINTTAB(2,12)"Has a blank formatted disc been"
500 INPUTTAB(2,14)"placed in Drive 1 ? "A$
510 IF NOT(A$="Y" OR A$="y") THEN480
520 CLS
530 PRINTTAB(2,10)"Please input the name of the file"
```

```
540 INPUTTAB(2,12)"that is to be created "file_name$
550 IFLEN(file_name$)>7THENVDU7:GOTO540
560 INPUTTAB(2,16)"How many fields in a record ? "
    field%
570 IFfield%<>9THENVDU7:GOTO560
580 DIMD$(field%-1):DIMI$(field%-1):dim_D_I=TRUE:CLS
590 FORfield=0TOfield%-1
600 PRINTTAB(2,12)"Please input the name of"
610 PRINTTAB(2,14)"field number";field+1
620 INPUTTAB(2,16)""N$:D$(field)=N$
630 CLS:NEXT
640 FORfield=0TOfield%-1
650 PRINTTAB(2,12)"Please input the initial values"
660 PRINTTAB(2,14)"of field number ";field+1
670 INPUTTAB(2,16)""N$:I$(field)=N$
680 CLS:NEXT
690 first_date$=date$
700 last_date$="999999"
710 N%=999
720 *DIR D
730 *TITLE "STAFF FILE"
740 FILE=OPENOUT(file_name$)
750 PRINT#FILE,last_date$,first_date$,field%,N%
760 FORfield=0TOfield%-1
770 PRINT#FILE,D$(field),I$(field)
780 NEXT
790 CLOSE#FILE
800 *DIR $
810 CLS:PRINTTAB(2,10)"PLEASE WAIT FOR THE BEEP"
820 PRINTTAB(2,12)"Initialised records are now"
830 PRINTTAB(2,14)"being placed on the file disc"
840 FILE=OPENOUT(file_name$)
850 FORR%=0TON%-1
860 PRINT#FILE,R%
870 FORfield=0TOfield%-1
880 PRINT#FILE,I$(field)
890 NEXT:NEXT
900 CLOSE#FILE
910 CLS:VDU7
920 FORfield=0TOfield%-1
930 PRINTTAB(3)D$(field);TAB(20);I$(field)
940 NEXT:PRINT
950 PRINTTAB(3)"The initial record details are"
960 PRINT:PRINTTAB(3)"given above. Press any key
    to return"
970 PRINT:PRINTTAB(3)"to the menu to correct
    or continue."
980 PROCreply
990 ENDPROC
```

In lines 490 to 510 inclusive, the user is requested to place an empty, but formatted, disc in Drive 1 because the new file is to be stored using that drive. The file name, of no more than 7 characters length, is asked for by lines 530 to 550 inclusive. The name used should obviously be as informative as possible and, once chosen, must be used in all file operations on that disc. The number of fields to be used in a record is asked for by line 560. In this demonstration package, there is not a choice and so the value "9" is the only acceptable input and any other value will be rejected by line 570. The reason for including this feature is to indicate how all the necessary and relevant information could be gathered by a package that was being developed. The value is used to dimension the two arrays, D$ and I$ - line 580. Readers will recall that D$ holds the field names and I$ the initial values that are used to create an empty file. In addition, the indicator "dim_D_I" is set to TRUE and this will prevent problems if the package is used for other options without first using the END option.

The field names that are to be used in a record are requested and loaded into the array D$ by lines 590 to 630 of the program. Similarly, the array I$ is loaded using lines 640 to 680 inclusive. The date that was input at the start of the program run is given to the variable "first_date$" in line 690 and this date will remain with the file as its creation date. As there will have been no previous file-accessing operations on a file that is being created, it is necessary to insert a dummy date for the variable, "last_date$" - line 700. A file of 1000 records is a manageable size and should a greater number of records be required it is advisable to use more than one disc. Line 710 limits the file size to 1000 records.

The information that constitutes the file details which, excepting "last_date$", will not be changed during the existence of the file is then stored on the disc using lines 720 to 790 inclusive. The directory "D" is selected in line 720, D being a mnemonic for "details", and a name for the disc is allocated in line 730. Should more than one disc be used for the file, this name could be "STAFF FILE n" where the value "n" is input during the file-creation routine. This procedure would allow a number of different discs to be used for the complete file, each using the same file name but having different identifiers. Thus, if three discs were required for the file "EMPLOY1", the first could be identified as "STAFF FILE 1", the second as "STAFF FILE 2" and the last as "STAFF FILE 3". The advantage of this method of identification is that up to 12 characters can be used for the title.

Line 750 will store the date, field and file-size details and the following FOR...NEXT loop will store the field names and initial values. After the file has been closed in line 790, the selection of directory "$" follows. The file is then initialised, lines 840 to 890 inclusive, while an explanatory message is being displayed - lines 810, 820 and 830. On completion of the initialisation of the file, the file is closed and an informative "beep" is sounded - lines 900 and 910 respectively. Readers should note that lines 740 and 840 both use the same file name but, as explained previously, with a different directory. The last part of this procedure displays the record details for approval - lines 920, 930 and 940. The message that is also displayed will allow a return to the menu for a repeat of the complete file-creation procedure or a further choice from the menu. The purpose of PROCreply, dealt with later, is to prevent further action by the program until the user is ready.

PROCadd_record

Listing 9.4 is based on the record-addition routine developed in chapter 8 but includes a link to a routine that results from the need of a number of procedures to access, that is OPENin, a file.

```
LISTING 9.4
1000 DEFPROCadd_record
1010 CLS
1020 PRINTTAB(2,12)"What is the name of the file"
1030 INPUTTAB(2,14)"that is to gain records ?
     "file_name$
1040 IFLEN(file_name$)>7THENVDU7:GOTO1010
1050 PROCaccess_file(file_name$)
1060 R%=record%
1070 PROCload_record(file_name$,field%,
     total_record_length,R%)
1080 PROCcreate_record:IFfile_end=TRUE THEN1130
1090 PROCsave_record(R%)
1100 CLS:PRINTTAB(2,12)"Record No ";R%;
     " has been saved"
1110 INPUTTAB(2,16)"Are more records to
     be added ? "A$
1120 IFA$="Y" OR A$="y"THEN1070
1130 CLS:INPUTTAB(2,12)"Are the additions to be
     examined ? "A$
1140 IF NOT(A$="Y" OR A$="y") THEN1160
1150 PROCexamine_record
1160 CLS:PRINTTAB(6,10)"RECORD ADDITION IS COMPLETE"
1170 PRINTTAB(2,16)"Press any key to return
     to the menu"
1180 PROCreply
1190 ENDPROC
```

A file name that is too long will be rejected by line 1040. The new procedure referred to above is named in line 1050 but will be detailed later. Four procedures that were detailed in chapter 8 are used in this procedure, lines 1070,1080,1090 and 1150, and the remainder of the procedure is concerned with the display of information to the user and the provision of choices for further action.

PROCamend_file

Apart from the new file-access procedure mentioned previously, there is nothing else in this procedure that requires a descriptive treatment. · Unacceptable values of the number of the record that is to be amended will be trapped in either line 1260 or 1280.

LISTING 9.5

```
1200 DEFPROCamend_file
1210 CLS:PRINTTAB(2,12)"What is the name of the file"
1220 INPUTTAB(2,14)"that is to be amended ? "file_name$
1230 IFLEN(file_name$)>7THENVDU7:GOTO1210
1240 PROCaccess_file(file_name$)
1250 CLS:INPUTTAB(2,12)"Which record is to be
     amended ? "N%
1260 IFN%>record%THEN1270ELSE1280
1270 VDU7:GOTO1250
1280 IFN%<1THEN1290ELSE1300
1290 VDU7:GOTO1250
1300 R%=N%-1
1310 CLS:PROCload_record(file_name$,field%,
     total_record_length,R%)
1320 PROCamend_record(R%):R%=R%+1
1330 PROCsave_record(R%)
1340 CLS:PRINTTAB(2,12)"Record No. ";R%;" has
     been amended"
1350 INPUTTAB(2,16)"Are more records to be
     amended ? "A$
1360 IFA$="Y" OR A$="y"THEN1090
1370 CLS:PROCexamine_record
1380 ENDPROC
```

One feature that readers may notice about this procedure and the previous one is the contents of lines 1030 and 1220. Both are concerned with an input of the file name and this task is a feature of other options. The reason why the file name is requested by each option is to cater for unpredictable user choices. Readers will, no doubt, realise that this feature could be satisfied by introducing a procedure that would be linked-to, for all but options 1 and 8, in order to obtain the file name. The resulting input could then be used by any of the other options but, unless designed with care, would not give the user any information about the chosen option such as is given in lines 1030 and 1220. The final decision in such cases must, of course, lie with the program writer after consultation with the user, should they not be the same person.

PROCdelete_record

Information to the user is provided in this procedure to explain what is happening during a period when no change to the screen display is taking place. As mentioned in chapter 8, record deleting can be a lengthy operation on a large file particularly if the records to be deleted are not selected by the user in descending order, that is the highest numbered record first and then the next highest numbered and so on.

```
LISTING 9.6
1390 DEFPROCdelete_record
1400 CLS:PRINTTAB(2,12)"What is the name of
     the file"
1410 INPUTTAB(2,14)"that is to lose records ? "
     file_name$
1420 IFLEN(file_name$)>7THENVDU7
     :GOTO1400
1430 PROCaccess_file(file_name$)
1440 CLS:INPUTTAB(2,12)"Which record is to be
     removed ? "N%
1450 IFN%>record%THEN1460ELSE1470
1460 VDU7:GOTO1440
1470 IFN%<1THEN1480ELSE1490
1480 VDU7:GOTO1440
1490 R%=N%
1500 CLS:PRINTTAB(2,12)"RECORD ";N%;" IS ABOUT
     TO BE REMOVED"
1510 INPUTTAB(2,14)"Is this acceptable ? "A$
1520 IF NOT(A$="Y" OR A$="y") THEN1590
1530 CLS:PRINTTAB(2,12)"PLEASE WAIT FOR THE BEEP."
1540 PRINTTAB(2,14)"The record is being removed."
1550 PROCremove_record(R%)
1560 CLS:VDU7:PRINTTAB(2,12)"Record ";N%;" has
     been removed."
1570 INPUTTAB(2,14)"Are any more records to be
     removed ? "A$
1580 IFA$="Y" OR A$="y"THEN1440
1590 CLS:PROCexamine_record
1600 ENDPROC
```

As well as the error traps that have been described earlier, this procedure allows the user to abort a record removal even after selection of the record number has been made - lines 1500, 1510 and 1520. In this package, such an act will return the user to the menu, line 1520, but if further deletions were required, either 1440 or 1570 could be substituted for 1590.

PROCsort_the_file

This procedure links to PROCsort which readers will recall is another lengthy operation that requires user information to be displayed in order to allay fears that something has gone wrong. The usual error traps have been incorporated and a "beep" is sounded after the sorting operation has been completed.

LISTING 9.7

```
1610 DEFPROCsort_the_file
1620 CLS:PRINTTAB(2,12)"What is the name of
     the file"
1630 INPUTTAB(2,14)"that is to be sorted ? "
     file_name$
1640 IFLEN(file_name$)>7THENVDU7:GOTO1620
1650 PROCaccess_file(file_name$)
1660 CLS:PRINTTAB(2,12)"What field is the file"
1670 INPUTTAB(2,14)"to be sorted on (1-9) ? "N%
1680 IFN%<1 OR N%>field%THEN1690ELSE1700
1690 VDU7:GOTO1660
1700 CLS:PRINTTAB(7,12)"PLEASE WAIT FOR
     THE BEEP."
1710 PRINTTAB(2,14);file_name$;" is being sorted
     on field ";N%
1720 PROCsort_file(N%)
1730 VDU7:CLS:PRINTTAB(2,12)"The file has now
     been sorted."
1740 INPUTTAB(2,14)"Is a record examination
     required ? "A$
1750 IF NOT(A$="Y" OR A$="y") THEN1770
1760 CLS:PROCexamine_record
1770 ENDPROC
```

Although this point will be dicussed later, it should be mentioned that it is usual to maintain several versions of the file, each sorted on a different field. This is to avoid lengthy sort operations on a regular basis - there are, of course, disadvantages to this feature and these will be highlighted.

PROCsearch_file

In the development phase of this procedure, the opportunity of sorting the file was given to the user but this is no longer necessary. This procedure is, in fact, used by two options because it is likely that a search will be required before printing individual or multiple records.

LISTING 9.8

```
1780 DEFPROCsearch_file
1790 CLS:PRINTTAB(2,12)"What is the name of the file"
1800 INPUTTAB(2,14)"that is to be searched ? "
     file_name$
1810 IFLEN(file_name$)>7THENVDU7:GOTO1790
1820 PROCaccess_file(file_name$)
1830 CLS:PRINTTAB(2,12)"What field is to be used in"
1840 INPUTTAB(2,14)"the search (1-9) ? "N%
1850 IFN%<1 OR N%>field%THEN1860ELSE1870
1860 VDU7:GOTO1830
1870 CLS:PRINTTAB(2,12)"What item is to be
     searched"
1880 INPUTTAB(2,14)"for ? "search$
1890 PROCpack_string(N%,search$)
1900 CLS:PRINTTAB(2,12)file_name$;" is being
     searched"
1910 PRINTTAB(2,14)"for ";search$
1920 PROCsearch(N%,Search$)
1930 VDU7
1940 INPUTTAB(2,16)"Is an examination
     required ? "A$
1950 IF NOT(A$="Y" OR A$="y") THEN1970
1960 CLS:PROCexamine_record
1970 CLS:PRINTTAB(2,12)"Are any more searches
     required"
1980 INPUTTAB(2,14)"in this field ? "A$
1990 IFA$="Y" OR A$="y"THEN1870
2000 IFprint1=TRUE THEN2010ELSE2030
2010 PROCprint_file
2020 print1=FALSE
2030 ENDPROC
```

Choosing the printing option will set the indicator "print1" to TRUE - see line 240. As mentioned above, the present search procedure is linked-to and then, in order to provide the print option, the print procedure must be followed. This is not, however, an automatic process because selecting the search option should not provide the printing option as well. The indicator, sometimes called a "flag" or "marker", will determine the action to be taken as appropriate. In line 2000, line 2010 is selected only if "print1" is TRUE meaning that printing is required. If it is FALSE, printing is not required and line 2030 is selected instead. To allow further printing before the use of the package is terminated, "print1" is set to FALSE again in line 2020. If this was not done, printing of records would be made available for every search option chosen.

PROCprint_file
Another indicator, "print2", is sensed in this procedure. This is to overcome the problem that is created if a program attempts to dimension an array more than once. If it is necessary to dimension an array when entering a procedure, any subsequent entries to that array cannot include a DIM statement for the same array. Thus, when the print procedure is first entered, "print2" is set to TRUE - line 2060 of listing 9.9. All subsequent print-option selections will sense that the indicator is TRUE and link to line 2070 thus missing the DIM statement in line 2060.

LISTING 9.9
```
2040 DEFPROCprint_file
2050 IFprint2=TRUE THEN2070
2060 DIMF(8):print2=TRUE
2070 CLS:INPUTTAB(2,9)"Is the printer ready (Y/N) ? "A$
2080 IF NOT(A$="Y" OR A$="y")THEN2090ELSE2100
2090 VDU7:GOTO2070
2100 CLS:PRINTTAB(2,6)"Please input the required
     order"
2110 PRINTTAB(2,76)"of printing the fields":PRINT´´
2120 FORprint_field=0TO8
2130 PRINT"Print field ";print_field+1
     ;" is Record field ";:INPUTF%
2140 F(print_field)=F%
2150 NEXT
2160 INPUT´´"Is the order correct (Y/N) "A$
2170 IF NOT(A$="Y" OR A$="y") THEN2100
2180 CLS:PRINTTAB(2,12)"Please input ´S´
     for a single"
2190 PRINTTAB(2,13)"record printout"
2200 PRINTTAB(2,15)"or ´M´ for a multiple record"
2210 PRINTTAB(2,16)"printout ";:INPUTA$
2220 IF NOT(A$="S") THEN2410
2230 CLS:PRINTTAB(2,12)"Please input the
     number of the"
2240 INPUTTAB(2,14)"record that is to be
     printed "N%
2250 IFN%>record%THEN2260ELSE2290
2260 VDU7:PRINTTAB(2,16)"Record No.";N%;" has"
2270 PRINTTAB(2,17)"not yet been created"
2280 PRINTTAB(2,18)"Press any key to continue"
     :PROCreply:GOTO2230
2290 IFN%<1THEN2300ELSE2320
2300 VDU7:PRINTTAB(2,16);N%" IS OUT OF RANGE"
2310 GOTO2280
2320 R%=N%-1
2330 CLS:PROCload_record(file_name$,field%,
     total_record_length,R%)
2340 PROCprint_record(R%)
```

```
2350 PRINTTAB(2,14)"Are any more single records"
2360 INPUTTAB(2,16)"to be printed (Y/N) ? "A$
2370 IF NOT(A$="Y" OR A$="y")THEN 2380ELSE2230
2380 CLS:PRINTTAB(2,12)"Are multiple records"
2390 INPUTTAB(2,14)"to be printed (Y/N) ? "A$
2400 IF NOT(A$="Y" OR A$="y")THEN 2540ELSE2410
2410 CLS:PRINTTAB(2,8)"Please input the record"
2420 PRINTTAB(2,10)"sequencee details"
2430 PRINTTAB(2,13)"The first record in the"
2440 INPUTTAB(2,14)"sequence is "F%
2450 PRINTTAB(2,16)"The second record in the"
2460 INPUTTAB(2,17)"sequence is "L%
2470 FORR%=F%-1TOL%-1
2480 PROCload_record(file_name$,field%,
     total_record_length,R%)
2490 PROCprint_record(R%)
2500 NEXT
2510 PRINTTAB(2,14)"Are more sequences to"
2520 INPUTTAB(2,16)"be printed (Y/N) "A$
2530 IF NOT(A$="Y" OR A$="y")THEN 2540ELSE2410
2540 ENDPROC
```

In line 2070, the user is asked to indicate whether or
not the printer is ready for use. Should the answer not
be "Y" or "y", the routine will return to line 2070
after sounding a "beep". If, however, an affirmative
answer is given incorrectly, there is no way by which
the micro can sense the fact, but a safeguard exists
because only a certain amount of data can be sent to
the printer before the micro is prevented from further
output. In the development version of the procedure,
the field printing order was not capable of selection
by the user, but that feature now exists in the
package. This is contained in lines 2100 to 2150 and
lines 2160 and 2170 allow corrections to be made to the
printing order.

It should be noted that the order that is selected
will apply both to single and multiple record printing
but array F could be loaded again if necessary. The
printing of dummy records is prevented by line 2250 and
line 2290 will prevent problems caused by the selection
of a non positive record number. The opportunity of
printing multiple records after all single records have
been printed is given in line 2380 and should this
feature be required, lines 2410 to 2500 will be used to
print the sequence of records. The printing of more
sequences can be selected by an affirmative response to
the question produced by lines 2510 and 2520.

PROCend

This procedure will ensure that when the file handling routines have been used, all the files are closed, the date of use is recorded and that the disc system is returned to the default values.

LISTING 9.10
```
2550 DEFPROCend
2560 *DIR D
2570 PROCload(file_name$)
2580 last_date$=date$
2590 FILE=OPENIN(file_name$)
2600 PRINT#FILE,last_date$,first_date$,field%,N%
2610 FORfield=0TOfield%-1
2620 PRINT#FILE,D$(field),I$(field)
2630 NEXT
2640 CLOSE#0
2650 *DIR $
2660 *DRIVE 0
2670 CLS:PRINTTAB(17,6)"THE"
2680 PRINTTAB(8,8)"FILE HANDLING PROGRAM"
2690 PRINTTAB(15,10)"HAS NOW"
2700 PRINTTAB(16,12)"ENDED"
2710 PRINTTAB(7,16)"THE DISCS MAY BE REMOVED"
2720 ENDPROC
```

As the date information is in directory D, this directory must be selected before the file details can be loaded into the micro´s memory. Lines 2560 and 2570 will carry out this function and then the value of "last_date$" is replaced with the date that was input when the file-handling routine was run by the user - line 2580. As only one item in the details file is being changed it is obviously unnecessary to obtain all the details and then put most of them on file again without change. However, to keep the procedure as simple as possible, this is what has been done.

The file has to be opened again because the procedure for loading the file, see line 2570, closes the file after use. Lines 2600 to 2630 put all the details onto the file again and all files are closed in line 2640. In this package, only two files have been opened and all the procedures that accessed files also closed them afterwards. Thus line 2640 is not actually required - it is, as always in this work, better to be safe than sorry and so the retention of "CLOSE#0" is advocated. The default disc drive situation is restored in lines 2650 and 2660. Finally, the user is informed that the routine is complete in lines 2670 to 2710 inclusive.

PROCcheck_date
This procedure has been described previously and is detailed below for the benefit of those readers who do not have access to the program cassette.

LISTING 9.11
```
2730 DEFPROCcheck_date(date$)
2740 date=TRUE
2750 D$=LEFT$(date$,2)
2760 IFD$<"01"THENdate=FALSE:GOTO2860
2770 Y$=RIGHT$(date$,2)
2780 M$=MID$(date$,3,2)
2790 IFM$>"12" OR M$<"01"THENdate=FALSE:GOTO2860
2800 IFM$="02"THEN2840
2810 IFM$="04" OR M$="06" OR M$="09" OR M$="11"THEN2830
2820 IFD$<"32"THEN2860ELSEdate=FALSE:GOTO2860
2830 IFD$<"31"THEN2860ELSEdate=FALSE:GOTO2860
2840 IFD$<"29"THEN2860
2850 IFVAL(Y$)MOD 4=0 ANDD$="29"
     THEN2860ELSEdate=FALSE:GOTO2860
2860 ENDPROC
```

FNenter_data
Like the previous procedure, this function requires no further explanation.

LISTING 9.12
```
2870 DEFFNenter_data(across%,down%,size%,S_N$)
2880 LOCAL char$,length,input$
2890 length=0:input$=""
2900 PRINTTAB(across%,down%)
     ;STRING$(size%,"")+STRING$(size%,CHR$(127));
2910 GOTO2930
2920 VDU7
2930 char$=GET$
2940 IFchar$=CHR$(127)THEN3040
2950 IFchar$=CHR$(13)THEN3080
2960 IFlength=size%THEN2920
2970 IFS_N$<>"S"THEN2990
2980 IFchar$<CHR$(65)ORchar$>CHR$(90)THEN2920ELSE3000
2990 IFchar$<CHR$(48)ORchar$>CHR$(57)THEN2920
3000 input$=input$+char$
3010 length=length+1
3020 PRINTchar$;
3030 GOTO2930
3040 IFinput$=""THEN2920
3050 length=length-1
3060 input$=LEFT$(input$,lenqth)
3070 GOTO3020
3080 NIL=(length=0)
3090 =input$
```

PROCreply

This three line program hardly merits the name of procedure but does, nevertheless, perform in the same way that other procedures do.

LISTING 9.13
```
3100 DEFPROCreply
3110 R$=GET$:*FX15,1
3120 ENDPROC
```

The GET$ function will wait for a key to be pressed and then the string variable, R$, takes the string that corresponds to the pressed key. If required, the string could be used to determine which key had been pressed but in this case the information is not required. The procedure serves only to hold up the running of the program until the user initiates a continuation by pressing any key. The input buffer is flushed by *FX15,1.

PROCload

Readers should note that another procedure with the name PROCload_record is used in the package. This procedure is used to obtain the file details and is linked-to by PROCend, already described, and the function that calculates the total record length.

LISTING 9.14
```
3130 DEFPROCload(file_name$)
3140 FILE=OPENIN(file_name$)
3150 INPUT#FILE,last_date$,
     first_date$,field%,N%
3160 IFdim_D_I=TRUE THEN3190
3170 DIMD$(field%-1)
3180 DIMI$(field%-1):dim_D_I=TRUE
3190 FORfield=0TOfield%-1
3200 INPUT#FILE,name$,char$
3210 D$(field)=name$
3220 I$(field)=char$
3230 NEXT
3240 CLOSE#FILE
3250 ENDPROC
```

If the D$ and I$ arrays have been dimensioned before, the indicator, dim_D_I, will be TRUE and lines 3170 and 3180 will be missed. If it is FALSE, the arrays will be dimensioned and the indicator set to TRUE. The two arrays will then be loaded with the file details - lines 3190 to 3230 inclusive.

PROCaccess_file

This procedure is an amalgamation of the various routines that formed the main programs for the different developments in chapter 8. It is linked to by five of the option procedures and it is used to provide the user with information about the file.

LISTING 9.15

```
3260 DEFPROCaccess_file(file_name$)
3270 CLS:PRINTTAB(2,12)"Place the disc
     holding ";file_name$
3280 PRINTTAB(2,14)"in Drive 1"
3290 PRINTTAB(2,20)"Press any key to
     continue"
3300 PROCreply
3310 CLS:PRINTTAB(5,12)"PLEASE WAIT
     FOR THE BEEP."
3320 PRINTTAB(2,14);file_name$;" is
     being interrogated."
3330 *DIR D
3340 total_record_length=FNlength
     (file_name$)
3350 IFdim_E=TRUE THEN3370
3360 DIME$(field%-1):dim E=TRUE
3370 file_end=FALSE
3380 *DIR $
3390 PROCcount_lengths
3400 CLS:VDU7:PRINTTAB(2,4)"The file"
     ;file_name$;" was created"
3410 PRINTTAB(2,6)"on ";first date$;
     " and was last accessed"
3420 IFlast_date$="999999"THEN
     last_date$=first date$
3430 PRINTTAB(2,8)"on ";last_date$;".
     It has a capacity"
3440 PRINTTAB(2,10)"of ";max_file%
     ;" records and holds"
3450 PRINTTAB(2,12);record%;" records
     at the moment."
3460 IFNOT(record%=max_file%)
     THEN3480
3470 PRINTTAB(2,14)"NOTE!!   NO MORE
     RECORDS CAN BE ADDED"
3480 INPUTTAB(2,16)"Is a record
     examination required ? "A$
3490 IF NOT(A$="Y" OR A$="y")
     THEN3510
3500 CLS:PROCexamine record
3510 ENDPROC
```

After the statements that provide the user with instructions and information, lines 3270 to 3320 inclusive, the file details are obtained by lines 3330 and 3340. Line 3340 links to the record length function that, in turn, links to the procedure for loading the file details. If a record has not been obtained before, the array E$ will not have been dimensioned and thus the indicator, dim_E, will be FALSE. If so, line 3360 will be obeyed but, if not, line 3360 will be missed. The indicator that is used in record creation, file_end, will be set to FALSE in readiness for such a routine, line 3370, and then the default directory is selected in line 3380.

The procedure for counting the file length and the number of records that was developed in chapter 8 is used in line 3390. Lines 3400 to 3470 inclusive will display the important details of the file to the user. A warning about a full file is given by line 3470 and, finally, a record examination option is offered.

FNlength

This function provides the means by which the length of the records on the file is calculated. The result is used with the PTR statement when random access of the file is required. It was developed in chapter 8 and is used in this package without change.

LISTING 9.16
```
3520 DEFFNlength(file_name$)
3530 PROCload(file_name$)
3540 total_record_length=0
3550 FORfield=0TOfield%-1
3560 total_record_length=LENI$(field)+
     total_record_length
3570 NEXT
3580 total_record_length=2*field%+
     total_record_length+LENSTR$(N%)+2
3590 =total_record_length
```

PROCcount_lengths

This procedure calculates the number of records that the file holds and also the capacity of the file. Again, it was developed in chapter 8 and is used without change.

LISTING 9.17
```
3600 DEFPROCcount_lengths
3610 C%=0:max_file%=0
3620 FILE=OPENIN(file_name$)
3630 REPEAT
```

```
3640 PTR#FILE=(C%)*total_record_length
3650 INPUT#FILE
3660 C%=C%+1:max file%=max_file%+1
3670 UNTIL EOF#FILE
3680 max file%=max_file%-1
3690 record%=0:C%=0
3700 REPEAT
3710 PTR#FILE=(C%)*total record_length+5
3720 INPUT#FILE,employee_no$
3730 record%=record%+1:C%=C%+1
3740 IF(record%=max_file% AND employee_no$=
     "999")THEN3780
3750 IF(record%=max file% AND employee_no$<>
     "999")THEN3760ELSE3770
3760 record%=max_file%:GOTO3790
3770 UNTILemployee_no$="999"
3780 record%=record%-1
3790 CLOSE#FILE
3800 ENDPROC
```

PROCexamine_record

Readers will recognise this procedure, and the two that
it calls, as being almost unchanged since the initial
development took place. They are listed without further
comment.

LISTING 9.18
```
3810 DEFPROCexamine_record
3820 INPUTTAB(2,14)"Which record is to be
     examined ? "R%
3830 CLS:R%=R%-1 3840 PROCload_record(file_name$,
     field%,total_record_length,R%)
3850 PROCdisplay_record(R%)
3860 INPUTTAB(2,22)"NEXT RECORD NO., 0 TO END "R%
3870 IFNOT(R%=0)THEN3830
3880 ENDPROC
```

PROCload_record

A procedure that uses the value of PTR to obtain a
record from the file.

LISTING 9.19
```
3890 DEFPROCload_record(file_name$,
     field%,total_record_length,R%)
3900 FILE=OPENIN(file_name$)
3910 PTR#FILE=(R%)*total_record_length
3920 INPUT#FILE,R%
3930 FORfield=0TOfield%-1
3940 INPUT#FILE,char$
3950 E$(field)=char$
```

```
3960 NEXT
3970 CLOSE#FILE
3980 ENDPROC
```

PROCdisplay_record

This is a procedure that produces a screen display of the contents of a record together with field names and the number of the record.

LISTING 9.20
```
3990 DEFPROCdisplay_record(R%)
4000 PRINTTAB(8,2);"** EMPLOYEE RECORD ";R%+1;" **"
4010 PRINTTAB(1,4);"1";TAB(3,4);D$(0);TAB(22,4);E$(0)
4020 PRINTTAB(1,6);"2";TAB(3,6);D$(1);TAB(22,6);E$(1)
4030 PRINTTAB(1,8);"3";TAB(3,8);D$(2);TAB(22,8);E$(2)
4040 PRINTTAB(1,10);"4";TAB(3,10);D$(3);TAB(22,10);
     E$(3)
4050 PRINTTAB(1,12);"5";TAB(3,12);D$(4);TAB(22,12);
     E$(4)
4060 PRINTTAB(1,14);"6";TAB(3,14);D$(5);TAB(22,14);
     E$(5)
4070 PRINTTAB(1,16);"7";TAB(3,16);D$(6);TAB(22,16);
     E$(6)
4080 PRINTTAB(1,18);"8";TAB(3,18);D$(7);TAB(22,18);
     E$(7)
4090 PRINTTAB(1,20);"9";TAB(3,20);D$(8);TAB(22,20);
     E$(8)
4100 ENDPROC
```

PROCcreate_record

This procedure uses the indicator, file_end, that is set to TRUE by an input of "999" during the input of record details, to update the value of the record number and the number of records on the file. It will also be set to TRUE when the file becomes full.

LISTING 9.21
```
4110 DEFPROCcreate_record
4120 PROCupdate_attributes(R%)
4130 record%=record%+1
4140 R%=R%+1:IFfile_end=TRUE THEN4170
4150 IFR%=max_file%+1THEN4160ELSE4170
4160 file_end=TRUE:record%=record%+1
4170 record%=record%-1
4180 ENDPROC
```

PROCsave_record

This procedure will print the record details resident in the array, E$, onto the file.

```
LISTING 9.22
4190 DEFPROCsave_record(R%)
4200 FILE=OPENIN(file_name$)
4210 PTR#FILE=(R%-1)*total_record_length
4220 PRINT#FILE,R%
4230 FORfield=0TOfield%-1
4240 PRINT#FILE,E$(field)
4250 NEXT
4260 CLOSE#FILE
4270 ENDPROC
```

PROCamend_record

Like the previous six procedures, this was developed in
chapter 8 and is not changed in this presentation. It
is similar in many respects to the procedure that is
used for updating the attributes of a record, that is,
the field details, but acts only on existing records.
It offers the opportunity of changing any of the field
details from the values that were recorded originally.

```
LISTING 9.23
4280 DEFPROCamend_record(R%)
4290 *FX4,1
4300 *FX229,1
4310 LOCAL A$
4320 CLS
4330 PROCdisplay_record(R%)
4340 PRINT:PRINT"Do you wish to amend"
     ;CHR$(136);D$(0)
4350 PRINT:INPUT"Y/N",A$:IFA$<>"Y"THEN4470
4360 employee_no$=FNenter_data(22,23,3,"N")
4370 IFemployee_no$="999"THENfile_end=TRUE
     ELSE4390
4380 GOTO5310
4390 IFVAL(employee_no$)>=1THEN4400ELSE4360
4400 IFLEN(employee_no$)=3THEN4460
4410 IFLEN(employee_no$)=2THEN4440
4420 E$(0)="00"+employee_no$
4430 GOTO4470
4440 E$(0)="0"+employee_no$
4450 GOTO4470
4460 E$(0)=employee_no$
4470 CLS
4480 PROCdisplay_record(R%)
4490 PRINT:PRINT"Do you wish to amend "
     ;CHR$(136);D$(1)
4500 PRINT:INPUT"Y/N",A$:IFA$<>"Y"THEN4580
4510 REPEAT
4520 surname$=FNenter_data(22,23,16,"S")
4530 UNTIL NOT NIL
4540 REPEAT
4550 surname$=surname$+" "
4560 UNTILLENsurname$=16
```

```
4570 E$(1)=surname$
4580 CLS
4590 PROCdisplay_record(R%)
4600 PRINT:PRINT"Do you wish to amend"
     ;CHR$(136);D$(2)
4610 PRINT:INPUT"Y/N",A$
     :IFA$<>"Y"THEN4680
4620 REPEAT
4630 initials$=FNenter_data(22,23,2,"S")
4640 UNTIL NOT NIL
4650 IFLENinitials$=2THEN4670
4660 initials$=" "+initials$
4670 E$(2)=initials$
4680 CLS
4690 PROCdisplay_record(R%)
4700 PRINT:PRINT"Do you wish to amend"
     ;CHR$(136);D$(3)
4710 PRINT:INPUT"Y/N",A$:IFA$<>"Y"THEN4770
4720 sex$=FNenter_data(22,23,1,"S")
4730 IF sex$="M" OR sex$="F" THEN 4760
4740 VDU7
4750 GOTO4720
4760 E$(3)=sex$
4770 CLS
4780 PROCdisplay_record(R%)
4790 PRINT:PRINT"Do you wish to amend"
     ;CHR$(136);D$(4)
4800 PRINT:INPUT"Y/N",A$:IFA$<>"Y"THEN4870
4810 REPEAT
4820 born$=FNenter_data(22,23,6,"N")
4830 UNTIL LEN(born$)=6
4840 PRCCcheck_date(born$)
4850 IFdate=FALSE THENVDU7:GOTO4810
4860 E$(4)=D$+M$+Y$
4870 CLS
4880 PROCdisplay_record(R%)
4890 PRINT:PRINT"Do you wish to amend"
     ;CHR$(136);D$(5)
4900 PRINT:INPUT"Y/N",A$
     :IFA$<>"Y"THEN4970
4910 REPEAT
4920 dept$=FNenter_data(22,23,2,"N")
4930 UNTIL NOT NIL
4940 IFLENdept$=2THEN4960
4950 dept$=" "+dept$
4960 E$(5)=dept$
4970 CLS
4980 PROCdisplay_record(R%)
4990 PRINT:PRINT"Do you wish to amend"
     ;CHR$(136);D$(6)
5000 PRINT:INPUT"Y/N",A$
     :IFA$<>"Y"THEN5070
```

```
5010 REPEAT
5020 joined$=FNenter_data(22,23,6,"N")
5030 UNTIL LEN(joined$)=6
5040 PROCcheck_date(joined$)
5050 IFdate=FALSE THENVDU7:GOTO5010
5060 E$(6)=Y$+M$+D$
5070 CLS
5080 PROCdisplay_record(R%)
5090 PRINT:PRINT"Do you wish to amend"
     ;CHR$(136);D$(7)
5100 PRINT:INPUT"Y/N",A$
     :IFA$<>"Y"THEN5170
5110 REPEAT
5120 job$=FNenter_data(22,23,2,"N")
5130 UNTIL NOT NIL
5140 IFLENjob$=2THEN5160
5150 job$=" "+job$
5160 E$(7)=job$
5170 CLS
5180 PROCdisplay_record(R%)
5190 PRINT:PRINT"Do you wish to amend"
     ;CHR$(136);D$(8)
5200 PRINT:INPUT"Y/N",A$:IFA$<>"Y"THEN5260
5210 salary$=FNenter_data(22,23,5,"N")
5220 IF VAL(salary$)<3500 THEN 5210
5230 IFLENsalary$=5THEN5250
5240 salary$=" "+salary$
5250 E$(8)=salary$
5260 CLS
5270 PROCdisplay_record(R%)
5280 PRINTTAB(6,22);"Are details
     correct? (Y/N)"
5290 A$=GET$:*FX15,1
5300 IFA$="Y" OR A$="y"THEN5310ELSE4280
5310 *FX4,0
5320 *FX229,0
5330 ENDPROC
```

PROCupdate_attributes

As mentioned in connection with the previous procedure, this procedure creates a record but, with the exception of the final display before saving to file, allows no possibility of changing the details. The complete set of details must then be input again.

LISTING 9.24

```
5340 DEFPROCupdate_attributes(R%)
5350 *FX4,1
5360 *FX229,1
5370 LOCAL A$
```

```
5380 CLS
5390 PROCdisplay_record(R%)
5400 PRINTTAB(13,22);"Please input"
5410 PRINTTAB(1,24);D$(0)
5420 employee_no$=FNenter_data(22,23,3,"N")
5430 IFemployee_no$="999"THENfile_end=TRUE ELSE5450
5440 GOTO6370
5450 IFVAL(employee_no$)>=1THEN5460 ELSE540
5460 IFLEN(employee_no$)=3THEN5520
5470 IFLEN(employee_no$)=2THEN5500
5480 E$(0)="00"+employee_no$
5490 GOTO5530
5500 E$(0)="0"+employee_no$
5510 GOTO5530
5520 E$(0)=employee_no$
5530 CLS
5540 PROCdisplay_record(R%)
5550 PRINTTAB(13,22);"Please input"
5560 PRINTTAB(1,24);D$(1)
5570 REPEAT
5580 surname$=FNenter_data(22,23,16,"S")
5590 UNTIL NOT NIL
5600 REPEAT
5610 surname$=surname$+" "
5620 UNTILLENsurname$=16
5630 E$(1)=surname$
5640 CLS
5650 PROCdisplay_record(R%)
5660 PRINTTAB(13,22);"Please input"
5670 PRINTTAB(1,24);D$(2)
5680 REPEAT
5690 initials$=FNenter_data(22,23,2,"S")
5700 UNTIL NOT NIL
5710 IFLENinitials$=2THEN5730
5720 initials$=" "+initials$
5730 E$(2)=initials$
5740 CLS
5750 PROCdisplay_record(R%)
5760 PRINTTAB(13,22);"Please input"
5770 PRINTTAB(1,24);D$(3)
5780 sex$=FNenter_data(22,23,1,"S")
5790 IFsex$="M"ORsex$="F"THEN5820
5800 VDU7
5810 GOTO5780
5820 E$(3)=sex$
5830 CLS
5840 PROCdisplay_record(R%)
5850 PRINTTAB(13,22);"Please input"
5860 PRINTTAB(1,24);D$(4)
5870 REPEAT
5880 born$=FNenter_data(22,23,6,"N")
```

```
5890 UNTILLEN(born$)=6
5900 PROCcheck_date(born$)
5910 IFdate=FALSE THENVDU7:GOTO5870
5920 E$(4)=D$+M$+Y$
5930 CLS
5940 PROCdisplay_record(R%)
5950 PRINTTAB(13,22);"Please input"
5960 PRINTTAB(1,24);D$(5)
5970 REPEAT
5980 dept$=FNenter_data(22,23,2,"N")
5990 UNTIL NOT NIL
6000 IFLENdept$=2THEN6020
6010 dept$=" "+dept$
6020 E$(5)=dept$
6030 CLS
6040 PROCdisplay_record(R%)
6050 PRINTTAB(13,22);"Please input"
6060 PRINTTAB(1,24);D$(6)
6070 REPEAT
6080 joined$=FNenter_data(22,23,6,"N")
6090 UNTILLEN(joined$)=6
6100 PROCcheck_date(joined$)
6110 IFdate=FALSE THENVDU7:GOTO6070
6120 E$(6)=Y$+M$+D$
6130 CLS
6140 PROCdisplay_record(R%)
6150 PRINTTAB(13,22);"Please input"
6160 PRINTTAB(1,24);D$(7)
6170 REPEAT
6180 job$=FNenter_data(22,23,2,"N")
6190 UNTIL NOT NIL
6200 IFLENjob$=2THEN6220
6210 job$=" "+job$
6220 E$(7)=job$
6230 CLS
6240 PROCdisplay_record(R%)
6250 PRINTTAB(13,22);"Please input"
6260 PRINTTAB(1,24);D$(8)
6270 salary$=FNenter_data(22,23,5,"N")
6280 IF VAL(salary$)<3500 THEN 6270
6290 IFLENsalary$=5THEN6310
6300 salary$=" "+salary$
6310 E$(8)=salary$
6320 CLS
6330 PROCdisplay_record(R%)
6340 PRINTTAB(6,22);"Are details correct? (Y/N)"
6350 A$=GET$:*FX15,1
6360 IF A$="Y" OR A$="y" THEN 6370 ELSE 5340
6370 *FX4,0
6380 *FX229,0
6390 ENDPROC
```

PROCremove_record
This is a procedure that removes a record by replacing
it with the next higher-numbered record in the file.
The process will be repeated for the remaining records
and the final record is replaced, in its original
position, by a dummy record.

```
LISTING 9.25
6400 DEFPROCremove_record(R%)
6410 FORR%=N%TOrecord%-1
6420 PROCload_record(file_name$,field%,
     total_record_length,R%)
6430 PROCsave_record(R%)
6440 NEXT
6450 PROCdummy_record
6460 R%=record%
6470 PROCsave_record(R%)
6480 record%=record%-1
6490 ENDPROC
```

PROCdummy_record
This is a procedure that loads a copy of the field
details, held in array I$, into the array E$ so that a
record can be replaced by a dummy record.

```
LISTING 9.26
6500 DEFPROCdummy_record
6510 FORfield=0TOfield%-1
6520 E$(field)=I$(field)
6530 NEXT
6540 ENDPROC
```

PROCsort_file
This procedure is based on that which was developed in
chapter 8 but includes certain features that are
necessary when it is used in this package.

```
LISTING 9.27
6550 DEFPROCsort_file(N%)
6560 S%=INT(record%/2)+1:E%=record%:N%=N%-1
6570 IFsort=TRUE THEN6590
6580 DIMS$(8):DIME1$(8):DIME2$(8):sort=TRUE
6590 IFS%=1THEN6610
6600 S%=S%-1:R%=S%-1:PROCload_record(file_name$,
     field%,total_record_length,R%)
     :W$=E$(N%):FOR F%=0 TO 8
     :S$(F%)=E$(F%):NEXT:GOTO 6650
6610 R%=E%-1:PROCload_record(file_name$,
     field%,total_record_length,R%)
     :FOR F%=0 TO8:S$(F%)=E$(F%):NEXT
```

```
      :W$=S$(N%):R%=0:PROCload_record
      (file_name$,field%,total_record_
      length,R%):R%=E%
      :PROCsave_record(R%):E%=E%-1
6620  IFE%=1THEN6630ELSE6650
6630  R%=1:FOR F%=0 TO8
      :E$(F%)=S$(F%):NEXT:PROCsave_record(R%)
6640  GOTO 6760
6650  J%=S%
6660  I%=J%
6670  J%=2*J%
6680  IFJ%<E%THEN6710
6690  IFJ%=E%THEN6730
6700  IFJ%>E%THEN6750
6710  R%=J%-1:PROCload_record(file_name$,
      field%,total_record_length,R%)
      :FOR F%=0 TO8
      :E1$(F%)=E$(F%):NEXT:R%=J%
      :PROCload_record(file_name$,
      field%,total_record_length,R%)
      :FOR F%=0 TO8
      :E2$(F%)=E$(F%):NEXT
6720  IFE1$(N%)<E2$(N%)THENJ%=J%+1
6730  R%=J%-1:PROCload_record(file_name$,
      field%,total_record_length,R%)
      :FOR F%=0TO8:E1$(F%)=E$(F%):NEXT
      :IFW$>=E1$(N%)THEN6750
6740  R%=I%:PROCsave_record(R%):GOTO6660
6750  R%=I%:FOR F%=0TO8:E$(F%)=S$(F%)
      :NEXT:PROCsave_record(R%):GOTO6590
6760  EN
```

A number of arrays used in the original development of this procedure did not cause objections to be raised by the operating system of the micro as a result of not being dimensioned. The arrays were S$, E1$ and E2$. In developing this package, it was found necessary to correct this feature in order to prevent "BAD DIM" messages being produced. The consequence of dimensioning arrays is that any further attempts to dimension them will produce a further message, as previously discussed. This is overcome by using the indicator "sort" that is set to FALSE in line 20. On first using the sort procedure, this indicator is set to TRUE, line 6580, after the arrays have been dimensioned. All subsequent use of the procedure will miss out this line by virtue of the state of the indicator. Apart from this aspect, the procedure is the same as was developed in chapter 8.

PROCsearch

The incorporation of this procedure did not require changes to be made, apart from message-display details which do not require explanation.

LISTING 9.28

```
6770 DEFPROCsearch(N%,Search$)
6780 L%=1:H%=record%+1:up=FALSE:prevM%=0
6790 IFN%=1THENA%=5
6800 IFN%=2THENA%=10
6810 IFN%=3THENA%=28
6820 IFN%=4THENA%=32
6830 IFN%=5THENA%=35
6840 IFN%=6THENA%=43
6850 IFN%=7THENA%=47
6860 IFN%=8THENA%=55
6870 IFN%=9THENA%=59
6880 M%=INT((H%-L%)/2)+1
6890 IFM%=prevM%THEN6970
6900 prevM%=M%
6910 R%=M%-1:PROCload_field(A%,R%)
6920 IFfield$=Search$THEN6980
6930 IFfield$<Search$THEN6950
6940 H%=M%:M%=INT((H%-L%)/2)+1
     :IFup=TRUE THEN6960ELSE6890
6950 L%=M%
6960 M%=L%+INT(H%-L%)/2:up=TRUE:GOTO6890
6970 CLS:PRINTTAB(2,12)search$;" NOT FOUND":
     GOTO6990
6980 PROCrepeated_entries(A%,M%,Search$)
6990 ENDPROC
```

PROCpack_string

This procedure is different from the version developed in chapter 8 because of the need to avoid attempts to dimension arrays more than once. In this procedure, the array Search$ was originally dimensioned to a size that was determined by the length of the item being searched for. In the present version, the array is dimensioned to the maximum size that has to be accommodated, that is 16 - see line 7020, and the indicator "search" is set to TRUE. Future links to this procedure will thus miss out line 7020.

LISTING 9.29

```
7000 DEFPROCpack_string(N%,search$)
7010 IFsearch=TRUE THEN7030
7020 DIMSearch$(16):search=TRUE
7030 IFN%=1THEN7120
7040 IFN%=2THEN7170
```

```
7050 IFN%=3THEN7210
7060 IFN%=4THEN7260
7070 IFN%=5THEN7260
7080 IFN%=6THEN7210
7090 IFN%=7THEN7260
7100 IFN%=8THEN7210
7110 IFN%=9THEN7240
7120 IFLENsearch$=3THEN7260
7130 REPEAT
7140 search$="0"+search$
7150 UNTILLENsearch$=3
7160 GOTO7260
7170 REPEAT
7180 search$=search$+" "
7190 UNTILLENsearch$=16
7200 GOTO7260
7210 IFLENsearch$=2THEN7260
7220 search$=" "+search$
7230 GOTO7260
7240 IFLENsearch$=5THEN7260
7250 search$=" "+search$
7260 Search$=search$
7270 ENDPROC
```

The result is that the procedure is more simple to understand because, whatever field is selected, the appropriate packing routine is followed and then, finally, the array Search$ is given the value of search$ - note the use of "S" for the array.

PROCrepeated_entries
The procedure used in the package is the same as was developed in chapter 8 apart from the screen-display details.

```
LISTING 9.30
7280 DEFPROCrepeated_entries(A%,M%,Search$)
7290 C%=0
7300 IFM%-1=0 OR M%=record%+1THEN7440
7310 Z%=M%-1
7320 REPEAT
7330 Z%=Z%-1:IFZ%<0THEN7360
7340 R%=Z%:PROCload_field(A%,R%)
7350 UNTILfield$<>Search$
7360 B%=Z%+2
7370 REPEAT
7380 Z%=Z%+1:C%=C%+1
7390 R%=Z%:PROCload_field(A%,R%)
7400 UNTILfield$<>Search$
7410 IFC%-1=1THEN7440
```

```
7420 CLS:PRINTTAB(2,12)"There are"
     ;C%-1;" records containing"
7430 PRINTTAB(2,14)search$;", beginning
     at RECORD NO ";B%:GOTO7450
7440 CLS:PRINTTAB(2,12)search$;" found
     at RECORD NO ";M%
7450 ENDPROC
```

PROCload_field
This procedure will load a selected field from the
designated record using the value of R% and A% in the
calculation of PTR. There are no changes from the
chapter 8 version.

LISTING 9.31
```
7460 DEFPROCload_field(A%,R%)
7470 FILE=OPENIN(file_name$)
7480 PTR#FILE=R%*total_record_length+A%
7490 INPUT#FILE,field$
7500 CLOSE#FILE
7510 ENDPROC
```

PROCprint_record
This version of the procedure that was developed in
chapter 8 is different by virtue of left-justification
being used for the field values - see lines 7590 and
7600. This is a consequence of the use of the packing
procedure that was dealt with earlier. As the surname
string has trailing spaces inserted, the calculation of
the spaces required for right-justification will move
the surname left so that the sixteenth character is
right-justified.
    In this case, only single character versions of
"initials", "department no." and "job code" and
four-figure "salary" values will be out of alignment
but this feature is not such a visual distraction as a
short surname that is incorrectly positioned.

LISTING 9.32
```
7520 DEFPROCprint_record(R%)
7530 CLS:VDU2:PRINT´´
7540 FORN%=1TO9
7550 X%=F(N%-1)
7560 IFX%=0THEN7620
7570 X%=X%-1
7580 PRINTSPC(2);D$(X%);
7590 X=20-LEND$(X%)
7600 PRINTSPC(X);
7610 PRINTE$(X%)
7620 NEXT
7630 VDU3
7640 ENDPROC
```

This procedure is the last of those used in the file-handling package. Readers should enter the complete set of procedures and make a backup copy that is then "locked" using the "ACCESS" command. This will prevent the need to enter the package again in the event of disaster. Readers using the program cassette will need to key in *TAPE and LOAD"L9" to load the package and then select the disc system by keying in *DISC. RUNning the package will, unless errors have been entered, provide screen displays that guide the user through the various inputs that are required.

The employee details should be entered and then the ability of the package to perform the various options should be tested. As the package is used in this manner, readers should make notes of features that are appropriate to their own design of package or of features that need to be modified for particular requirements. The use of top-down-design methods will be of value during the development phase and the importance of making a backup copy of a routine as it is being developed cannot be stressed encugh.

10 Extending and Adapting the Package

As a result of testing the package, readers will have decided that certain features must be altered before it can be used in their own particular situation. The most likely area for change is the number and type of fields in a record and readers will be taken through such an activity so that the changes can be introduced as easily as possible.

To run the package, readers will probably have used a LOAD"file name" command followed by RUN. This may not be acceptable to unskilled users and neither is the use of CHAIN"file name" because both commands need the name of the package to be known by the user. The name can be obtained by using "*." but, for security reasons, such methods may not be divulged to users. A method by which the program can be used without its name being known to the user has the extra advantage of being quicker.

BOOTing Programs

Such a method is provided on the BBC micro and is known as the AUTO-START method. To obtain auto-start facilities, the disc holding the package must be placed in Drive 0. Next, type *OPT 4 3 after first selecting the $ directory using *DIR $. After typing *BUILD !BOOT and pressing RETURN, the digit "1" will appear to the left of the flashing cursor. A special program can now be built from the keyboard and this will be stored on the disc in Drive 0 under the name "!BOOT".

The program to be used is as follows - after each command, press RETURN.

```
1 CLS
2 VDU21
3 CHAIN"file name"
4 Now press ESCAPE
```

The disc drive will rotate for a few seconds and if "*." is keyed in and followed by RETURN, readers will see something like the following

```
(36)
Drive 0              Option 3 (EXEC)
Directory :0.$       Library :0.$

    !BOOT                file name
```

This indicates that the file called "!BOOT" is now stored on the disc although it cannot be listed. The option value of 3 was produced by the *OPT command used earlier. To complete the preparations, the package should now be listed and the following statement inserted - 5 VDU6. The modified package should, of course, be saved before doing anything else.

BOOTing the File-handling Package

The effect of these activities is that the !BOOT file will be obeyed by the micro when the following action is taken with the package disc in Drive 0. Press **both** the SHIFT and BREAK keys together but keep the SHIFT key held down for about 2 seconds after releasing the BREAK key. The disc drive will start and then the screen will clear except for the characters "VDU21". This is the result of lines 1 and 2 of the !BOOT file.

The disc drive will now LOAD and RUN the program with the name given in line 3 of !BOOT - this name should, of course, be the same name as that of the package. This information will not be displayed on the screen because the VDU21 statement prevents output being sent to the screen. The first statement in the package is now in line 5, that is VDU6. This statement reverses the effect of the VDU21 statement and thus the screen can receive output again.

The aspect of security will not be pursued because it is of no consequence in situations where the user is also the owner of the system. Discs can always be removed from the vicinity of the micro and stored in, say, a safe if a possible danger exists. It must be stressed again, however, that the best security against loss of data is the use of backup discs that are kept in a DIFFERENT location from those in daily use.

Choosing a Monitor

Readers may have obtained or be considering the use of a colour monitor instead of a monochrome device. The use of colour instead of black and white or of black and green is something that cannot be decided without full consideration of the expected use of the micro. If the only expected use is for file handling of the type dealt with in this book, then a monochrome output is satisfactory. However, the usual result of putting work onto a micro is a rapid realisation by the user of its ability to do other work.

In these circumstances, a satisfactory commercial software package may well be obtainable and it might well be written for use with a colour monitor. In such cases, using a monochrome monitor may present difficulties because of poor screen contrast. The real answer is to obtain a colour monitor only if commercial software is to be used or if readers expect to develop their own packages with a colour output. The package described in this book does not include colour because it is not felt to be essential for the envisaged purposes.

Programming Languages
The language used for the package, as readers are undoubtedly aware, is called BASIC and is one of the numerous **high level** languages that computers use. Because these languages were developed to allow non-computer people to write programs in what is, essentially, a form of English, the result is that they are slow in use. Without being too technical, this is because of the need to convert the English-like phrases into the language that the computer, whether micro or not, uses to do its work. The conversion process takes time and this increases the time that the micro takes to do a particular job.

In this package, the data has to be obtained from the disc or put onto the disc and the amount of work that is done by the micro in between these operations is carried out in a relatively short time. The largest delay is caused by the disc or printer because they use moving parts. When a lot of work is done in the memory in between disc or printer operations, there is some justification in writing the relevant procedures in the language that the micro can understand without conversion - this is known as assembly language.

Readers may feel that their packages would benefit from running at a higher speed and would, therefore, like to investigate the use of assembly language. Ian Birnbaum´s book "Assembly Language Programming for the BBC Microcomputer" (Macmillan, second edition, 1984) contains a number of listings that could be incorporated into a BASIC program.

Modifying the File-handling Package
The requirements for modifying the package to make it suitable for particular situations will be examined now. Basically, all variations of the package will concern the number of fields in a record and the details of those fields. These details are apparent to users when the contents of a record are displayed and readers will probably remember that considerable importance was given to the presentation of those details. A cluttered display may make the rapid extraction of information difficult and long field names will reduce the space available for the field details.

Readers may, however, consider that the presence of more fields has greater importance than absolute clarity of presentation. The present records have nine fields and they are presented with alternate spaces. If each of the spaces is used to hold a field, this will make eight more fields available. If the number of fields is restricted to this total, that is seventeen, the modifications to the package are not too lengthy. This is because the other information that is presented with a record, such as that which appears when a record is being created, amended or examined, does not need to be repositioned.

With this constraint imposed on the modification, there are three procedures that will require attention. These are PROCdisplay_record, PROCamend_record and PROCupdate_attributes. Lines 560 and 570 can be replaced with an assignment of the appropriate value to "field%" and thus eliminate a user input requirement. The details presented by the record-display procedure are obtained from arrays E$ and D$ and these are dimensioned in line 580. The largest amount of work will be in the modification of the amend-record and attribute-update procedures.

This is because they both carry out certain data-validation work and the type of validation will depend on the actual field being dealt with. Thus, any changes to the record structure will necessitate extensive changes to both of these procedures.

Some of the other changes are of a minor nature only and really constitute a cosmetic exercise on the package. Thus, if changes to the number of fields were not being considered there would be no need to make the following changes. Lines 6580, 6600, 6610, 6630, 6710, 6730 and 6750 in PROCsort_file all use the value "8". This is, of course, related to the number of fields and corresponds in the package to the variable "field%-1". The replacement of the constant "8" by the variable will save work in any subsequent modifications of the package. As a further example of this point, line 7540 can be changed to "FOR N%=1 TO field%" but not to FOR N%=0 TO field%-1". Readers should be able to establish the reason why the latter is not acceptable.

Line 1670 will require changing because it prints the value "9" as part of a text string. An easy solution is to remove the brackets and their contents from the text string. If the field number range is considered to be desirable information for the user, however, the bracketed part could be replaced by (1-";field%;"). Line 1840 can be treated in exactly the same way. The last of the cosmetic changes applies to line 2120 in which "8" should be replaced by "field%-1".

Listing 9.28 will require additions to the list of "IF...THEN" statements so that A% can be correctly assigned. Finally, listing 9.29 will require similar additions and also the construction details for "search$" will need modification to suit the new field details.

If a printer is available when readers start to incorporate their changes, the use of a printed copy of the complete package is recommended. Readers should remember to indent the listing, before printing, by using LISTO 7 as described earlier. The resulting listing can then be annotated with the changes and fault finding, should this be necessary, is then much easier.

Sorted Files

The long time taken to sort a file will prove to be unacceptable in situations in which a data search using a different field is required. The problem can be overcome by sorting the file on those fields that are used regularly or, if all are used regularly, by producing a sorted file for each field. If seventeen fields are being used, this will mean that seventeen different discs will be required, one for each sorting.

This procedure will have the obvious advantage that to search a file that has been sorted on a different field from that presently in use, only a few seconds are needed to change the disc and boot up the file handling package again. This method will require that all the file discs have the same file name as far as the micro is concerned but they will need to have different labels for easy and rapid identification during use.

File Security

When a file is altered by addition, deletion or amendment, all of the sorted files can be recreated from the altered file but a word of caution about loss of data is not out of place here. The cost of recreating a file from scratch will be more expensive than the purchase of a triplicate set of discs. The first set can then be used to create a second set, or generation, using *ENABLE and *BACKUP - see the disc manual for details of these commands.

The first generation should then be used as a backup set and all normal file-handling carried out with the second-generation discs. When alterations are carried out on the file, these should be on a disc from the second generation. When the alterations have been carried out, a third-generation file is then created by using *ENABLE and *BACKUP again and the second-generation discs used as a backup.

When further alterations become necessary, a third-generation disc should be used and a fourth generation created using a disc from the first generation and so on. This procedure, usually described as the Grandfather, Father, Son method always ensures that a file can be recreated using a disc from the previous generation and the latest-alteration details for the file.

File Merging

Finally, if additions are carried out on a daily basis, the subsequent sorting procedure - required for all the sorted files - may be too time-consuming to be acceptable. A different method of incorporating additions is desirable and one method is to use a procedure that merges a sorted file of additions held in memory into a disc file that is sorted on the same sort key. If only one disc drive is available, the procedure is not particularly straightforward. With two disc drives, however, the file on the disc can be read, record by record, and each record that is read is written onto the second disc if no new record is to be inserted - this is just copying the existing file, record by record, from the file disc to the second disc.

When the correct place for a record insertion is found, the record in memory is written onto the second disc. This procedure is repeated until all the new records in memory have been merged into, as opposed to added onto, the new file. Readers should have no difficulty in appreciating that this procedure will be much faster than that which the package uses. The difficulty may be seen to exist in the writing of the procedure but the methods of top-down-design and the use of structured programming will make the task easier.

Final Note

All that remains now is to wish readers every success in their future programming.

Appendix I Answers to Self-test Questions

Self-test 1.1

```
 10 REM TEST PROGRAM 1
 20 N$="TESTFILE1"
 30 FILE=OPENOUT(N$)
 40 READ NUMBER
 50 PRINT# FILE,NUMBER
 60 FOR V=1 TO NUMBER
 70 READ NAME$,C,DELIV$
 80 PRINT# FILE,NAME$,C,DELIV$
 90 NEXT V
100 CLOSE# FILE
110 DATA 10
120 DATA "PLATES,LARGE",1278,"EX STOCK"
130 DATA "PLATES,SMALL",1279,"4 WEEKS"
140 DATA "GLASSES,SHERRY",823,"SPECIAL ORDER"
150 DATA "CUP",771,"EX STOCK"
160 DATA "SAUCER",772,"EX STOCK"
170 DATA "BOWLS,SOUP",473,"2 WEEKS"
180 DATA "BOWLS,FRUIT",1280,"3 WEEKS"
190 DATA "SPOONS,DESSERT",079,"SPECIAL ORDER"
200 DATA "SPOONS,TEA",080,"EX STOCK"
210 DATA "SPOONS,SOUP",081,"SPECIAL ORDER"
220 END
```

Model Answer 1

```
 10 REM MODEL ANSWER 1
 20 N$="TESTFILE1"
 30 FILE=OPENIN(N$)
 40 INPUT# FILE,NUMBER
 50 FOR V=1 TO NUMBER
 60 INPUT# FILE,NAME$,C,DELIV$
 70 PRINTTAB(3);NAME$;TAB(19);C;TAB(25);DELIV$
 80 NEXT V
 90 CLOSE# FILE
100 END
```

Self-test 2.1

a)   This is a valid record for the employment agency
record structure.

b)   This is not a valid record because there are two
name-type entries and the number-type and price-type
entries are incorrectly positioned.

c)   This is not a valid record because the price-type
and date-type entries are incorrectly positioned and
there are two date-type entries.

Self-test 2.2

There is no single correct answer to this question
because readers will have their own views on what is
essential or not.
     Some easily identifiable requirements are

                    Membership number
                    Members´s name
                    Members address
                    Date of joining
                    Video format used
                    First hire date
                    Film identity
                    First hire return date
                    Second hire date
                    Film identity
                    Second hire return date
                    Third hire etc.

It is likely that three sets of records are used in
practice because some of the data is changing regularly
but other data changes very seldom. Thus one record
structure would cater for those membership details that
change infrequently, another would cater for   the
membership details that change frequently and there
would be a record structure linking film title, format,
purchase cost, purchase date, censorship grading, hire
cost grading and film identity number.

Possible answers for this arrangement are

Field No.	Identifier	Type
1	Member Number	Number
2	Member Name	Name
3	Member Address 1	Name
4	Member Address 2	Name
5	Member Address 3	Name
6	Joining Date	Date

Field No.	Identifier	Type
1	Member Number	Number
2	Film Number	Number
3	Hire Date	Date
4	Return Date	Date
5	Film Number	Number
6	Hire Date	Date
7	Return Date	Date

and so on

Field No.	Identifier	Type
1	Film Number	Number
2	Film Title	Name
3	Film Format	Name
4	Purchase Cost	Price
5	Purchase Date	Date
6	Hire Cost Grading	Price

Self-test 2.3

1a. There will be 4 sets of data, on the left-hand side of the screen, as follows

BLOGGS	75-00	2	4/1/83
14/1/83	SMITH	25-00	10
5	20/12/82	JONES	300-00

1b. There will be 6 sets of data, on the left-hand side, as follows

BLOGGS	5	SMITH	2	JONES	10
14/1/83	75-00	20/12/82	25-00	4/1/83	300-00

1c. In this case, all the data is printed as a single column with no line separation between fields.

1d. The result will be a single column again but with a single-line separation between each of the 16 fields.

2 An "Out of DATA at line..." message will be printed for each attempt to RUN the program. This is because the result of multiplying the field value by the record value will give an answer that is greater than 16 and the program contains only 16 data items - lines 50 to 80 of listing 2.3.

3 The results to part 1 indicate that it is pointless to provide user-input facilities for field and record values unless the user is aware of the amount and type of data held within the program as DATA statements.

Self-test 3.1

```
1 - Set up the file in memory
 1.1 - Initialise all variables
 1.2 - Put dummy data into all records on the file
    1.2.1 - Define dummy record details
          1.2.1.1 - Define the field names
          1.2.1.2 - Define the initial field values
    1.2.2 - Repeat
    1.2.3 - Place dummy data on a record
    1.2.4 - Until all records are initialised
 1.3 - Put actual data into records
    1.3.1 - Initialise keyboard for data entry
    1.3.2 - Repeat
    1.3.3 - Input actual data
          1.3.3.1 - Display dummy record on the screen
          1.3.3.2 - Repeat
          1.3.3.3 - Enter the field data
                  1.3.3.3.1 - Repeat
                  1.3.3.3.2 - Input a character
                  1.3.3.3.3 - Validate the character
                  1.3.3.3.4 - Until all field data is valid
          1.3.3.4 - Verify the data visually
          1.3.3.5 - Store the record
          1.3.3.6 - Until all the records are created
    1.3.4 - Until all data is on record
2 - Save the file
 2.1 - Display the file-size message
 2.2 - Request the file name
 2.3 - Store the file
 2.4 - Inform user that file has been stored
```

Self-test 3.2

There are two places in listing L3 that are required
to call PROCcheck_date(date$). L3 is not, however,
given as a complete listing and thus reference will be
made to listing 3.7 - this appears on page 33. The
first call can be inserted as follows

```
1143 PROCcheck_date(born$)
1146 IF date=FALSE THEN VDU7:GOTO 1120
1150 E$(4,R%)=D$+M$+Y$
```

Similarly, the second call is provided as follows

```
1303 PROCcheck_date(joined$)
1306 IF date=FALSE THEN VDU7:GOTO 1280
1310 E$(6,R%)=Y$+M$+D$
```

Self-test 3.3

Two possible solutions are given here but readers may
well have produced alternatives that reflect their own
perception of the problem.

First, the procedure for requesting input data can
be modified to present the date request as "DDMMYY" and
then reverse the order of the values that are stored.

Second, as the most likely user error is to input
the "DD" figures before either of the "MM" or "YY"
figures, it is feasible to inspect the entry and decide
whether or not it is a "DD" or "YY" entry. For example,
if the first figure is greater than "3", it is a
feasible decade value for an employee since employment
could have commenced after 1939. The routine could then
make a decision regarding the possible interchange of
the "DD" and "YY" so as to produce the right format.

Self-test 4.1

a) The problem is caused by the fact that the sorting
routine examines each key field item from left to right
and, in the case of alphabetic ordering, takes the
length of each item into account. Thus, "A" will be
positioned before "AA" and "B". With numeric ordering,
however, the leftmost digit will be ordered first and
then ordering will be made on the next digit to the
right and so on. This ordering means that a 4-digit
number such as 4321 will be ordered after a 5-digit
number such as 12345 even though 4321 is of lower value
than 12345.

b) By inserting a leading zero before a 4-digit number, the sorting routine would place such a number before any 5-digit number and thus overcome the problem of incorrect sorting. The presence of one or more leading zeros in front of everyday numeric data is, however, not desirable. As all the fields in the record are treated as string variables such as "born$", "salary$" and "sex$", it is possible to concatenate such strings with a space string placed in front of the item. The irritation of leading zeros is thus overcome. This is the method that is used in listing 9.24.

Self-test 4.2

1 - Load the file into memory
  1.1 - Define field names
    1.1.1 - Initialise array
    1.1.2 - Put field names into array
  1.2 - Define initial field values
    1.2.1 - Initialise array
    1.2.2 - Put dummy values into array
  1.3 - Set up memory space for file
    1.3.1 - Initialise array
    1.3.2 - Put dummy records into memory-based file
  1.4 - Retrieve file from tape
    1.4.1 - Open file
      1.4.1.1 - Obtain file name
      1.4.1.2 - Open channel
    1.4.2 - Obtain file
      1.4.2.1 - Repeat
      1.4.2.2 - Obtain a record
      1.4.2.3 - Until all records obtained
    1.4.3 - Close file
2 - Sort file
  2.1 - Input field for sort key
  2.2 - Use key for sorting file
    2.2.1 - Initialise variables
      2.2.1.1 - Start value, S, set to half file
           length (rounded down) plus 1
      2.2.1.2 - End value, E, set to file length
  2.3 - Build heap
    2.3.1 - If value of S is 1, use step 2.4
    2.3.2 - Reduce S by 1 and put record(S) into
         temporary store
    2.3.3 - Set index J to value of S
    2.3.4 - Set index I to value of J
    2.3.5 - Set index J to twice the value of J
    2.3.6 - Swap so that record(I) is equal to or
         greater than record(2*I) and is equal to
         or greater than record(2*I + 1)

2.3.6.1 - If J is less than E link to level
          2.3.7
2.3.6.2 - If J is equal to E link to level 2.3.8
2.6.3.3 - If J is greater than E link to level
          2.3.10
2.3.7 - If key value of record(J) is less than key
        value of record(J+1) set index J to value
        J+1
2.3.8 - If key value of record in temporary store is
        equal to or greater than key value of record
        J link to level 2.3.10
2.3.9 - Replace record(I) by record(J) and link to
        level 2.3.4
2.3.10 - Replace record(I) by record in temporary
         store and link to level 2.3.1
2.4 - Sort heap
2.4.1 - Place record(E) in temporary store
2.4.2 - Put record(1) in place of record(E)
2.4.3 - Reduce E by 1
2.4.4 - If value of E is 1 place record in temporary
        store into record(1) position and link to
        level 3.1
2.4.5 - If value of E is greater than 1 link to
        level 2.3.3
3 - Examine file
3.1 - Repeat
3.2 - Offer record selection
3.3 - Display chosen record
3.4 - Until no more records are to be examined
4 - Permit further sorting
4.1 - Offer further sorting
4.2 - Input response
4.3 - Act according to response
5 - Finish of program

Self-test 5.1

The first time that line 160 is obeyed, no problem
results, After line 190 has caused the selected record
to be displayed, line 160 is obeyed again but without
first clearing the screen. Thus the question in line
160 is superimposed on the text in line 22 of the
screen display instead of replacing it.
   The corresponding line in listing 5.5, that is line
210, does not use a TAB command to position the print
line and thus the text in line 22 of the screen display
is overwritten when line 210 is obeyed on the second
and later occasions.

Self-test 6.1

Lines 850 and 860 could be combined as a procedure if it was not for the alternative provided by the IF...THEN statement - procedures are not used in this way. However, a global variable, RESPONSE say, could be set to TRUE within the procedure and tested to determine subsequent action after the procedure call had ended.

Self-test 6.2

a) When PROCremove_record is called in line 100, it is preceded by a CLS statement and thus no problem is created if an acceptable value for R% is input. An unacceptable value will cause a return to line 770 for a further input and if line 770 starts with a CLS statement, the unacceptable input will be erased. This will remove the need for the CLS statement in line 100.

b) A solution to this problem is based on the fact that the value of record% indicates the length of the file. If the file contains ten records, the correct value of record% is also ten but if that value is changed to nine, the file will have only nine records that are accessible even though ten records were saved.

Thus, to "remove" record ten, the last record in this example, it is necessary only to change the value of record% to nine and no records need to be moved down the file. In general terms, inserting the following new line will handle the requirement.

785 IF R%=record%-1 THEN 830

Self-test 7.1

The order of the composite statement in line 1530 indicates that the screen will be cleared before the printer is switched on by the VDU2 statement. However, if line 1530 is presented as

1530 VDU2:CLS:PRINT´´

the printer will be switched on before the screen is cleared. The CLS statement is received and interpreted by the printer as a form feed instruction. Thus the paper in the printer will be advanced by the length that the printer has been set to deal with.

Self-test 7.2

In this case the printer is switched on after the
screen has been cleared and so no form feed of the
paper takes place. In addition, the PRINT ´´ statement
is obeyed before the printer is switched on and so no
line feed instructions are given to the printer even
though the screen display will be correct. Thus a
continuous column of four-field records will be
printed.

Self-test 7.3

A FOR...NEXT loop will always execute the instructions
between FOR and NEXT once - see page 261 of the User
Guide. Thus, if F% is input with a larger value than
L%, the result will be that only the last record of the
desired sequence will be printed.

A possible solution to the problem is to insert

    343 IF L%<F% THEN 350
    346 PRINT "ERROR - PLEASE INPUT AGAIN":GOTO 330

Self-test 7.4

Referring to listing 7.5, array F is dimensioned to the
value 8, thus initialising all the array elements to
zero. When the sequence of records is printed only four
fields are selected and the remaining elements in the
array are left containing zero. The zero value is used
as a print terminator in line 1560.

When single records are printed while still in the
same RUN, and thus without DIMensioning array F again,
the remaining elements of the array are used,
Subsequently, when a sequence of printing is requested,
four elements are loaded, line 320, but the remaining
elements do not contain zero and thus an unexpected
printout is obtained.

As will be explained later on page 165, arrays
cannot be dimensioned more than once and so it is not
possible to zero the elements of array F again in this
manner. A possible solution is to amend line 320 as
follows

    320 F(0)=1:F(1)=2:F(2)=6:F(3)=8:F(4)=0:
        F(5)=0:F(6)=0:F(7)=0:F(8)=0

Self-test 7.5

If the error is not corrected, sensitive information such as salary and date of birth will be revealed inadvertently.

Self-test 7.6

Line 250 of listing 7.5 allows input of a variable N% that will be used, after conversion to R%, by the print-record procedure. There is no check on the validity of the value of N% and a non-existent record may be requested as a result. This is not, of course, desirable and a suitable data-check routine should be incorporated.

Self-test 7.7

User-selection of fields can be obtained as follows

```
220 PROCselect_fields
320 PROCselect_fields

DEFPROCselect_fields
CLS:INPUTTAB(0,6)"How many fields are to be
printed ",N%
PRINTTAB(0,9)"Please input the field numbers in
the required order of presentation":PRINT´
REM Clear array F
FOR N=0 TO 8:F(N)=0:NEXT
REM Set up N% fields of array F
FOR I=1 TO N%:INPUT F(I-1):NEXT
ENDPROC
```

Self-test 8.1

a) Line 60 of listing 8.5 uses the value given by LEN(D$(field)) in the calculation of the total record length. This value of total record length is larger than necessary because the field names do not need to be saved with each record.

b) More space will be available for saving variable data, as opposed to static data such as field names, if line 60 is written as

```
60 total_record_length=
   LEN(I$(field))+total_record_length
```

Appendix II   Analysis of Printer Types

The range of printer types that is available for the small-business market presents a confusing picture for those who are just entering the world of computing. As well as trying to unravel the often-bewildering specifications that manufacturers provide, the prospective buyer has to decide what the widely varying prices indicate in terms of quality or features.

As usual, the differing requirements of various users make it difficult to generalise on what constitutes the ´best buy´ but one coarse distinction that can be made is between those users who need a printout mainly for internal office use and those who will produce invoices, orders, etc. for subsequent use by other organisations.

Dot-matrix Printers
For the first type of use, the dot-matrix printer has a lot to offer in terms of low cost, reliability and speed of printing. The printing of graphics displays is also possible as is the production of what is known as near-letter-quality, or NLQ, printing but the descenders, or tails, of letters such as p,q,y and g are not always of an acceptable standard for certain requirements. The speed of printing in the NLQ mode is about 30 characters per second - 30cps - but in the draft mode that is usually available on such printers, the speed can be as high as 200cps.

These features are available on printers costing a few hundred pounds and another feature would be the option of using cut sheets, continuous stationery or roll paper. More expensive dot-matrix printers offer letter-quality, LQ, printing at about 60cps, NLQ printing at about 125cps and draft printing at about 300cps.

Daisy-wheel Printers
The second requirement is normally met by using a daisy-wheel printer in which the character sets and/or fonts are user-selectable by substituting different daisy-wheels. The characters are produced in the same way as on a typewriter and thus the quality is higher than on the low to medium-priced dot-matrix printers. The printing speed is unlikely to exceed 30cps unless prices in excess of a thousand pounds are paid but if

price is not important, speeds approaching 100cps are
obtainable. If speed is less important than printing
quality, 10 to 20cps daisy-wheel printers can be
obtained for prices similar to those of dot-matrix
printers.

General Comments

Single or multi-ply continuous stationery, also called
fan-fold or Z-fold paper, can be obtained with
pre-printed user-based information but requires a
printer that has tractor or sprocket feed facilities.
Various maximum column widths are available and range
from 80 columns up to nearly 200 columns.

The lower-priced dot-matrix and daisy-wheel printers
tend to be noisy and this might present problems in
certain environments although sound-proofing cabinets
are available.

If noise reduction is of importance, the ink-jet and
thermal printers may be considered but speed of
printing is usually reduced and the special paper used
with thermal printers is an expensive consumable item.
The prices are, typically, in the same range as the
dot-matrix types.

There are, of course, several more printer types
available but these are less likely to be used with the
BBC micro because they usually cost several thousand
pounds - examples are band printers, laser printers and
line printers. Thimble printers are similar to
daisy-wheel printers in operational features and cost.

One feature that may cause needless confusion
concerns the interface arrangements that exist for
printers. As mentioned in chapter 7, both serial and
parallel printer interfaces are available on the BBC
micro and so both types of printer may be used. The
usual printer configurations are for Centronics, a
parallel arrangement, or for RS232, a serial
arrangement and typically, dot-matrix printers are of
the parallel type while, again typically, daisy-wheel
printers are of the serial type. Other arrangements
such as ASCII, C-loop and TTL are quoted in the
literature and purchasers should always state that the
printer is for use with a BBC micro and obtain
confirmation that the proposed purchase is suitable.

Conclusion

This review of printers for the BBC micro is based on
the information available in the latter quarter of 1984
and, because of the almost daily advances in the
technology, cannot reflect the future situation
regarding printing speeds and costs - the predicted
shipping of over 13 million printers in 1985 will
undoubtedly mean lower prices and more features.

Appendix III: Floppy Disc Drive Units

A wide variety of disc drives is available for use with
the BBC micro but the manufacturer's specifications do
not always help the prospective buyer to make the
choice that is most suitable for the particular need.
Statements about disc sizes, capacities, dual and
single drive, single and double density, integral PSU,
etc. only serve to confuse rather than clarify the
situation. Hopefully this review will enable readers to
compare the various features and make a reasoned choice
that will satisfy their particular requirement.

Disc Sizes
The most common size of disc used with personal
computers like the BBC micro has a diameter of five and
one quarter inches or, in decimal fraction form, 5.25
inches. The non-metric unit of "inch" indicates the
origin of the design and is, in fact, perpetuated in
all the sizes of discs in common use. Other sizes are 8
inch and, more recently, 3.5 inch and 3 inch.

In the same way that cassette sizes such as C30,
C45, etc., are an indication of capacity, so an 8 inch
disc will, typically, hold more information than a 5.25
inch disc. This similarity does not exist in the case
of the 3 and 3.5 inch discs which, because of advanced
technology, hold at least as much information as the
lower-capacity 5.25 inch discs.

Disc Capacities
As implied in the previous section, the capacity of a
disc is not purely a function of its diameter. Again,
this is a result of improved technology being applied
to an existing design. In the same way that audio
cassettes can now hold stereo recordings on both sides
of the cassette, so 5.25 inch discs can be used on
improved-design equipment to hold more information than
the original design would allow.

When a 5.25 inch blank disc is being prepared to
hold magnetically recorded information, a process known
as "formatting", the surface of the disc is "divided"
into 10 sectors, each of which can hold 256 bytes. Each
byte holds a code to represent a letter, a digit, a
punctuation symbol, etc.

Simple multiplication produces a byte-capacity
figure of

$$40 \times 10 \times 256 = 102400 \text{ bytes}$$

for a 40 track disc. In a similar manner to the use of
kilo, abbreviated to "k", to mean 1000, computer users
refer to the value 1024 as "K" - note that a capital
letter is used for the computer-based version. Thus the
40 track capacity figure obtained above is equivalent
to 100Kbytes, usually abbreviated to 100Kb.

A single 40 track disc can, therefore, hold over one
hundred thousand characters or about 35 pages of this
book.

Single and Double Density

A 40 track disc uses single density recording and thus
if 80 tracks are recorded on the same area of the disc,
double density recording is required. Discs are sold as
single or double density and the price usually reflects
the quality control checks that are necessary to
guarantee double density operation. A double density
disc will have twice the capacity of a single density
disc, usually quoted as 200Kb.

Single and Dual Drives

In order to obtain increased capacity, double density
drive systems can be used but some programs, including
the package developed in this book, require that the
operating program is held on one disc and another disc
is used to hold the data on which that program is
operating. It is necessary, therefore, to use a dual,
or double, drive system which can be 40 track or 80
track based. Some systems, however, allow for switching
between 40 and 80 track so that it is possible for one
drive to operate as a 40 track and the other as an 80
track system.

The maximum capacity of such a dual-drive,
double-density system is four times that of a
single-drive, single-density system, that is 400Kb.

Single and Double Sided Drives

A further method of increasing capacity is to use both
sides of the disc and, again, either single or double
density recording can be obtained. If a dual drive,
double sided, double density disc drive system is used,
the capacity is 800Kb or 0.8Mb. The use of a capital M

as a prefix indicates the value of one million or Mega
- abbreviated to "M".

Combined Units

The configuration of the dual drive systems provides
for user convenience by offering two drives as separate
units, or as stacked units - one above the other or as
tandem units - side by side. In addition, the units may
be half height instead of standard height and can thus

be placed under the BBC micro to make a compact computing system.

Power Supplies
Although the BBC micro has sufficient power capacity to cope with the requirements of dual drive systems, not all disc drive systems, whether single or dual drive, rely on power being supplied by the computer. Instead the disc drive system is powered from the mains supply just as the computer is. If the power supply of the BBC micro is overloaded by using a disc drive system that is not really suitable, operating errors may occur on a random basis and thus corruption of data may result.

General Comments
This review has concentrated on 5.25 inch disc drive types because, at the time of writing, this is the size used by most of the personal computer owners who use disc systems. 8 inch disc systems are not widely used with personal computers although it is possible to obtain such systems for use with the BBC micro.

The recent introduction of the 3 and 3.5 inch disc systems is likely to make an impression on the 5.25 inch disc market because of the improved technology which allows for large capacity in more compact units. Figures available in late 1984 are 500Kb for 3 inch systems, 1Mb for 3.5 inch systems and 1.6Mb for some 5.25 inch systems.

Index